PRAISE FOR *THE FISCAL FEMINIST*

"Gaining control over your financial situation is one of the most important things you can do to gain confidence in yourself and your future. Kimberlee unlocks the knowledge and mindset needed to do just this."

—**AMY JO MARTIN,** founder and CEO, Renegade Global, investor, and *New York Times* bestselling author

"What Kimberlee has done with this powerhouse of a book is pack biography, authentic care, and true financial lessons into one highly readable and digestible work. Each page reflects her own story and journey, her care for the message of financial empowerment, and the practical lessons necessary for women of all backgrounds and circumstances to find fiscal responsibility. A must-read!"

—**DAVID L. BAHNSEN,** Managing Partner, The Bahnsen Group, and author of *There's No Free Lunch: 250 Economic Truths*

"A refreshing, timely, and insightful strategic guide to motivate all women to achieve empowerment in their personal finances, money relationships, and career development despite the challenges and demands they experience. It is a call to action for women to embrace self-care and seize control of their financial futures."

—**COCO BROWN,** founder and CEO, Athena Alliance

THE FISCAL
FEMINIST

THE FISCAL FEMINIST

A FINANCIAL WAKE-UP CALL FOR WOMEN

KIMBERLEE DAVIS

WONDERWELL

Library of Congress Control Number: 2021919412

ISBN 978-1-63756-000-6 (paperback)
ISBN 978-1-63756-001-3 (EPUB)

Editor: Ariel Curry
Cover design and interior design: Morgan Krehbiel
Author photo: Jessica Schramm

Published by Wonderwell in Los Angeles, CA
www.wonderwell.press

WONDERWELL

Distributed in the US by Publishers Group West and in Canada by Publishers Group Canada

Printed and bound in Canada

To my three daughters—Allison, Claire, and Merrill—who continually inspire me to be the best version of myself

and

to all women who are ready to join the Fiscal Sisterhood

CONTENTS

INTRODUCTION

EARLY ONE MORNING in the autumn of 2011, I woke up with the sudden urge to check my email. The universe was warning me that something was up. Much to my chagrin, I saw a message from my divorce lawyer in London. My first reaction was, *Why on earth am I receiving an email from her—my divorce was finalized over six months ago?* And then I read her note, and my world unexpectedly and mercilessly changed forever.

Six months prior to "the email," I was divorced in a court in London, England, from my husband of twenty-three years. We had spent the last thirteen years in England, and he remained living there even though I decided to move back to Southern California during the several years of divorce proceedings. The divorce decree awarded me a settlement, alimony, and child support for my three daughters, two of whom were in high school at the time, and one who had just started at university. I was satisfied with the terms of the divorce decree, and all looked secure for my and my children's future. My daughters and I got on with trying to get acclimated to our new lives and figuring it all out. My plan was to go back to work and reestablish myself in the United States professionally, which in my midfifties was going to be a challenge, but doable in some way.

I thought it was just going to take time. But I no longer had time, because "the email" informed me that my ex-husband would not be paying alimony anymore, and he was going to court to revise the divorce decree due to his "circumstances." Suddenly, our future looked very bleak indeed.

There I was with no real professional game plan; no job at that point; and children who needed to be housed, educated, and fed. It was a wake-up call, a real bullhorn in my ear. The message I heard was: *Get with it, make a plan, and execute the plan—because otherwise you and your family are going to be living a very different life.*

For six months, I would get some money from my ex-husband by agreement, but after that I'd be on my own. Negotiating this revision of our agreement through the court process took almost three years— during which I received no alimony or support whatsoever. And in the end, he won the appeal; alimony and child support were reduced to a negligible sum. Fear and desperation took over. I had to downsize in all ways and severely cut costs in short order. I made finding a job in my wheelhouse my job for the foreseeable future. I sent applications furiously, stressed out beyond belief, unable to sleep. I stayed that way until I got fed up with the fear and decided that I would take every opportunity the universe put in front of me to escape this nightmare of fear and feeling powerless.

Enough with the drama, you might be thinking—*this is supposed to be a book about women and money!* Let me wrap up my saga by saying that eventually I did find a job as a financial advisor, and that changed my life. It took a long time for me to build up my resources, pay down debt incurred when the alimony stopped, and build my professional standing—but I did it. You may be on a similar journey, trying to navigate an uncertain world with no safety net. I know what it is like to live paycheck to paycheck, because I used all the money from my settlement for rent, living expenses, and education for my daughters.

During this time of struggle, I had some very dark moments, and my eldest daughter sent me a poem she read in her college English class. I hope it's as encouraging to you as it was to me:

"Invictus" by Willian Ernest Henley

Out of the night that covers me,
    Black as the pit from pole to pole,
I thank whatever gods may be
    For my unconquerable soul.

In the fell clutch of circumstance
    I have not winced nor cried aloud.
Under the bludgeonings of chance
    My head is bloody, but unbowed.

Beyond this place of wrath and tears
    Looms but the Horror of the shade,
And yet the menace of the years
    Finds and shall find me unafraid.

It matters not how strait the gate,
    How charged with punishments the scroll,
I am the master of my fate,
    I am the captain of my soul.

The Problem with Women and Money

I have been pondering the relationship between women and their fiscal responsibility to themselves for quite some time because of my own experience navigating financial problems. My story turned out alright, but it could have had a very different ending—a *sad* ending where my future and my children's futures were negatively impacted and my retirement a nightmare. I would never do anything to purposefully put myself and my children at risk, but it almost happened because I did not have my priorities straight, was not vigilant, didn't take preventive action, and didn't know how to have "uncomfortable" money conversations. I now realize that the fear and uncertainty I felt in those years could have been avoided, or at the very least minimized. My life was the perfect storm of problems that most women face with money:

We don't have the right training.

Women have unique financial issues and concerns that they must confront over the course of their lives, and that differ from men's. Many of our beliefs about money are formed by our upbringing and the people in our lives. Often, women don't get the benefit of the same "money talks" and education that their male counterparts receive, and the playing field is still not equal. But with that said, we are not born with preconceived notions about money, and it is within our control to reprogram our mindset and secure our financial futures.

We are busy.

I have had many roles and worn many hats. I have been a mother, wife (again), ex-wife, daughter of elderly parents, a professional woman, and a stay-at-home mom (SAHM). My career began as a Wall Street corporate lawyer. I then transitioned into investment banking and corporate finance, and finally wealth management. I was a stay-at-home mom when my three daughters were young. My experiences have covered the gamut of the diverse roles that women fulfill throughout their often very complex lives. Given my professional background, one might assume that I had the correct mindset and skill set to traverse multifaceted personal financial challenges with knowledge and ease.

Unfortunately, I let my busyness prevent me from seeing what was really happening with my finances. I took my eye off the ball, telling myself that someone else had it covered and allowing someone else to dictate my financial future. It is risky to live in denial, and in this book, I am asking you to get uncomfortable in the short term by asking the right questions and taking preventive action to secure future calm financial waters, however life unfolds for you.

We put everyone else first.

As women, we often put the needs of others—children, husbands, partners, parents, and friends—before our own. I did not do any premarital or postmarital financial planning, and I never took the necessary time to keep my eye on my financial situation, leaving that to my husband. Yes, I was responsible for paying the monthly bills, but I did not have a grasp on the overall picture. I never fully understood that the many sacrifices I made without planning were beyond detrimental to my financial future.

I experienced a "gray divorce," a growing trend among couples over the age of fifty who split later in life. A gray divorce is a financial double whammy for women, who have less time to recoup lost earnings for the time they devoted to their families earlier in life. As a result, many women who experience a gray divorce have a much lower quality of life in their later years. During the course of my marriage, I had three children, two years apart each; supported the career of my husband; moved to a foreign country for my husband's career; and was the primary caregiver to the children. It was a very hectic life, and my primary focus was the family and its needs. Everyone and everything came before understanding my own financial situation. *Sound familiar?*

What I failed to recognize was that this behavior could ultimately cause great problems for me and my children, the very people I spent so much time trying to protect and nurture. Due to my lack of attention and preventive planning, I spent a long time fraught with uncertainty.

The Real Deal

My mission is to help all of you who are reading this book—mothers, daughters, professional women, single women, married women, divorced women, widowed women, women of all ages and wealth levels—embrace your financial responsibility to yourselves and achieve security in both calm and turbulent times. I want you to give yourself permission to be financially strategic, intentional, and knowledgeable, while still enjoying all the things that money can't buy.

Whether we like it or not, the reality is that money plays a big part in life. We can't survive without it, so we might as well learn how to have a healthy relationship with it. There is no Prince Charming or fairy godmother. William Ernest Henley had it right: We are the masters of our fates. We should be the chief executive officer of our own life, even if we share that life with a partner or a parent or somebody else. We have a personal responsibility to ourselves to understand how to be financially organized, savvy, and responsible; this will give us peace of mind, control of our lives, and freedom of choice. To me, this is about self-love and self-care. If you love yourself and respect yourself, whatever your age or situation, you will make sure that you are knowledgeable about your financial life; you will be proactive and relish every minute of it because you are protecting yourself from unforeseen harm and reducing future stress and worry in the event of unforeseen circumstances.

In this book, I'll help you understand how we got to where we are today. We'll explore our complex history with finances and the ways in which our work, relationships, and technology influence our power over our financial lives. I'll introduce you to the tools for organizing your finances and planning for your future. We'll get tactical about personal finance, retirement planning, buying property, making investments, managing relationships with others, navigating divorce, and estate planning.

We are all smart, capable women with many complex, competing demands—relationships, family, career, health, money—and they are all intertwined. If we can reduce the stress of financial turmoil and hardship, then we can be healthier and clear-minded, and have energy for all the other demands without worrying that our financial situation is about to crumble. That is a stress we don't need.

Let's be role models for other women—younger women, our daughters, our granddaughters, our nieces, our coworkers, and our friends.

Let's seize control of our financial futures and enjoy it! It is a great feeling to be CEO of your life.

So, let's get to it!

CHAPTER 1

The Evolution and the Revolution: Women's Financial Health, Past and Present

"And one day she discovered that she was fierce, and strong, and full of fire, and that not even she could hold herself back because her passion burned brighter than her fears."

—Mark Anthony, *The Beautiful Truth*

N 1860, ELIZABETH PACKARD, a housewife and mother of six living in Illinois, was committed to an insane asylum by her husband for having opinions and promoting religious beliefs that differed from his own. Unbelievably, nineteenth-century laws permitted men to silence their wives by confinement to mental institutions, for virtually any cause. At the time, simply disagreeing with your husband was all the "proof" doctors needed to lock a woman up indefinitely. But Elizabeth's abuse had begun years before that, when her husband sold property she had inherited against her will, and then denied her access to her funds.

Technically, under Illinois law at the time, they weren't hers anyway—they were his.

In *The Woman They Could Not Silence*, author Kate Moore tells Elizabeth's haunting story of abuse and her fight for freedom and equality. When she finally was released from the asylum, three years after being committed, Elizabeth returned home only to find that her husband had sold all of her possessions and moved her children to a new state. She took him to court, and eventually won back her right to parent her youngest children. She found a way not only to provide for herself but to fight for other women's freedom as well. Elizabeth challenged the misogynist norms of her time, changing women's rights and the medical science of that era.[1]

Women have been on a long and often arduous journey to acquire financial rights. We take a lot for granted today and often forget that it wasn't so long ago that women were denied many basic financial rights—a situation that made it impossible for them to be independent economic actors. It is true that women's rights have evolved over many years, and women can now independently manage their own financial lives if they choose to. But the playing field is still not even. As you'll see in this chapter, women are still disadvantaged in a number of ways, and there is still substantial work to be done in order for women to achieve true financial equality and independence.

Financial independence and empowerment are the means to fulfilling our responsibilities, taking care of ourselves and our families, achieving our goals, and having freedom and choice in our lives. Unfortunately, it's not just given to us. Thankfully, in most parts of the world, no one has the authority or power to wrongfully lock us away or sell our belongings without our permission. But women must claim their right to be financially in charge of their lives, and to be CEO of their financial futures and financial security. We should no longer rely on others to chart our financial course; it is up to us to be our own financial stewards. It is time for us to be fierce with our finances.

The Fight for Financial Freedom

Despite Elizabeth Packard's experience, the financial status of women had started to evolve during the 1800s in the United States, when states began enacting laws that expanded women's financial rights. In 1884, Maine became the first state to guarantee women the right to "separate economy." In 1848, New York passed the Married Women's Property Act, which gave married women the same financial rights as unmarried women and no longer held a woman liable for her husband's debts. If only Elizabeth had lived in New York! The New York legislation was used as a model for other states, but it wasn't until 1900 that the rest of the country caught up with these particular ideas. In 1862, the Homestead Act decreed that American women could own land in their own name. That same year, California passed a law establishing a state savings-and-loan industry that also guaranteed that a woman who made deposits in her own name was entitled to keep control of her money (that is, it was no longer under her husband's control), and the San Francisco Savings Union approved the first loan to a woman.

During this time, there were many women trailblazers who helped to push societal mores and expectations. Victoria Woodhull and her sister, Tennessee Claflin, became the first female stockbrokers in 1870. Woodhull was a suffragist, and in 1872 became the first woman to run for president, choosing Frederick Douglass, the abolitionist, as her running mate. Although Woodhull's campaign was unsuccessful—women didn't even have the right to vote at that time—the sisters' brokerage firm was a success, and Cornelius Vanderbilt invested with them.

Henrietta "Hetty" Green, often referred to as the "Witch of Wall Street," was another trailblazer of the late 1800s; she became a successful businesswoman and financier, and was known as the "richest woman in America during the Gilded Age." Green was born into a rich family that made its money in whaling and shipping, and she had a strong interest in accounting and finance from a young age. When Green was twenty, her father bought her "a wardrobe full of the finest dresses of the season . . .

in order to attract a wealthy suitor," but Green sold her new wardrobe and bought government bonds with the proceeds.[2] During a time when married women were still subject to coverture, a legal doctrine that ceded a woman's legal rights to her husband, Hetty Green had different notions. Before she would marry, she made her husband sign a prenuptial agreement! According to Hetty, "It is the duty of every woman, I believe, to learn to take care of her own business affairs." She also noted that "a girl should be brought up as to be able to make her own living . . . ."[3] These words were true then, and they are still true today.

Even with this progress, however, women continued to have many of their rights either denied or minimized into the early 1900s. In 1875, the United States Supreme Court upheld a state court decision in Missouri that refused to register a woman as a lawful voter because state laws only allowed men to vote; and in 1908, Oregon limited the number of hours a woman could work. Finally, after years of suffragist protest and agitation, the Nineteenth Amendment to the Constitution of the United States was passed, and women finally had the right to vote.

You might think that this finally gave women equality in other areas of their lives as well; unfortunately, no. Even with the right to vote, women were, and still often are, up against the system financially— though many things have gotten better. However, as recently as 1971, a woman could **NOT**:

- **Get an Ivy League education.** It wasn't until the late 1960s and early 1970s that undergraduate women meaningfully broke into Ivy League schools. Only Cornell University and the University of Pennsylvania admitted women undergraduate students earlier.[4]

- **Get a credit card in her own name.** Until the mid-1970s, banks and other financial institutions denied married women in the United States credit cards or loans in their name, and single women also had difficulty getting credit. Thanks to the efforts of Ruth Bader Ginsburg and her work as an attorney, the Equal

Credit Opportunity Act of 1974 was enacted. It "prohibits discrimination on the basis of race, color, religion, national origin, sex, marital status, or age in credit transactions."[5] That means that if you apply for a loan or a credit card, banks and financial institutions can now only consider factors relating to your creditworthiness, and women no longer need male cosigners.

- **Take legal action against workplace sexual harassment.** The first time a court recognized sexual harassment as grounds for legal action was in 1976 in *Williams v. Saxbe*. The U.S. District Court for the District of Columbia ruled that quid pro quo sexual harassment was a type of gender-biased or sexual discrimination after Ms. Williams refused a sexual advance by her supervisor, was repeatedly harassed and humiliated, and was ultimately fired a year later.[6]

- **Get health insurance at the same rates as men.** Prior to 2014 and the enactment of the Affordable Care Act, more than half of individual insurance plans charged higher premiums for a forty-year-old female nonsmoker than a forty-year-old male nonsmoker. This practice of charging women more than men for the exact same coverage cost women $1 billion per year in 2012. Yet despite these higher premiums paid by women, 90 percent of individual health plans didn't provide maternity benefits; and in most states, pregnancy was a preexisting condition that prevented women from purchasing health insurance.[7]

- **Get any protection for being discriminated against in the workplace for being pregnant.** The Pregnancy Discrimination Act, passed in 1978, prohibits discrimination based on pregnancy, childbirth, or medical conditions related to either. However, there is still plenty of pregnancy discrimination afoot in the workplace.[8] Between 1997 and 2011, the U.S. Equal Employment Opportunity Commission saw a 50 percent increase in the number of pregnancy discrimination charges filed, and the number of charges haven't changed significantly since then. In 2012, Congress introduced the Pregnant Workers Fairness Act, which clarified that employers cannot force pregnant workers off the job or deny them reasonable accommodations that would allow them to continue working while maintaining healthy pregnancies.[9] However, this bill did not pass, no progress was made on the federal level, and a persistent form of pregnancy discrimination continues to occur when an employee's pregnancy conflicts in some way with her job duties.[10] Unfortunately, in 2020, pregnant workers were still being pushed off the job for being pregnant. As of September 2020, thirty states had passed stronger laws providing stronger protections for pregnant workers. In 2021, the House of Representatives passed the Pregnant Workers Fairness Act in a bipartisan vote. As this book went to press, it was still awaiting passage in the Senate.[11]

For centuries, women have been fighting for equal pay, financial autonomy, leadership opportunities, and the eradication of gender-based discrimination. The changes over the years as a result of these efforts have increased women's economic presence and have had a positive impact on the economy. There is still a long way to go, but we must press on and fight the good fight! Let's NOT go quietly back to the 1950s . . .

Right Here, Right Now: The Fight Continues

Every woman is different, with a unique path, goals, and preferences. Today, women have more freedom to make life choices without others controlling these decisions. With this freedom and choice, there has also been a shift toward growing financial power for women. But in order for each individual woman to have financial independence and the freedom that comes with it, *we* must make the decision to take responsibility to do so for ourselves. Given the historical context, we can see that the cards are sometimes stacked against us, but we must continue to make strides both individually and collectively.

Seventy percent of women believe that women and men have fundamentally different life journeys, according to a Merrill Lynch report.[12] And that is true. First, we are often the primary caregivers for family members, and although this is very fulfilling, we will probably experience financial setbacks as we make accommodations for providing this care. Although there are now more stay-at-home dads, they remain the minority. In 2016, dads comprised 17 percent of all stay-at-home parents, according to the Pew Research Center.[13] Second, we live on average five years longer than men. Critical to any long-term financial outlook is ensuring that we plan for our life in retirement, as we may be alone.

The data can be sobering, but it's absolutely essential to understand exactly what we're up against and why it's so important to be savvy and shrewd when it comes to our financial future. It starts with being aware, and in chapters 2 through 11, we'll talk about what action you can take now to ensure your security and financial wellness in life. There is so much potential waiting for you! But first, let's look at the facts.

The Gender Pay Gap: It's a Fact

In 2020, women earned eighty-one cents for every one dollar earned by a man—in other words, an average women's annual salary is 81 percent of an average man's salary.[14] Currently, women account for 57 percent of college- and graduate-degree earners, and although women have comprised the majority of college-educated adults for almost four decades, they still continue to earn less than men.[15] The good news is that due to this rise in education, there has been a dramatic increase in women's earnings, which grew by 75 percent, compared to only 5 percent for men, between 1970 and 2015.

However, even with the dramatic increase in women's wages, there is still a significant gender pay gap due to historical trends in employment. According to a 2018 Census Bureau report, "The average worker, between ages 25 and 64, earned $41,900 in 2017, compared to a worker with at least a bachelor's degree who earned $61,300. When specifically comparing gender pay differences, the earnings vary greatly between men and women. The median income of a man with a college degree is $74,900. A college-educated woman on the other hand will earn just $51,600."[16] The estimated lifetime earnings of a college-educated woman are 70 percent of that of her male counterpart.[17] That in turn affects Social Security benefits, with the average benefit collected by a sixty-five-year-old woman being 20 percent less than the annual benefit collected by a sixty-five-year-old man.[18] There is a negative financial ripple effect from the gender pay gap.

Some may argue that the pay gap is mainly the fault of women, because they don't negotiate forcefully, ask for raises, or behave aggressively enough in the workplace. I dispute this argument wholeheartedly. Historically, as discussed, women were not exposed to the workplace, had few economic rights, and were caregivers who were treated as dependents. Remember Elizabeth Packard, who was put in a mental institution for having opinions? The historical narrative has not cultivated an environment where women could learn to negotiate aggressively without ridicule. Even today, when women assert themselves, they are often viewed as being overbearing or aggressive, while their male counterparts are considered confident for the same behavior.

Women's Employment Rates: The Uphill Battle

From the end of the Great Recession in July 2010 to the beginning of the COVID-19 crisis in February 2020, women gained 11.1 million jobs. According to *The Washington Post*, in January 2020, before the pandemic, "For just the second time, women outnumbered men in the U.S. paid workforce, with their new majority buoyed by fast job growth in health care and education over the past year, as well as the tight labor market."[19] Progress was being made, but now women must deal with the fallout from the COVID-19 pandemic.

In April 2020, 100 percent of women's job gains were wiped out.[20] Men, however, saw only 85 percent of their job gains wiped out in 2020. Women of color were especially hit hard by job losses during the pandemic. The unemployment rate increased to 16.4 percent for Black women and 20.2 percent for Latina women, compared to an overall unemployment rate for all women of 15.5 percent. Younger women between the ages twenty and twenty-four experienced unemployment rates reaching 28 percent, compared to 24 percent for men in the same age group.[21]

There was some job recovery for women in 2021, with the August 2021 unemployment rate for women at 4.8 percent, but it has been slow progress, and women's participation in the workforce remains well below pre-pandemic levels. According to a September 2021 report from the National Women's Law Center, we will need almost nine straight years of job gains at the August 2021 rate of employment for women to recover the jobs lost since February 2020. Further, reported unemployment rates do not include people who have left the workforce voluntarily, since these people are no longer counted as unemployed. The women's labor participation rate of 57.4 percent in August 2021 remains well below the pre-pandemic participation rate of 59.2 percent in February 2020; that rate has not been as low since December 1988. If the women who have left the labor force since February 2020 were included in the unemployed, women's unemployment in August 2021 would have been 6.9 percent.[22]

During the pandemic, the domestic burden of caring for children and relatives and homeschooling children has fallen predominantly on women, which is widely believed to account for the record number of women departing the workforce.[23] According to a recent study from Washington University in St. Louis, the pandemic placed a heavy strain on women's work, with enduring consequences. The research emphasizes the Herculean demands place on women "who are expected to work like they don't have children, and raise children like they don't work."[24]

The research also reveals that there is measurable discrimination against mothers in the job market for both college-educated women in managerial roles and women in low-wage roles. Callback rates were much lower for mothers than for childless women. In low-wage sectors, the callback rate for mothers was 21.5 percent compared to 26.7 percent for childless women; and in the professional sector, the callback rate was 22.6 percent for childless women compared to 18.4 percent for mothers.

The Invisible Labor Issue

What is "invisible labor"? It's the childcare and care for elderly family members, coupled with domestic work, that women often do. You know, the work nobody pays you to do!

Women do almost three times as much unpaid care and domestic work as men, and they provide 70 percent of childcare during standard working hours. This unseen economy has a real impact on the formal economy and on women's lives. This is unpaid work. The COVID-19 pandemic has highlighted that the maintenance of our daily lives is built on the invisible, unpaid labor of women. Increased demand for childcare and care of elderly family members is deepening the already existing inequalities in the gender division of labor.

In September 2020, 865,000 women dropped out of the workforce, compared to 216,000 men! In other words, 80 percent of the 1.1 million people who dropped out of the workforce in September 2020 were women. Why this disparity? According to Emily Martin, vice president for education and workplace justice at the National Women's Law Center, "This is the devastating impact of the ongoing breakdown of our nation's caregiving infrastructure in the face of COVID-19. As families across the country struggle to figure out how to keep their jobs while also making sure their children are cared for, safe and learning every day, it's women who are being pushed out of work."[25]

Parenting is extremely rewarding, but as the mother of three daughters, I have experienced lost opportunities and long breaks in my career. My children have always come first, and yet sometimes I think I could have better served them and myself through some key financial and career decisions along the way. With hindsight, I believe I should not have left employment completely when having children. I also regret agreeing to move to another country for an undefined period of time to support my husband's career aspirations, which severely limited my ability to work. Those choices prevented me from exploring my own career aspirations, achieving self-realization, and developing my independence. After all is said and done, children grow up and sometimes marriages end. You may be left charting your own course, so it's best to be prepared.

The work/parenting balance is difficult and often requires us to make difficult choices. The loss of career advancement and salary growth during my career breaks caused a lot of financial stress for me and my daughters when I got divorced, and then I had to make up for lost time out of my profession. I am not alone in this, as 41 percent of mothers, versus 21 percent of fathers, believe that being a working parent makes it harder to advance their careers.[26]

Adding to that, two-thirds of the care provided to our elderly parents and relatives is done by women.[27] Caregivers are often sandwiched between caring for their children and their elderly relatives, which leads to major time demands on their lives. Although parenting and caregiving are fulfilling and purposeful, these obligations can be stressful and add to the financial challenges that women confront. Caregiving responsibilities often result in work interruptions and increased financial responsibilities—a double whammy. As the only child of two elderly parents whom I am blessed to still have, I understand this dilemma intimately.

The Cumulative Pay Gap

Taking breaks in a career journey can lead to a cumulative pay gap. Essentially, the already-existing gender pay gap coupled with interruptions in working causes women to earn much less in their lifetimes than men. According to the Merrill Lynch Age Wave study, women often experience three key work interruptions:

- On average, women in their twenties and thirties take eight years out of the workforce to care for two children.
- A woman in her late forties and fifties may stop working for four years to care for a parent.
- A woman in her early sixties may retire two years earlier than planned to care for an ailing spouse.[28]

The study also states that when a woman reaches her retirement age, she will have earned $1,055,000 less than a man who stayed continuously in the workforce, due to these factors.[29]

We need legislation that supports women with childcare and eldercare. Without it, as we have seen, women will work less or be forced to step away from the workforce due to these responsibilities. This exodus will have a detrimental financial effect on them, their children, society, and the economy in general. With fewer women in the labor force, the economy does not benefit from the talents and abilities of 51 percent of the population. Research suggests that the economy becomes more productive and competitive with women participating and providing a unique set of skills and perspectives.

The pay gap, coupled with gender segregation in industries that often pay less, and with the average women's life span, results in women being more vulnerable in retirement. Women are giving care and making personal sacrifices that benefit society, yet they are being financially punished for their efforts!

We can turn this around with our voices and votes, with intentional and strategic career choices, by being confident in our competence, and by negotiating for ourselves. In chapter 2, I will provide some tools and tips for taking charge of your pay equity and career growth and longevity.

Longer Lives, but Less Wealth

The fact that women are living longer lives is a great thing that should be celebrated, yet it isn't all good news. Here are some interesting facts, according to the United Nations Population Division (2019):

- On average, women live five years longer than men.
- By age eighty-five, women outnumber men two to one.
- Eighty-one percent of centenarians are women.[30]

But with this great news about women's longevity comes the reality that women are more likely to be alone and financially self-reliant during their elder years.

> "Longevity is a critical issue for women, probably one of the biggest reasons why women's needs are so different than men's in terms of financial saving and investing."
>
> **—Annamaria Lusardi, PhD, Academic Director, Global Financial Literacy Excellence Center, George Washington University**

Most women (60 percent) worry that they will run out of money if they live to be one hundred years old, and 42 percent of women are afraid they will run out by eighty years old. These are legitimate fears. Only 9 percent of American women have $300,000 or more put aside, but according to the Merrill Lynch Age Wave study, a typical retirement costs $738,000.[31] In addition, a woman's longer life span means she will accrue nearly $200,000 more in medical expenses in her later years. The sobering out-of-pocket cost for healthcare through retirement (including long-term care) is $494,000 for men, but $688,000 for women. And yet, 30 percent of women between the ages of thirty and forty-four—the critical years for contributing to retirement savings—say they have not planned at all for their future.[32]

Another fact to consider is that women in two-income households face more challenges in saving for retirement than those in one-income households, according to a report from Prudential Financial and the Center for Retirement Research.[33] About 46 percent of women in two-income households are on track to save less than they need for a comfortable retirement, compared with 32 percent of married women in single-income households and 39 percent of all single women. This is in part because of a lack of planning that can occur when only one earner in a two-income household has access to a workplace retirement plan.

Longevity for women is a blessing, but it could turn into a curse if women don't plan for it financially. By acknowledging the facts and confronting them head-on, we can ensure we get to enjoy our longevity. None of this is insurmountable! I will address the solutions throughout this book; and we will take a deep dive into how to start saving, retirement planning, and investing. With planning and action, we've got this!

The Women Wealth Gap

Women's long-term financial security is not just about pay, it's about overall wealth. It's about women's net worth. What's net worth? When you subtract your liabilities (such as mortgages, credit card debt, student loans, and car loans) from your assets (for example, checking and savings accounts, investment portfolios, and real estate), you get the value of your net worth. It's your own personal balance sheet.

Women have less access to "wealth escalators"—like fringe benefits, promotions, and government benefits—that help people create wealth beyond their typical income. Five times more women live paycheck to paycheck, without any emergency savings, compared to men. This is because women get paid less than men for comparable jobs, and because women tend to enter fields that are paid less than traditionally male-dominated professions. Interruptions in careers cause women to have lower Social Security benefits, pre-tax savings opportunities in 401(k)s and health savings accounts, and interruptions in employer-paid medical insurance. As you will see as you read on, with proper planning and informed choices, there are actionable solutions to address the effects of career interruptions. Women have more options today to protect their futures, and it's up to us to know them and exercise them.

Now more than ever before, we need to start focusing on creating wealth by acknowledging the unique challenges we face due to work interruptions, longer lives, increased healthcare costs, and family care responsibilities. Planning your personal finances, saving, and investing can be effective tools in staving off long-term financial stress.

Women on Investing

Women invest less money because they *have* less money, but when they do invest, studies have shown that they are more successful investors than men.

Given the wealth gap, women must strive to make investing part of their financial strategy. Investing is essential to grow assets over time to ensure long-term financial security. Holding cash balances in savings accounts and investment accounts will not get you to the finish line, because cash has no growth potential. Typically, we women like to hoard our cash rather than invest, and that just isn't going to increase our wealth over time when interest rates are low and inflation exists. Cash loses value daily because of inflation, nibbling away at the value of your dollars. The best way to grow your money is through prudent investing and the benefits of compound growth.

Often, women are said to be risk averse. A study by the German Institute for Economic Research (DIW) concluded that because women have generally half as much to invest as men, they are compelled to be more cautious.[34] One could argue that this makes women more aware of risk, but not necessarily risk averse.

A 2016 BlackRock study reported that men as a group are more interested in investing than women, and enjoy managing their money more than women do.[35] Men put a greater priority on growing their wealth than women (35 percent versus 28 percent, respectively), and men are more likely to hold stocks, whereas women hold 71 percent of their assets in cash. Only a fraction of American women (26 percent) invest in the stock market, but women are more likely than men to participate in workplace retirement plans. When women do invest in the stock market, they do more research, trade less, and remain calmer during market upheavals.

This gender difference in investor behavior essentially comes down to women's perceptions of their financial knowledge. Women are more likely than men to say they have lower levels of financial knowledge relating to markets and investing in general, and hence they are more cautious and less likely to make trades. Women are also more focused on managing risks to financial stability over the short term, whereas men tend to focus on long-term money goals.

Focusing on growing their wealth in the long term will definitely help women to achieve financial security. Among women who have made growing their wealth a priority, 63 percent have investments, and they are twice as likely to contribute to savings and regularly invest. Although women are less engaged investors, they are more likely than men to seek professional advice for their investments and savings decisions.

The upshot is that we need to have a greater sense of urgency with respect to saving for retirement, and we need to confront our investment phobia to attain financial independence. Although holding cash has its place, if the preponderance of our investable money is in cash, it will not keep pace with inflation over time and grow enough to take us through retirement—especially in the current interest rate environment. Financial independence requires a lifetime commitment to prudent investing; it is not a one-and-done situation. It needs to be informed and intentional. We'll discuss investing more in chapter 7.

Women and Spending

A study by the Wharton business school titled "Men Buy, Women Shop" found that women tend to view shopping as a recreational activity, whereas men focus on the goal, wanting to make their purchase and be done.[36] Because of that, women are better at comparison shopping and finding good deals. A couple additional fun facts:

- Men tend to carry more debt than women. A Vanguard report found that men had borrowed an average of $10,424 to women's $8,755, a difference of about 16 percent; a 2017 study by GOBankingRates found that men had an average of $95,057 in debt compared to $31,037 for women—more than three times as much.[37]

- A report from the Center on Philanthropy found that women across all income groups are more likely to donate to charity than men—and the more money they have, the more they donate. Female-headed families earning more than $100,000 a year actually donate twice as much as men in the same income bracket.[38]

I think we can dispel the myth that women are crazy, irresponsible spenders compared to men! Time to stop buying into the myths and lean into the truth. Women have sound financial instincts, and we should not believe any stereotypes that say otherwise. Now is the time to have an intentional focus on our financial behavior and make it a priority, because time is of the essence, and small first steps can lead to game-changing results in your financial life and security.

THE UPSHOT

The female trailblazers before us cast off the chains of tradition and restriction to carve out a path for women to achieve political and financial independence. We need to continue to walk that path and take care of ourselves. We've come far, but there's still much work to be done.

In this book, I invite you to get honest about your financial situation. Are you taking steps now to prepare for your future? Would you be taken care of if something unthinkable happened? If you're choosing to stay home, have you thought about the long-term impact of that decision and how to mitigate your risks? Considering these questions takes courage and vulnerability—but it's absolutely essential. Choose to be a financial warrior, a boss, your own CEO, and the queen of your finances! This book will help you take action, become knowledgeable, get financially organized, and fight the fear. Achieving financial wellness is the ultimate self-care and expression of self-love, and only you can do that for yourself. There is no knight in shining armor to save you . . . you have to save yourself!

"How wrong is it for a woman to expect
the man to build the world she wants,
rather than to create it herself?"
—Anaïs Nin

CHAPTER 2

Women's Challenges in the Workforce

"The best way out is always through."

—Robert Frost

SOMETIMES IN LIFE, we have to push through obstacles with per-severance, passion, and belief in ourselves to arrive at success. Usually, it isn't a linear journey, and that is the beauty of it! We learn so much about ourselves when we are challenged. Often, opportunities that can change our lives present themselves unexpectedly amidst turmoil or transition. It's up to us to act on these opportunities and not be fearful of change or leaving our comfort zone.

I have always been inspired by J.K. Rowling's story. J.K. Rowling is universally known for writing the Harry Potter book series, which has been a hugely successful publishing and film enterprise. And yet, when she was down on her luck—divorced, jobless, trying to take care of a dependent child, and living on government benefits—she probably didn't think that she would someday be a world-renowned author. During this period, she took a teacher training course and wrote her book in cafés. She submitted her first Harry Potter manuscript to twelve publishing houses; all but one rejected it. Although that one publisher agreed to publish the book, they also told her to get a day job because she probably wasn't going to make much money writing for children! Now Rowling is one of the most successful authors of all time and was named the world's highest-paid author by *Forbes* in 2017 and 2019. Even with all the ups and downs in her personal and professional life, she followed her passion to write, come what may. Rowling put herself out there, challenged herself with a goal of writing a novel in less-than-ideal circumstances, and didn't give up. She followed that goal through to completion. It's a great story of a woman who overcame the obstacles.

Reinvention and achieving new milestones are possible for all of us. I read a post on LinkedIn by a woman who described her journey from unemployment to getting a full-time position as a customer engineer at Microsoft. "I applied for over 150 jobs. Doubt, fear, insecurities most definitely started to build a cloud over my head," she wrote. "But I DID NOT GIVE UP! I had FAITH that I know change will come as long as I work hard, turn my negatives into positive . . . and keep pushing through. I made a profile on Microsoft career pages. I honestly did not imagine that a recruiter from Microsoft would take a chance on me. Thank you."[1]

Each of us has ups and downs along the way, but it is how we navigate them that counts. I applied for more than eighty jobs during my reinvention period and experienced *a lot* of rejection. Employers weren't clamoring to hire a woman of a "certain age," regardless of my experience. During my very uncertain period, I had no idea how it was all going to turn out, but I knew that I had the drive, capabilities, and desire to find a career I was passionate about, and one that would be the building block for my reinvention and salvation at fifty-four years of age! We women are strong and capable, so we must remember that we can make the changes in our lives to establish our financial independence. We just have to be determined and use all the tools available.

In this chapter, we'll discuss many of the challenges facing women in and out of the workplace. Many factors conspire to make our working lives difficult and sometimes less than rewarding—but, as was true for J.K. Rowling and the customer engineer at Microsoft, there is hope for the future. My goal is to give each of you a road map to navigate these challenges and to inspire you to stay positive and hopeful. Remember that Rome wasn't built in a day, and that each small step and effort will eventually lead to a positive shift. Patience and persistence are our friends.

The Rise of Working Women

In the early twentieth century, the United States Census Bureau reported that only 20 percent of all women were "gainful workers," which was defined as working outside the home; only 5 percent of married women were in that category. Most women were not afforded significant educational opportunities at that time, and formally educated women were few and far between. Hence, these women with little education labored as domestic workers or piece workers in factories, often in unsafe and unsanitary conditions. Fewer than 2 percent of eighteen- to twenty-four-year-olds were enrolled in higher education, and only one-third of them were women. Although these educated women did not have to engage in manual labor, their choices were severely limited, and most left the workforce upon marriage.[2]

By 1930, the participation of single women in the workforce reached 50 percent, and 12 percent of married women also worked outside the home. With mass high school education becoming the norm, graduation rates rose for women. New technologies were developed that required clerical workers, and women filled those positions. Although there remained a stigma for married women working, and most women were expected to have short careers, the barriers to doing so slowly began to erode after World War II. By 1970, 50 percent of single women and 40 percent of married women were participating in the workforce.

The 1970s were a turning point for women, with attitudes about women working changing as more women attended college and became equipped for careers as opposed to just jobs. The two-income family emerged during this time, and women learned to balance family and work responsibilities. As shared in chapter 1, better workplace protections slowly emerged, access to birth control increased, and, in 1974, women could apply for credit in their own name without a male cosigner. By 1999, the labor force participation rate of women increased to 60 percent.[3]

Sadly, U.S. women's workforce participation peaked in 1999 and then plateaued. In 2020, the participation rate for women was 58 percent, and it is projected to be 55 percent by 2024.[4] Why is that? In a nutshell, the continued lack of equal opportunity, the lack of affordable childcare and paid family leave, and the challenges of managing work and family responsibilities continue to deter women's advancement.

This is a real tragedy, because workplaces, families, women, and the economy would all benefit from continued progress for women in achieving greater workforce participation. A Brookings Institution study estimated that if women had the same participation rate as men, gross domestic product would increase by 5 percent![5] Women bring new and different skills into the workplace, which enhances macroeconomic growth not only through increased productivity but also by increasing overall wage levels for both women and men. Although women's labor force participation has stalled in the United States, other major developed nations, such as Iceland, New Zealand, Norway, and Switzerland, have seen continued growth because these countries make accommodations for childcare costs and responsibilities to enable women to participate in their workforces.[6]

The Effects of COVID-19 on Women's Employment

As discussed in chapter 1, the COVID-19 pandemic caused record-high unemployment for women, along with burgeoning life-work challenges for those who remained employed (the invisible labor issues). It also led women to reassess whether they want to remain in the workforce. COVID-19 exposed the many weaknesses that were inherent in the labor market—weaknesses that had been ignored when business was good and the economy was robust.

Many women are burned out and exhausted from their ongoing work and family responsibilities, essentially working the "double shift" with very little support, a situation that was greatly exacerbated during the pandemic. Women in frontline jobs with lower wages have had to choose between their careers and providing childcare. Many professional women have attributed their exit from the workforce to non-inclusive behavior such as discrimination, pay gaps, and toxic work environments, which became more apparent during the new equal rights movement of 2020.

The 2020 She-cession

In 2020, the sudden and unexpected outbreak of the coronavirus pandemic caused about 114 million people to lose their jobs, according to the World Economic Forum.[7] The Bureau of Labor Statistics also showed that unemployment resulting from the pandemic rose more acutely for American women than men, with an even bleaker picture for women of color.[8] The COVID-19 crisis highlighted the consequences of gender and racial inequities in the workforce, with women being particularly vulnerable on several fronts to the pandemic's aftermath.

Most jobs lost due to the pandemic were in industry sectors where women's participation is concentrated, such as hospitality and leisure, education, health services, retail, and government. In the hospitality and leisure sector (bars, restaurants, hotels), women accounted for 54 percent of the job losses even though they made up only 52 percent of that sector's workforce. In the education and health services sectors (teachers and nurses), women accounted for 83 percent of the job losses while making up 77 percent of the sector's workforce. Government employment declined substantially, driven by losses in education jobs in local and state government, with women losing 63 percent of those jobs, despite representing 58 percent of the workforce. According to the McKinsey Global Institute's calculations, women's jobs were 1.8 times more vulnerable to the pandemic crisis than men's jobs.[9]

In April 2020 in the United States, women accounted for 55 percent of the job losses and yet represented only 49 percent of the overall workforce. The unemployment rate for men aged sixteen years and older was 13.3 percent in April 2020, compared to an unemployment rate of 15.7 percent for women during the same period. Job losses in April 2020 erased a decade of job gains for U.S. women. Women suffered the same effect globally, with women making up 39 percent of global employment and accounting for 54 percent of overall job losses.[10] C. Nicole Mason, president and chief executive of the Institute for Women's Policy Research, said, "I think we should go ahead and call this a 'she-cession.'"[11]

The pandemic was not the ultimate cause of these unemployment inequalities, however. Betsey Stevenson, a former chief economist at the U.S. Labor Department, said, "This pandemic has exposed some weaknesses in American society that were always there, and one of them is the incomplete transition of women into truly equal roles in the labor market."[12]

The 2021 Great Resignation and Reassessment

Not only did women lose more jobs in the pandemic, but women are also voluntarily leaving the workforce at higher rates, contributing to what is now being called the Great Resignation. Although some women are leaving to pursue better opportunities, the majority are dropping out because of the increased pressures and responsibilities of trying to manage both home and work during the pandemic. This is especially the case for women who have young children. According to the McKinsey & Company and LeanIn.Org *Women in the Workplace* 2020 study, there are several predictive factors when it comes to whether a woman might downshift or leave the workplace:[13]

- Lack of flexibility at work
- Feeling like they need to be available to work at all hours (i.e., "always on")
- Housework and caregiving burdens due to COVID-19
- Worry that their performance is being negatively judged because of caregiving responsibilities during the pandemic
- Discomfort sharing the challenges they are facing with teammates or managers
- Feeling blindsided by decisions that affect their day-to-day work
- Feeling unable to bring their whole self to work

One woman who has two children, ages seven and eleven, was quoted in the study, saying:

> I feel like I am failing at everything. I'm failing at work. I'm failing at my duties as a mom. I'm failing in every single way, because I think what we're being asked to do is nearly impossible. How can you continue to perform at the same level as in the office when you had no distractions, plus being asked to basically become a teacher for kids and everything else with online learning? I'm doing it all, but at the same time I'm feeling like I'm not doing any of it very well. I also worry that my performance is being judged because I'm caring for my children. If I step away from my virtual desk and I miss a call, are they going to wonder where I am? I feel that I need to always be on and ready to respond instantly to whatever comes in. And if that's not happening, then that's going to reflect poorly on my performance.[14]

COVID-19 hasn't caused these challenges for women; it's merely the stressor to an already untenable situation. These issues affect all women in all jobs, with each woman experiencing her own distinct challenges depending on her own unique situation. We need to get creative in formulating solutions to our particular situation, and later in the chapter we will discuss some actionable steps.

Women's Ongoing Struggle for Equality

Several factors contribute to our ongoing struggle for gender equality in our careers and pay. The upheaval from COVID-19 shone a light on the disparities that have existed, and it gave women a chance to look at their lives from a different perspective. When our routines suddenly stopped due to the pandemic, it led to some self-reflection.

Another notable quote from the McKinsey/LeanIn study came from a mother of two. "There were times when I said to my husband, 'One of us is going to have to quit our job,'" she said. "And I remember thinking, 'How come I'm the only one thinking about this, and my husband isn't?' I don't think him leaving was ever in question."[15] This unequal expectation—that she would quit her job, rather than her husband—isn't just a COVID-19 problem, and it's not unique to that woman's marriage, either. Women still face occupational gender segregation, as well as greater unpaid care responsibilities.

Gender-Specific Work

Despite all the progress that has been made over the years, the nature of work continues to be significantly gender-specific. Occupational gender segregation is prevalent in the U.S. labor market and globally. While there has been some integration in occupations over time, many remain highly dominated by either men or women. A 2020 McKinsey Global Institute Report states that men and women tend to "cluster" in different occupations in both mature and emerging economies. They estimate that 4.5 percent of women's employment is at risk in the pandemic globally, compared with 3.8 percent of men's employment, just given the industries that men and women participate in.[16]

Women have more than the average share of employment in three of the four sectors most affected by COVID-19. Compared with the aggregate share of women in global employment—39 percent—women have 54 percent of global jobs in accommodations and food service, which are among the sectors worst affected by the crisis; 43 percent of jobs in retail and wholesale trade; and 46 percent in other services, including the arts, recreation, public administration, real estate, and business administrative jobs. Women comprise 70 percent of the global health workforce, on the front lines of the pandemic response.[17] Most of these jobs are not suitable for remote working, and hence have been most at risk.

Further, few companies have been proactive in adjusting norms and expectations for employees who are challenged by multifaceted care responsibilities from the fallout of the pandemic. Less than a third of companies adjusted their performance review criteria to account for the challenges created by the pandemic, and only about half updated employees on their plans for performance reviews or their productivity expectations during COVID-19. That means many employees—especially parents and caregivers—are facing a choice between falling short of pre-pandemic expectations that may now be unrealistic (and were probably unrealistic pre-pandemic anyway) or pushing themselves to keep up an unsustainable pace. A frontline worker quoted in the 2020 McKinsey/LeanIn study said, "We are still expected to meet, if not exceed, all of our targets. The Covid-19 pandemic hasn't affected anything as far as what we're required to get done. So far, we've been able to make our goals, but there is a lot of extra stress. They tell us, 'You just need to figure it out.' Delay is not an option."[18]

At the beginning of 2020, pre-pandemic, one area of good news for women was that their participation in corporate America was trending in the right direction. This was most pronounced in senior management:

between January 2015 and January 2020, representation of women in senior-vice-president positions grew from 23 to 29 percent, and representation in the C-suite grew from 17 to 21 percent. Women remained dramatically underrepresented—particularly women of color—but the numbers were slowly improving.[19]

Despite gains for women in leadership, the "broken rung" was still a major barrier in 2019. For the sixth year in a row, women continued to lose ground at the first step up to manager. For every one hundred men promoted to manager, only eighty-five women were promoted. As a result, women remained significantly outnumbered in entry-level management at the beginning of 2020—they held just 38 percent of manager-level positions, while men held 62 percent. Women are overrepresented in support functions like administration, while men tend to be concentrated in operations, profit and loss, and research and development—all viewed as critical experiences for CEO and board-level positions. In 2020, 40 percent of human resources directors were women, compared to 17 percent of chief marketing officers and 16 percent of chief information officers.[20]

Women in senior-level positions are held to higher performance standards, and they are often the only, or one of the only, women in senior positions, according to the McKinsey *Women in the Workplace* 2020 study.[21] These senior-level women feel pressure to work more to prove themselves and always be "on it," which inevitably leads to burnout. This phenomenon predates the pandemic. Women are forced to outperform because they are frequently held to higher standards than men and can face harsher standards and criticism, especially when they are one of the "onlys."

As a woman advisor in wealth management, an industry in which only 20 percent of financial advisors are women, I completely relate to this feeling. I knew early on in my career that I absolutely had to outperform my male counterparts to be successful. If truth be told, this frustrated and angered me. However, it also inspired and motivated me to be persistent and relentless in my efforts, and ultimately it was worth it. It isn't fair, but over time, women will overcome these barriers as they continue to pursue their professional aspirations.

The Burden of Unpaid Care Responsibilities

In 1980, the now-defunct Charles of the Ritz company came out with a commercial for Enjoli perfume (no longer made), known as the "8-hour perfume for the 24-hour woman." All these years later, I still remember this commercial because it represented the ideal of the "You Can Have It All" lifestyle. It sounds ridiculous, but although women at the time were breaking into corporate America, they were still expected to keep the fires burning on the home front as well. The commercial for this perfume featured a glamorous woman wearing a business suit that morphed into a satin nightgown as she sang these lyrics:

> 'Cuz I'm a woman.
> Enjoli!
> I can bring home the bacon.
> Enjoli!
> Fry it up in a pan.
> And never let you forget you're a man.
> I can work till 5 o'clock.
> Come home and read you tickety tock.
> Tonight I'm gonna cook for the kids.
> And if its lovin' you want, I can kiss you and give you the shiverin' fits.

Yes, those are the actual lyrics. In response to this commercial, author Jill Orr wrote, "The . . . Charles of the Ritz company were trying to attach their product to the now defunct idea that it's a breeze for any woman to be a successful professional, a doting wife, an attentive mother, a gourmet cook, a meticulous homemaker, and a satin gown wearing sex kitten—all at the same time."[22] This idea was emblazoned into our minds as the gold standard for how a working woman should act, and it set women up for untold anxiety and stress in achieving unrealistic and unfair goals.

In 1980, I was twenty-two and just entering law school. My dream had always been to become a lawyer and move to New York City—in that order. I wasn't really thinking about getting married and having children at that point, as I was so incredibly determined to be an independent woman with a serious profession. Still, that Enjoli commercial helped reinforce the expectation in my mind that if I did ever get married, I would have to be both a professional and an exceptional wife and mother, as defined by the traditional standards of the fifties and sixties.

"But," you might be saying, "it's 2020 and the Enjoli commercial is long gone." Unfortunately, some of these anachronistic ideas are still hanging around. Here are a few facts to ponder: Recent economic research indicates that among married couples who work full-time, women provide 70 percent of childcare during standard working hours, which has been exacerbated by the closing of schools and day care, and by cleaning and babysitting services being curtailed during the pandemic. A May 2020 Boston Consulting Group survey reported parents in the United States nearly doubled the time they were spending on education and household tasks before the coronavirus outbreak, to fifty-nine hours per week from thirty, with mothers spending fifteen hours more on average than fathers.[23] Even before the pandemic, women with children were more likely than men to be worried about their performance reviews at work and their mental well-being, and to be sleeping fewer hours. Mothers are 1.5 times more likely than fathers to spend an additional three or more hours per day on housework and childcare.[24] Sounds like the Enjoli commercial standards from pre-1980 are still present today.

In 2017, 70 percent of mothers with children under eighteen participated in the labor force, with more than 75 percent employed full-time. Mothers were the primary or sole wage earners for 40 percent of households with children under eighteen, compared with 11 percent in 1960. Being a single parent is no longer unusual, and most children who grow up in the United States in the twenty-first century will be raised by parents who work. One in five mothers don't live with a spouse or partner. Only a minority of children will grow up in families with a full-time stay-at-home parent throughout their childhood.[25] Despite the fact that working mothers are the norm, the notion still lingers that most families have someone to help them with caregiving, and that is just not true.

When someone needs to take time away from work to provide care, it will most likely be a wife, mother, or adult daughter who will do so.

More than 11 million children younger than age five are in some form of childcare in the United States, and parents pay a significant portion of their income for this care. For single mothers, this is a particularly burdensome expense. In most states, one year of infant day care in a day care center is more expensive than a year at a public university! In many states, the cost of childcare is prohibitive.[26] Over the last twenty years, the rising cost of childcare resulted in an estimated 13 percent decline in the employment of mothers with children under age five.[27]

The Motherhood Penalty

Being a mother can be a very rewarding experience, but unfortunately it causes unintended consequences for women who work and are trying to pursue a career to create a secure financial future for themselves and their families. The "motherhood penalty" is a real thing that affects women's financial security, and it is essential for women to consider. What is the "motherhood penalty"? Essentially, it is the notion that mothers aren't able to maintain their professional footing as well as their male colleagues or women who don't have children. This idea negatively affects their earning potential. According to a report from Third Way, a national think tank, the typical mother sees her earning power drop by 4 percent for each child she has. The opposite is true for men! Upon becoming a father, men see their income rise by 6 percent.[28] This suggests that employers may still largely view men and women in traditional roles, with women as caregivers and men as breadwinners.

Motherhood has a long reach throughout women's lives, and analysis has shown that its impact on women's careers attenuates over the expanse of their lives. Children reduce labor force participation, but this effect is strongest when women are in their twenties and thirties, when their children are younger. And yet later in life, as children age, there may be counterpressures for mothers to meet the financial needs of older children. This is what happened to me. After my divorce, when

I was in my midfifties, I had to pivot and earn money to support my children's endeavors. It certainly wasn't easy, but it can be done with determination, faith in your capabilities, and, most of all, resilience.

Our Power to Effect Change

Although the outlook may be bleak at times, and it may feel discouraging that we are still fighting this fight—it's absolutely essential that we keep pushing on, for our own benefit as well as our daughters' and other young women's. We need to believe in ourselves and be committed to achieving choice and independence in our lives. There are many practical steps we can take toward equality in the workforce.

> "Life has no remote . . .
> get up and change it yourself!"
> —Mark Cooper

Companies Need to Take Steps to Change

Companies are the key players in instigating change to address the challenges that women face. When choosing a place to work, look for companies that have favorable work policies and make an effort to address a sustainable work-life balance and flexible work options. If company leaders are modeling flexibility in their lives and careers, that is an encouraging sign. Investigate if company performance review metrics are based on performance, and not when, where, or how many hours are worked. During the pandemic, many companies are offering parenting resources, mental health counseling, and paid time off for homeschooling demands. For example, Adobe has given their managers the tools to make flexible schedules for their employees the new norm.

Be informed and understand the resources that your company or a potential employer has to offer you. Sometimes these policies aren't effectively communicated, so be proactive and ask questions.

Your Voice and Your Vote

We each have a vote and a responsibility to be informed. We can't leave it to others to vote in change to benefit our lives. On a macro level, we can use our votes and voices to push some governmental policy changes, such as:

- **Twelve weeks of paid family and sick leave.** This is something we desperately need, as the United States is the only developed country in the world that doesn't have some sort of paid family leave requirement.

- **Access to affordable childcare and universal preschool.** All working parents, especially mothers, who are bearing the brunt of homeschooling and childcare, would benefit from this. According to the U.S. Census Bureau, a third of women between the ages of twenty-five and forty-four say they aren't working because of childcare demands—almost three times more than their male counterparts.[29]

- **Wage gap transparency.** Requiring companies to disclose wage information by gender, race, and ethnicity would keep companies accountable and openly demonstrate inequities and biases that need to be addressed.

- **Increasing the minimum wage to $15 an hour.** This would help many women afford to both work and pay for childcare.

- **Providing caregiver credits.** Legislating caregiver credits that would credit individuals caring for dependent relatives deemed wages for up to five years of service. As of May 28, 2021, the proposed Social Security Caregiver Credit Act of 2021 would provide this compensation for lost retirement benefits.

We must be proactive to get these changes enacted by contacting our political representatives and exercising our voice with our vote. It's a win-win for women, families, and the economy. And on a personal level, there are many things you can do to be proactive in saving for your retirement and maximizing your employer's benefits. We'll discuss these options in chapter 6.

Intentional Career Choices

I believe that purposeful and intentional actions produce better results in our lives. In my opinion, this is especially true in our career development. Do you want to control your career, or would you rather it control you? In case you are in doubt, the correct answer is that you want to be in the driver's seat of your career progression. Remember, you are the CEO of your life! Know your career mission and implement a plan to make it happen.

Consider the following deliberate actions:

1. **Crystallize your goal.** Clarify where you want to be in one year, three years, five years, or in ten years. Once you set your goal, work backward and create a step-by-step plan as to how to achieve these goals. If you change your mind along the way, as many of us do, pivot and create another strategy. You must know your mission to determine the correct path. Think of it as your personal business plan.

2. **Network and communicate with others about your career mission and goals.** Human interaction is often key to opening up new opportunities. Don't be shy about putting yourself out there and networking.

3. **Prioritize and evaluate.** Focus on tasks that get you to your end goal, and don't waste time on tasks that take you off track. Always check in with yourself to ensure that you are on track and not getting diverted or wasting time.

4. **Be purposeful with your time.** Keep to a schedule. Your personal business plan for your career should have tasks tied to a timeline so you are not just drifting aimlessly and you can achieve set goals in a timely and meaningful manner. Each step will propel you to the next step.

> "I am not lucky. You know what I am? I am smart, I am talented, I take advantage of the opportunities that come my way and I work really, really hard. Don't call me lucky. Call me a badass."
>
> —Shonda Rhimes, *Year of Yes: How to Dance It Out, Stand in the Sun and Be Your Own Person*

Confidence vs. Competence

Women are an intelligent and hardworking group. Women have earned more bachelor's degrees than men since 1982, more master's degrees than men since 1987, and more doctorate degrees than men since 2006. Among all racial/ethnic groups, women outperformed men at all degree levels in the 2015/16 academic year. For the class of 2016/17, women earned more than half of bachelor's degrees (57.3 percent), master's degrees (59.4 percent), and doctorate degrees (53.3 percent). Some very impressive statistics! And yet, according to a 2019 Harvard Business School report, women bring home less pay and have fewer C-suite positions, especially in technology and finance.[30] Department of Labor statistics state that women represent only 26 percent of U.S. workers in computer and math jobs.[31]

Women are shying away from STEM (science, technology, engineering, and mathematics) professions in particular, even when they are high achievers, because they buy into the stereotypical belief that men perform more strongly in these areas. Harvard Business School assistant professor Katherine B. Coffman says, "This weak self-confidence may hold some women back as they count themselves out of pursuing prestigious roles in professions they believe they won't excel in, despite having the skills to succeed."[32] Clearly, we need to work on our self-confidence and self-belief. In *The Confidence Code: The Science and Art of Self-Assurance—What Women Should Know*, Katty Kay and Claire Shipman discuss the distinction between competence and confidence. They state that "confidence is the purity of action produced by a mind free of doubt."[33]

According to Kay and Shipman's research, even when women are very competent, they tend to dwell on failure and mistakes more than men, and they let setbacks linger longer than men do, which undermines their confidence. Their research revealed that men tend to tilt toward overconfidence and, on average, rate their performance 30 percent better than it actually is. The authors reference a study conducted by Hewlett-Packard to figure out how to get more women into top management positions: "The authors [of the study] found 'that women working at H-P applied for promotions only when they believed they met 100 percent of the qualifications for the job. The men were happy to apply when they thought they could meet 60 percent of the job requirements.'"[34]

In other words, women feel confident only when they are perfect! We are setting impossible standards for ourselves, and this is penalizing our professional growth. Good is good enough, ladies, and it is better than perfect because "perfectionism is not striving for excellence but being impaired by it."[35] Let's focus on being good enough and daring to compete, because confidence is the characteristic that distinguishes those who imagine and dream from those who do.

Practicality vs. Passion

I have had several careers throughout my professional life. I started as a corporate securities lawyer; morphed into an investment banker; followed my passion for fashion and became an entrepreneur; realized that as much as I loved fashion, I wasn't a fan of the business of fashion; became a CFO of a different enterprise; and now I am a wealth manager. It has been a long and circuitous journey, and over the years, I was able to distill the elements of each job I enjoyed and those I did not. Being a wealth manager has allowed me to combine my interest in finance and the capital markets with my entrepreneurial spirit and my passion for helping people to achieve their financial goals. That said, along the way, I did sometimes need to take a step back and earn less, while I laid the foundation for a transition and built up experience in my profession.

The reality is that life choices need to be practical. I am not trying to quell any passions; I am just trying to keep it real. The fact is, we need to financially sustain our lives, and sometimes pursuing our passions just does not put food on the table. However, over time, we can work toward building a career that allows us to find the right balance of passion and practicality. Remember J.K. Rowling, doing whatever she needed to do to take care of herself and her child—*and* patiently working on her passion on the side until the right moment came.

We all need money to survive, but it shouldn't be the only decisive factor in job choice. There are plenty of options that can provide a decent standard of living and also allow you to be happy. You don't want to suffer from pursuing your passion professionally. It is wiser to have a solid financial foundation so that you can make small changes to get to your end goal without having the stress of financial turmoil. Most people can't quit their day job to follow their passion, at least not initially. But there may be jobs that are generally in the realm of your skills and passion, and that allow you to make a living while you continue to pursue your passion outside of your day job. For example, Toni Morrison was an editor at a publishing company for many years before she became a novelist herself. As we transition, we might need to compromise.

Ask yourself: What matters to you? What intrinsic qualities are you looking for in your work? Evaluate your core values, too, because it is significant in career satisfaction that you live your principles, and that your career affords you the opportunity to do so.

Choosing the Right Career

We all look for different qualities when it comes to our career choices. Some women seek well-paying jobs, others want a work-life balance, and still others may want to make a difference in the world or focus on their creative talents. We also want to have a supportive and inspiring work environment. In our analysis of what suits us for career choices, we need to weigh these factors with job resilience during recessions.

Recession-proof professions include medical professionals, legal professionals, accountants and auditors, IT workers, pharmacists, actuaries, veterinarians, grocery store workers, eldercare workers, mental health professionals, and social workers.

In 2020, the online community Fairygodboss compiled a list of the best careers for women by categories:[36]

- **Highest-paying careers:** The highest-paying careers are CEO, pharmacist, lawyer, computer and information systems manager, physician/surgeon, nurse practitioner, software developer, management analyst, operations research analyst, human resources manager, education administrator, marketing and sales manager, market research analysts and marketing specialist, producers and directors, physical therapist, occupational therapist, psychologist, financial analyst, medical and health services manager, post-secondary teacher, financial manager, and editor.

- **Low-stress careers for work-life balance:** Jobs identified as lower stress (although all jobs can be stressful at times) are audiologist, dental hygienist, geologist, food technologist, and librarian.

- **Careers that women rate as having overall job satisfaction:** These include program manager, product manager, sales rep, recruiter/ HR manager, and managing director.

- **Careers for those who want to make a difference:** For those who want to be impactful, some options are GED teacher, education director, roles related to the clergy, psychologist, and optometrist.

- **Careers with a creative slant:** For women who are more creative, a few possibilities are art director, industrial engineer, multimedia artist or animator, fashion designer, communications director, and public relations specialist.

STEM professions remain great career choices for women. Most of these fields are currently dominated by men, but that doesn't mean it's hard for women to break in. In fact, many companies want to hire and keep qualified women for STEM jobs. Women should not be put off from engaging in the STEM professions. Find mentors through professional associations such as the Association for Women in Science, the Society of Women Engineers, or the Association for Women in Mathematics. Explore companies with female-friendly policies, and educate yourself on how best to communicate. Not all STEM fields are dominated by men, with some fields having an equal mix of men and women or women having a higher representation—for example, accountants and auditors, registered nurses, clinical laboratory technicians, biological scientists, and database administrators.

Recession-Proof Jobs

The pandemic shone a spotlight on just how vulnerable many women's jobs were to an unexpected event or a recession. Having a profession that is resilient to recessions will ensure your financial security and peace of mind. No job is 100 percent recession-proof, but some careers are better than others in terms of not being eliminated during hard times.

What is a recession? As defined by the National Bureau of Economic Research, a recession is a significant decline in economic activity, normally visible in production, employment, and other indicators. This contraction in the economy typically occurs when there is a financial crisis, a large-scale natural disaster, the bursting of an economic bubble, an external trade shock, an adverse supply shock, or a pandemic, like COVID-19. When the United States experiences two consecutive quarters of declining gross domestic product, it's in a recession.

Keeping your job skills honed and fresh is also important for career growth during economic instability and uncertainty. Our communication, negotiation, leadership, creative-thinking, time-management, self-motivation, productivity, and networking skills are as important as our technical skills. Continually audit your skills and determine where there is room for further development of transferable skills. Stay ahead of the curve by being current with your relevant skills by reading related articles and newsletters, and by pursuing continuing education. Keep your digital presence fresh by updating LinkedIn, your website, or your social media. Network with leaders in your industry even when you are not looking for a job. Maintaining relationships and keeping your finger on the pulse of your industry can unlock future opportunities. Networking is probably the most important recession-proof job skill. In addition to networking, conducting informational interviews to learn about other industries, companies, and roles is an effective way to learn about new options without the stress of a formal interview.

Making a Career Change

If you decide that you do want to pursue a career more in line with your passions and goals (and that is also recession-proof), it's often worth it. Changing careers is never easy or immediate, especially if you have been working in a certain field for a long time. It can be intimidating and frightening to contemplate making a big change. But have faith and keep your resolve, because the right choice is there for you. The following actions can help you effectuate the change:

- **Free up your own time.** Delegate or prioritize the responsibilities you would like to handle while giving yourself time to develop outside of the workplace.

- **Embrace the change.** This space in between your current situation and a future that is still uncertain may be disconcerting, but this unsettled stage is a necessary part of the journey. As William Bridges states in his book *Transitions*, "You should not feel defensive about this apparently unproductive time-out during your transition points, for the neutral zone is meant to be a moratorium from the conventional activity of your everyday existence . . . . Only in the apparently aimless activity of your time alone, can you do the important inner business of self-transformation."[37]

- **Ask yourself why you are craving a change.** What are the short-term goals that you can achieve that will add up to your long-term goal? First things first: do a little soul-searching and ask yourself, "Why now?" "Find out what's actually driving your decision to switch careers," says certified professional career coach David Wiacek.[38]

- **Consider further education.** Pursuing further education can facilitate a pivot into a new industry and will make you a competitive candidate.

- **Create an advisory board for your career.** Lawler Kang, author of *Passion at Work*, suggests creating your own personal board of advisors with people from the industry that you are interested in who can act as mentors and give you feedback on your plans and strategy. Be proactive and seek out people who can help you get clarity in your vision and strategy, which will empower you to forge ahead.

- If you have the financial ability, **consider getting a career coach**. Coaches can explore with you what is missing in your current employment/profession, and they can help you crystallize what you are searching for.

- **Consider pursuing your passion** as a side-hustle as you build up your experience in that area enough to make a permanent change.

- **Manage your expectations.** If you have a senior position, you may have to take a step back and accept a pay cut, because your previous experience may not translate into the context of your new field. This is something I have encountered myself, but as I built up my experience and persevered, I was able to surpass my previous earning potential. It takes time.

- **Prepare financially.** Since it is possible that in the early days of your new career your income may drop slightly or even significantly, you need to have your financial house in order. Examine your expenses closely and reduce or eliminate any unnecessary spending. Separate your needs from your wants, and prioritize your long-term goals over short-term desires. Build up your savings prior to making a move so you have a cushion to get you through the transition.

Change of any kind requires planning, perseverance, patience, and resilience. But if you are strategic and intentional, it can be accomplished. Keep the faith and never give up until you reach your desired goal, because professional fulfillment will be your ultimate reward.

Advocating for Yourself

By cultivating effective negotiating skills, women can achieve greater success in their chosen profession. Often women are reluctant to negotiate forcefully for themselves for fear of being viewed as "pushy" or "aggressive." This fear is understandable, but advocating for ourselves is one of the most important things we can do for career progression.

In her book *Lean In: Women, Work, and the Will to Lead*, Sheryl Sandberg describes her negotiation with Facebook CEO Mark Zuckerberg after he offered her the position of chief operating officer. Sandberg was very eager to accept, but her husband encouraged her not to take the first offer and to negotiate fiercely for what she thought she deserved, given the duties she would be taking on. She explained to Zuckerberg that he was hiring her to run deal teams, and if she couldn't negotiate aggressively for herself, she probably wouldn't be successful at the job. She told him what she wanted, and the next day he made her a better offer.

If we don't ask, we won't get.

Women face immense social pressures when trying to advocate for themselves, in the form of the likability bias. The likability bias is the tendency to find women "less likable" when they transgress traditional gender roles and exhibit what are typically viewed as male traits.

How do we address the likability bias? How do we trade agreeableness for assertiveness without being viewed as demanding and unlikable? According to a 2016 study published in the *European Journal of Work and Organizational Psychology*, agreeable women are compensated less.[39] However, when women trade their agreeableness for assertiveness, they can be viewed as unlikable and demanding. This is the essence of the "likability bias." When a woman asserts herself, she is often called "aggressive," "ambitious," or "out for herself." When men do the same thing, they are seen as "confident" and "strong." Women end up paying a much higher cost for career growth than men do.

So how do we trade agreeableness for assertiveness without losing social standing? The following are a few tips for confronting this bias and asserting your opinions, beliefs, and ideas with confidence:

- **Stop apologizing:** This kind of language steals the focus from your accomplishments and makes your arguments personal. If you're in a position to speak up for yourself, remember that you're not asking for a personal favor. There's no need to make excuses for your request.

- **Practice being assertive:** The easiest way to do so is when the stakes are low. Get comfortable standing up for yourself over the little things, and it will gradually become second nature in other parts of your life.

- **Frame your arguments communally:** Research has found that women have an easier time negotiating when they're advocating for other people. State how your request or argument is in the best interest of the company or your department.

- **Ask for feedback:** Preemptively and regularly ask for feedback from supervisors and management. The goal is to show your employer that you want to do your job better, and then execute on it. Commit to improving, and then check back a few months later after having made those improvements.

- **Get the most out of meetings:** Men tend to talk more and make more suggestions in meetings than women do, while women are interrupted more, given less credit for their ideas, and have less overall influence. Work toward actively engaging in meetings and conversations. Don't be invisible: speak up and be heard.

In Barbara Stanny's book *Secrets of Six-Figure Women*, she lists traits of underearners, or women who undervalue their earning potential. These traits include a high tolerance for low pay, a willingness to work for free, and living in financial chaos. It breaks my to heart to know that any woman might fail to recognize her worth and continue to accept less than she deserves for her hard work and brilliant abilities.

Harvard Law School research states that deeply ingrained societal gender roles are the root cause of the gender gap in negotiated outcomes.[40] Women are expected to be accommodating and relationship-oriented, more concerned with the welfare of others than for themselves. These characteristics clash with the more assertive behaviors required for successful negotiations, and which are more in line with societal expectations for men, such as being competitive, assertive, and profit-oriented. As a result, many women are uncomfortable and reticent to strongly negotiate on their own behalf, and are fearful of a backlash in the workplace if they do so.

Research shows that 20 percent of women never negotiate. The consequences of this avoidance are shocking: according to the *Harvard Business Review* article "How Women Can Get What They Want in Negotiation," "a woman who opts not to negotiate her starting salary upon graduation will forgo an average of $7,000 the first year and will lose between $650,000 and $1 million over the course of a 45-year career."[41] So, do you want to potentially lose a great deal of money over your lifetime because you are uncomfortable negotiating or are afraid of a backlash? Not negotiating is a real economic cost that can be a game changer to your standard of living throughout your life! We simply cannot afford *not* to negotiate.

Negotiating must be the norm, *not* the exception. It is up to each of us to take responsibility for advocating and negotiating for ourselves. We need to capitalize on experience and training to reduce the gender gap in negotiating skills. According to the Harvard Law School Program on Negotiation Daily Blog *Women and Negotiation, Narrowing the Gender Gap in Negotiation*, women achieve more favorable outcomes at the bargaining table with more negotiating experience because they develop a greater sense of negotiating protocol and shed traditional gender expectations as they gain experience. That makes sense, right? The more you do it, the better you get!

Here are a few pointers for negotiation I've learned over my career:

- **Don't let a lack of power get to you.** You may not be in a managerial role or a position of power in your current position, but you can use visualization to bolster performance and outcomes at the bargaining table by thinking about times when you had power in a negotiation in other life situations with family or friends, or when you are a customer. Remember that mindset.

- **Take practical steps to boost your power.** You can improve your actual power at the bargaining table by taking a proactive approach, being prepared to make mistakes and learning from them as opposed to being deterred by them, and practicing your negotiating skills as much as possible, even with friends and family.

- **Stand up to a hard bargainer.** These are the toughest negotiators, the ones who make everyone want to succumb. Don't be intimidated. Have your facts in order, be confident, and state your case.

Here are a few tips on how to tackle salary negotiations in particular:

- **Quantify your accomplishments.** Prepare, prepare, prepare. Try to put a number on your contribution to your workplace. If it's possible to put a dollar figure to these accomplishments, do it. Research the typical salary range in your field, and reference these facts during your negotiations.

- **Bring documentation.** Don't rely on memory or your manager to simply trust that you're being underpaid. If you believe you're being paid below the market rate, you might print out salary information from similar positions and companies. If you believe you deserve a raise based on merit, you might save an email thread about your last workplace achievement.

- **Show improvement.** Here's where collected feedback about your work and your progress comes into play. Implement the feedback and improve your skills, then follow up, and be prepared to make your case.

In order for women to begin closing the gender equity gap in their professional lives—and, frankly, in all aspects of their lives—we must take responsibility for ourselves and enhance the skills needed to compete and level the playing field. Nobody is going to do it for us, and once enough of us start doing it, we can shift from viewing assertive, confident women as pushy to seeing them as strong and courageous (you know—the same way men are characterized now when they stand up for themselves) and effective negotiators. We must gather our confidence, recognize our strengths, have the courage to negotiate on our own behalf, and not give in at the slightest of pushbacks. We can be confident in our own authentic way; we don't have to mimic men. We can act like our authentic selves and still be effective negotiators!

Women's Entrepreneurship

Maybe a regular job isn't how you want to experience work in your life. More and more women are choosing entrepreneurship to escape the gender gaps in the traditional workforce altogether. In July 2020, the website Entrepreneur featured an article titled "10 Inspiring Women Entrepreneurs on Overcoming Self-Doubt and Launching Your Dream." It shared the stories of women entrepreneurs who overcame obstacles. One of them was Laura K. Inamedinova, a public relations innovator and founder of LKI Consulting. She believes that "entrepreneurship is a life philosophy where you allow yourself to explore different possibilities while being agile and reactive to new opportunities that arise." She adds that gender shouldn't play a role in your success as an entrepreneur. "What does play instead are personality traits and attitude towards business, and overcoming the inner barriers that hold women back from making it big," she says. "Young women should accept their fears and push fiercely towards their goals. Yes, it's going to be hard. You will feel stressed and anxious, but just keep going."[42]

According to a 2019 study by American Express, American women started an average of 1,817 new businesses per day between 2018 and 2019, down only slightly from the record-setting 2018 number of 1,821.[43] These women-owned businesses represented 42 percent of all American businesses—nearly 13 million—employing 9.4 million workers and generating revenues of $1.9 trillion. The report, which is based on U.S. Census Bureau data, found that from 2014 to 2019:

- The number of women-owned businesses increased 21 percent, while all businesses increased only 9 percent.
- Total employment by women-owned businesses rose 8 percent, while for all businesses the increase was far lower, at 1.8 percent.
- Total revenue for women-owned businesses also rose slightly above all businesses: 21 percent compared to 20 percent, respectively.

Over that same five-year period, the number of women who were operating side-gigs or -hustles also grew significantly. The report calls these women "sidepreneurs," and says they've grown at a rate that is nearly twice as fast as the overall growth in female entrepreneurship: 39 percent compared to 21 percent, respectively. Much of that growth comes from minority women, where sidepreneurship is two times higher than all businesses: 65 percent compared to 32 percent, respectively

Women are motivated to create their own businesses from a combination of necessity, flexibility, and opportunity. Necessity entrepreneurs can't find quality employment, so they decide to start their own businesses to increase their income. Flexibility entrepreneurs start their own businesses because workforce policies do not accommodate their caregiving responsibilities, or they desire more control over when and where they work. Opportunity entrepreneurs see possibilities in the market that they want to exploit. They are more likely to enter the market in good economic times than in bad. These businesses tend to have a higher rate of survival and better growth prospects than their necessity and flexibility counterparts. During good economic times, opportunity entrepreneurship rises.

Women entrepreneurs are facing challenges during the aftermath of the pandemic, but they can take a few steps to improve their chances of making it through the pandemic intact:

- Get your business certified as a "woman-owned small business," which is a business at least 51 percent owned by a woman. With this certification, you will qualify for certain federal contracts that aren't available to other businesses. If you are economically disadvantaged, explore the special certification for economically disadvantaged woman-owned small businesses to determine if you meet the economic requirements for support.

- Seek out service providers that specifically are looking to help women entrepreneurs. For example, Mastercard has been working to strengthen relationships with female business owners by offering expanded access to cybersecurity protections, enterprise-level market intelligence data, and mentorship and networking programs.

- Join a women-focused entrepreneurial group that can provide access to numerous resources that exist specifically for women-owned businesses. The National Association of Women Business Owners or the Small Business Administration Office of Women's Business Ownership are good places to start.

Although there are challenges to female entrepreneurship, many successful women entrepreneurs have been very creative in forming alternative paths to success for themselves. The statistics support the fact that women make better entrepreneurs than men. According to *Forbes* data provided by First Round Capital, companies with female founders perform 63 percent better than those of their male counterparts.[44] Although women entrepreneurs historically have had less access to capital, they have been successful at crowdfunding, and organizations such as the Female Founders Fund can provide investment for women entrepreneurs.

Being an entrepreneur requires persistence, a sound business plan, strategy, and funding. According to a Bank of America Business Advantage report, more than half of women entrepreneurs identified experiencing adversity, obtaining a college degree, and having a mentor as experiences that contributed to their success. When asked what the most important character trait was in terms of having the greatest impact on their business success, they identified integrity, closely followed by perseverance. Other top qualities included passion, ambition, accountability, and creativity.[45]

THE UPSHOT

Women collectively still face an uphill battle when it comes to achieving gender parity in the workforce and as business owners. We have come a long way, though; we have clarity on what is holding us back, and we have more women mentors to look to for inspiration and guidance. It is so important that we continue to push forward, exercise our vote, raise our voices, and be intentional and strategic in our career choices so as not to be vulnerable. We can't be lackadaisical; time is of the essence. If every woman commits to having confidence in herself, believing in her capabilities, creating an intentional strategy, and making decisions from self-belief rather than fear, things will change.

CHAPTER 3

The Elusive Paradox: Money and Relationships

"Wanna see how people really are?

Wait till money is involved."

—Chouhan Saahab

ALTHOUGH WOMEN ARE making some progress in achieving greater participation in the workforce and inching toward gender parity, we also have to improve our ability to talk about money in our personal relationships. These relationships are the core of our lives; and if we can't be transparent, honest, and forthright in them, our personal infrastructure will be fractured. We need to take the same intention and strategy that we implement in the professional sphere and bring it to our personal lives, too. Money is intrinsic to our personal lives, whether we like it or not; and we shouldn't feel odd, embarrassed, or fearful about addressing it head-on in our personal relationships. It doesn't need to be a confrontational topic; if we are open and honest with our loved ones and partners about our money traits and goals, our relationships will be greatly improved, and our stress levels will be reduced.

The Elephant in the Room

Although we may not think about it or want to admit it, each of us has a "money personality" that influences our interpersonal relationships. Whether it is with a spouse, partner, father, mother, sibling, or friend, money topics will surface frequently, and our reactions will define how copacetic the conversation will be. We each need to consider how our money personality defines our approach and emotional response to finances. I know we often like to think that love and affection for our significant others and family members conquers all, but often that just isn't true.

A 2019 CNBC article reported that nearly 73 percent of people have money management styles that are different from their partners.[1] Personal disagreements over finances are one of the main reasons that couples end up in divorce court. Two studies by TD Ameritrade in 2018 found that 41 percent of Gen Xers and 29 percent of baby boomers attributed the end of their marriage to money disagreements.[2] More important, if a couple is arguing about money early on in their relationship, it may be the number one predictor as to whether they will get a divorce, according to the journal *Family Relations*.[3] The upshot is that financial conflicts with our significant others are often the result of difficult decision-making processes dovetailing with different goals and values.

My experience is a superlative example of how financial conflict can cause a divorce—after more than twenty years of marriage. From the beginning, my spouse and I did not share the same approach, goals, or values when it came to money and financial decision-making. Ninety percent of our arguments were about money or children, or some combination of the two. Every financial decision was a struggle of conflicting approaches, which resulted in anger, resentment, judgment, and a slow deterioration of the love we had for each other. When we did resolve a financial decision, it usually left me feeling exhausted from the back-and-forth required to reach some agreement. These feelings seeped into other aspects of our relationship, and after a long period of struggle, we decided to divorce. We even went to a financial therapist at one point and really did try to see it from the other person's perspective, but we just couldn't sustain a compromise; our values and approach were just too different and ingrained. If we had just had an open, honest, and direct conversation about money prior to marriage, it would have allowed us to explore these issues and solve them before we got married.

The problem is that it is often difficult to discuss money with our loved ones. There never seems to be a right time to do so, and we feel uncomfortable and perhaps shallow having the money conversation. Why is this, when money impacts so many aspects of our lives and can be a deal breaker in relationships? Shouldn't we get over the phobia about money conversations, recognize them for the necessity they are, and approach them accordingly? We each have our own beliefs, values, and emotions about money that have been shaped by our individual life and family experiences. And as money is essential to living, we need to speak about our thoughts on it with candor and clarity. It is okay to talk about money with our loved ones—it doesn't mean we love them less! In fact, approaching money conversations with clarity and confidence could be the key to saving some relationships.

Your Money Personality

Ken Honda, an expert in the psychology of money and happiness, and the author of *Happy Money: The Japanese Art of Making Peace with Your Money*, has identified seven money personality types. If you can identify which types resonate with you, and understand the nuances and pitfalls of each, you can improve your relationship with money by being aware of how you think. We should all do some deep diving into learning about our money personalities; this way, we won't be blindsided by our denial when issues arise. I was in denial about my relationship with money for a long time, and I didn't want to examine how I really felt about it and its role in my life. Money controlled me, instead of me controlling the money, and to be honest, I think I was afraid of it. When I finally had to confront my fears face-to-face, I was forced to take action in order to avoid financial turmoil. It was a do-or-die moment. Once I pondered my money personality and truly came to understand what motivates me, I was able to craft a strategy to move forward. It was not easy—I still had to fight fear—but I got in touch with my inner financial spirit. It inspired me to motivate other women to confront their money fears and find the same freedom.

Here is a short summary of Honda's seven specific money personality types; most of us fall into a combination of types.[4]

1. **The Compulsive Saver:** Compulsive Savers love to hold on to their money and find safety and security in having a nest egg. They are bargain hunters, very thrifty, and always looking out for new ways to save—sometimes at the expense of reasonable enjoyments.

2. **The Compulsive Spender:** Compulsive Spenders love to spend money, often impulsively on random purchases they don't need. When they are upset, they spend to get the immediate gratification high to assuage their distress. But this is often followed by regret and buyer's remorse.

3. **The Compulsive Money-Maker:** The Compulsive Money-Makers' main focus in life is to grow their wealth through working and increasing their earnings. They associate a happy life with making more and more money, and they yearn for recognition of their financial success.

4. **The Indifferent-to-Money:** This personality type does not give a second thought to money, and it doesn't play a role in their decision-making process. In their mind, money doesn't have a role in major life decisions. Usually, the Indifferents already have a lot of money, and they have a safety net.

5. **The Saver-Splurger:** The Saver-Splurger is the Dr. Jekyll/Mr. Hyde of money personalities. They are financially savvy and careful some of the time, but without warning they will indulge in an impulsive spending spree. They vacillate between these two modes of behavior.

6. **The Gambler:** The Gambler has Money-Maker traits, because they identify with being seen as having a lot of money, but they also have Compulsive Spender tendencies, because they like to gamble and take big risks; they are spenders on steroids. They revel in their financial wins but are devastated by their losses.

7. **The Worrier:** The Worrier is always in fight-or-flight mode because they think the sky is always falling and that they will lose all their money and be destitute. They don't have confidence in their ability to grow their wealth to achieve financial freedom. Worriers are always preparing for the worst.

Our money personalities are highly influenced by our parents' and families' approaches to money. I am a combination of the Compulsive Money-Maker and the Saver-Splurger. My father is a compulsive saver, and his extreme frugality loomed over me and made me feel guilty if I ever spent any money. He inadvertently imparted to me that saving money was significantly more virtuous than spending money, or even enjoying money that you earn.

I think I also was very much influenced by my first husband's money personality, likely because I had taken time out of my career to stay at home with the children and to support his career by moving to London. He was the only wage earner, so money conversations were awkward, and we both struggled to control the money narrative. When I was not working and earning, I was the Worrier, and although I don't think I was compulsive, I was also a spender who spent money when I was unhappy and then had immediate remorse. I would buy things and then hide them from my husband. This is not a healthy way for two adult people to interact with each other. I admit I was fearful of being caught and felt guilt about my purchases (buyer's remorse!), but once I got back to earning again and had control over how I saved, invested, and spent money, I was much happier and financially healthier. These are classic characteristics of the Compulsive Money-Maker personality. I need to earn money to feel control; that's my thing—and now that I understand that this is my money modus operandi, I embrace it and it helps me in my money relationships.

What is your money personality? Figuring out your money personality will help you navigate your money relationships with others because it will help you understand your motivations and communicate your values.

The Money Languages

In 1992, Dr. Gary Chapman wrote the book *The Five Love Languages: How to Express Heartfelt Commitment to Your Mate*.[5] This book's thesis continues to resonate with people today. It is unlikely that your partner's love language is the same as yours, and when two people have different primary languages, it usually leads to disagreements and disappointment. Understanding and prioritizing each other's love languages will lead to a happier relationship. According to Dr. Chapman, the five love languages are:

1. Words of affirmation
2. Quality time
3. Physical touch
4. Acts of service
5. Receiving gifts

Just like with love languages, there are money languages driven by our money personality types. According to Dr. Kenneth Doyle, a financial psychologist and professor at the University of Minnesota, there are four basic money language profiles. Generally, we assume that most money quarrels are about a lack of money. It turns out, however, that most quarrels are not about a lack of money at all but about *how* money is spent. They are about how to use shared resources. Our money languages answer an important question: "What shapes your spending patterns?" We feel happy when we can spend money in a way that is aligned with our values, and threatened when we aren't able to do so because a partner or loved one disagrees with us. This inevitably leads to conflict. Hence, it is important to reflect on our unique money personality, which influences our money language. Here is a summary of Doyle's four money languages:[6]

1. **Drivers:** A Driver equates money with significance. Having money protects them from the fear of being incompetent, and the more money they have, the more in control and successful they feel. Drivers manifest their love for others through the good their money can produce in the lives of others. It is important to them to provide a good lifestyle for their family. Drivers rely on money to define their self-esteem and can be materialistic, often rating people's significance based on their financial status. Drivers feel a deep sense of inadequacy when they lack money; it is what defines them.

2. **Analytics:** An Analytic views money as protection from the curveballs that life throws at us. They are more focused on securing future financial stability than on enjoying the present, and they manifest their love for family by saving and planning for the future. Analytics tend to be very structured and adhere to their budget at all costs. They communicate their love by saving and planning for the future well-being and interests of their loved ones. Often, Analytics can come off as insensitive to the immediate needs of others because they find it difficult to deviate from their structured money agenda for any unplanned expenditures, and their loved ones may feel that they are less important to the Analytic than money.

3. **Amiables:** An Amiable believes money is a vehicle for them to express love and affection. Relationships and people are the focus of their financial agenda. Amiables express their love to their family and friends by sharing what they have with them, and they enjoy spending money on others. Although Amiables are kind and generous souls, they are not good at managing their money because they don't possess long-term motivations and goals. They have such a desire to help others with their financial burdens that they sometimes put themselves and their families at financial risk.

4. **Expressives:** Expressives equate money with acceptance, respect, and admiration from others. It is a connector to "desirable" people and a basis for the Expressive's relationships with these people. Expressives manifest their love by spending to cultivate acceptance. Sometimes they use their money language to cover their deep insecurities and lack of self-belief. They believe that money is a panacea.

My money language, as with my money personality, has evolved over time. I probably started off as an Amiable in my younger days, but now I believe I am a Driver, with a good helping of the Analytic. After all the financial turmoil I experienced, my goal is to provide for myself and my family and to secure our long-term financial future. I don't think money necessarily defines me, but it is a very important part of my lexicon, and I am driven by the desire for future financial security. That said, what I value most are the intangibles in life that money can't buy, but I have a healthy respect for the role money plays in my life.

It is highly likely that you and your spouse, partner, family member, or friend will have different money languages, which is not necessarily a bad thing. To be aware of your respective money personalities and languages will enable you to openly discuss your values and desires and take steps to ensure harmony in handling finances. Differences will abound. A Driver may want to send their children to the best and most expensive schools, whereas an Analytic may think a less expensive alternative is a better option when you weigh cost and quality. The goal is to have a game plan to address these issues and a strategy for communication.

Money-Proofing Your Relationship

The statistics cited earlier on how money causes stress in relationships may seem like a forbidding prognosis for married couples and partners surviving the turmoil of money relationships. However, differences often introduce balance into relationships and can be a source of strength. Let's discuss a few tips, adapted from a 2019 *Forbes* article,[7] which might help navigate these tricky relationship waters.

1. **Bring out your skeletons.** Be honest about your financial situation with your partner before making a legal commitment, regardless of how uncomfortable you may be about doing so. Begin as you intend to end, with clear and forthright communication. Talk about any outstanding debt, loans, income, investments, financial assets, and obligations. If you are already married, now is the time for a fresh start to open communication and get the facts out there. If you are entering into a second or third marriage, be clear about alimony, child support, or financial responsibilities that you have for aging parents or adult children. I recently got married for the second time, and we had a very candid conversation about all aspects of our financial situation well before we wed, even though it was occasionally uncomfortable.

2. **Establish that you are both stakeholders.** As both parties have a stake in all financial outcomes of their partnership, you both should have a vote in how your joint finances are spent. Even if there is only one earner in the family, you still both have a stake, and you still both should have a say. It is not okay for one partner to dominate the other financially.

3. **Discuss your money personalities and money languages.** First, we need to accept that each money language has benefits and blind spots, and we should be open to our partner's perspective and explore balance. Remember the golden rule to treat your partner as you would want them to treat you! Sometimes it isn't what you say but how you say it. Matt Bell, associate editor at Soundmindinvesting.com, thinks a lot of fights between spouses that seem as though they're about money aren't about [money] at all. It's actually a clash of temperaments.[8] It really comes down to how you have the financial disagreement; it's okay to complain about something your partner is doing, but it is not okay to use judgmental or condescending labels such as *irresponsible, stupid,* or *careless* to describe their behavior. Accept your partner's money language and listen to their concerns and attempt to understand them. By listening and calmly discussing concerns and different approaches, you will validate the other person's point of view, and that will facilitate coming to an agreement. Really listening to each other is very important!

4. **Don't keep secrets!** Remember how I would hide my purchases from my first husband? Well, I should not have done that; it did not help our relationship, and my duplicitous behavior did not help our situation. I should have had the courage to be open, and he should not have reacted with judgment, which is what I was always trying to avoid. Keeping secrets from your partner puts your partnership on the fast track to "marital mayhem"—I promise you this is true. *Forbes* cited a 2012 poll by CreditCards.com that found 7 percent of the U.S. population concealed financial accounts such as checking accounts, savings accounts, credit cards, and debt from their partners.[9] This is a form of financial "cheating," like secret affairs, and it will damage trust in a relationship.

5. **Set financial goals together.** Goals need to be aligned in a partnership; and any savings, investing, debt, and spending strategies must take into consideration the needs and aspirations of both partners for a successful strategy. First, both partners need to understand where they stand financially in order to establish realistic goals. Because life isn't linear and things change, people's financial expectations and priorities shift and change over time; hence, partners need to revisit their priorities regularly, regardless of where they are on the financial spectrum. Every year, partners should set aside time to revisit their priorities, whether it's debt repayment, saving for retirement, or buying a home. If you're in a single-income household, these conversations are just as essential, so that the nonworking spouse doesn't feel dependent or powerless, and the working spouse doesn't become resentful.

6. **Set a budget.** According to a Gallup poll, only 32 percent of people have a budget.[10] It may not seem very romantic or fun, but having a household budget that you both put together and adhere to may just be the thing that saves your relationship. In chapter 5, we'll discuss how to create and implement a budget and have fun doing it, as it is the most effective way to keep track of your financial life and make progress toward your financial goals. Budgeting sounds boring and tedious, but it will prevent marital turmoil when one or the other partner has no clue where their money is going. Both parties should have an equal say, and nobody should pull rank and impose their will. You can make budgeting fun. I recommend discussing your budget in a relaxed environment. You can have wine or cocktails; just don't get drunk until after you agree on the budget!

7. **Maintain a healthy amount of autonomy.** Discussing every purchase made with your partner might feel claustrophobic, and there may be times when you want to buy something that your

partner just can't endorse. Each partner can set up a discretionary account that is funded by budgeting a certain amount of cash to it monthly. This will lessen any guilt about spending on personal items like clothing, beauty treatments, sports toys, whatever! It also keeps holiday and birthday gifts a surprise, and preserves the true feeling of gift-giving. I love this idea and wish we had done something like it in my first marriage. It allows for a collaborative joint decision on the funding of monthly allowance amounts, provides freedom for each spouse to spend as they like, and holds each individual accountable to avoid overspending.

8. **Get help when you need it.** If you and your partner are at the end of your tethers and ready to call it a day because money has hijacked your partnership, consider reaching out to someone to help you work through the issues. A financial planner is one option, although this is a more quantitative, fact-based, planning approach, and it is helpful to agree on your collective goals for planning implementation to be successful. However, if the underlying discontent is an emotional problem, such as overspending, underspending, debt, or gambling, consider enlisting the services of a couple's therapist who specializes in financial therapy; such a person can help you explore the emotional elements underlying the situation. As I mentioned earlier, my first husband and I did reach out to a financial therapist, but frankly, we were too far gone at that point. Don't wait too long to seek help.

"Don't look for a rich husband. Be a rich wife."
—Ishita Majumdar

Your Partner is NOT Your Financial Plan

I am a huge Jane Austen fan; and I have read *Pride and Prejudice* many, many times. Elizabeth Bennet and Mr. Darcy are the epitome of Victorian romance and idyllic marital happiness. Elizabeth is ahead of her time in that she wants to marry for love, not for money or social stature—much to her mother's chagrin (even though she ends up with Darcy, who just happens to come from one of the richest families in England). During the 1800s, a woman had to choose a partner for financial reasons; their partner determined their financial status and comfort because women had no independent earnings unless they came from a wealthy family.

This view persisted well into the twentieth century. In the 1950s, it was still common for mothers to tell their daughters to "marry well" in order to be financially secure. Most women didn't have many educational or professional options, and even the few college-educated women of that era ultimately became housewives. Divorce wasn't as common as it is today, and women had to rely on their spouse for security in all things financial. If you were unhappy with your partner, you probably weren't so quick to end the marriage, because you didn't have many options for surviving financially on your own.

But not so today! It's not the 1950s anymore, ladies, so we need to leave that mindset far behind in the rearview window. Women have educational and professional opportunities today that enable them to be independent financial souls and CEOs of their own lives. Even if a woman chooses to step out of the workforce to raise children or care for family members, there are tools today that can be implemented to ensure her financial security down the road (we will discuss these tools in chapter 9). We should want to be equal partners with our significant others and not dependents, and any work done for the benefit of the family should be valued economically.

I get it—right now you might be thinking, *Hey, I have so much to do* (because, as I have noted elsewhere in this book, women do 75 percent of the domestic chores, not to mention the emotional labor), *why can't I just let my husband/partner handle the money?* I thought that, too, because I was too busy to deal with the "money stuff." I abdicated my responsibility to myself, and when my marriage ended, I was at a real disadvantage. I suffered from that decision—big-time. No one likes to think about their relationship ending, but I have seen this head-in-sand approach backfire on too many women. Sometimes, being smart and wise means engaging in worst-case-scenario thinking to make sure that you, your children, and those who rely on you are taken care of.

Even if you don't agree with what I am saying philosophically, the facts should persuade you that it's dangerous to rely on your partner to be your financial plan. They should also underline why you should pro-actively choose to be CEO of your life, even if you are in a relationship or have been happily married for decades.

A 2019 UBS poll found that 85 percent of women manage their household's everyday expenses, but only 23 percent of them take the lead in long-term financial planning.[11] Even though women are proac-tive with managing the everyday household finances, it is critical that they set their focus on the future and their long-term financial success.

Here's why:

REASON #1: SH!T HAPPENS, AND YOUR PARTNER MAY NOT BE AROUND FOREVER.

Death, divorce, addiction, and abuse are common scenarios that may leave you on your own. This turn of events is usually not planned or expected or wanted, and yet for many it is an unfortunate reality. So, don't wait for it to hit the fan: position yourself to have money knowledge and the tools you need to navigate choppy waters. Be the captain of your fate.

REASON #2: WOMEN LIVE LONGER THAN MEN, AND RETIRED WOMEN LIVE IN POVERTY MORE THAN MEN.

Even if you have the best partnership in the world, if your partner is a man, it is likely that you will outlive him. Most women will become the sole financial decision maker in their household at some point. Many women are single or will become single—it is a fact. Women are 80 percent more likely than men to be impoverished at age sixty-five and older, and women between the ages of seventy-five and seventy-nine are 300 percent more likely than men to be living in poverty.[12] Need I say more to convince you? Regardless of what happens, it is highly likely that at some point you will be managing your household finances, and I want you to feel confident and competent when the time comes.

REASON #3: SOMETIMES PARTNERS DON'T HAVE A CLUE ABOUT MANAGING FINANCES.

According to a 2015 study, only half of Americans over the age of fifty answered three basic financial questions—asked by economists at Wharton and George Washington University—correctly. Less than a third of Americans overall got them all correct, with 44 percent of those with a college degree getting all three right and 31 percent with some college getting them right.[13] So, despite men being expected to manage finances, your partner may not be a financial genius and you may not want to rely on him to be the steward of your financial future and security. Your partner may be unsure about their own financial goals, but may not want to admit they don't know what's up. In a situation where two people are involved, two heads are better than one, with both parties formulating the common goal and strategy. Old-fashioned gender roles still linger, but with all the facts at hand, we can see how they are damaging on the financial front.

REASON #4: MEN ARE WORSE INVESTORS THAN WOMEN.

According to a Fidelity Investments client data analysis, women outperform men by 0.4 percent when it comes to investing, which may seem like a minor difference but actually has a huge impact over time.[14] Women also save more than men, with women saving 9 percent of their paychecks compared to men's savings rate of 8.6 percent. Why are women better at investing? Because women don't focus on performance alone, and they take a long-term view of investments. Remember, trading and investing are different, and men are 35 percent more likely to make trades than women. Men tend to be overly confident in the short term, while women's patience pays off in the long run. Women tend to think about finances holistically and in relation to their life goals. Fidelity also found that when women participate in financial educational programs/webinars, it spurs them to take action to control their financial situation. Women are good at this, so seize the day and lean into your financial instincts.

WHAT ARE YOU GOING TO DO ABOUT IT?

1. **Commit.** Make a commitment to learn about money through reading, podcasts, blogs, webinars, etc., and set a personal deadline to taking one step toward a financial goal. No more excuses about not having time or interest, because this is as important as taking care of your health. If you don't take control, the stress you might suffer if you aren't prepared for life's twists and turns will certainly negatively affect your health. They are inextricably related.

2. **Communicate!** Don't avoid financial discussions. Yes, disagreements are inevitable, but use your money language to communicate and understand your partner's point of view, and to collaborate. Money can no longer be a taboo topic.

3. **Check.** Know what you own, what you owe, and the status of your accounts as an individual and with your partner.

Women as Breadwinners

The Institute for Women's Policy Research defines a female breadwinner as "a single mother who heads a household (irrespective of earnings) or a married mother who earns at least 40 percent of the couple's joint earnings."[15]

Middle-Aged, Black, and College-Educated Wives Are More Likely to Be Breadwinners (%)

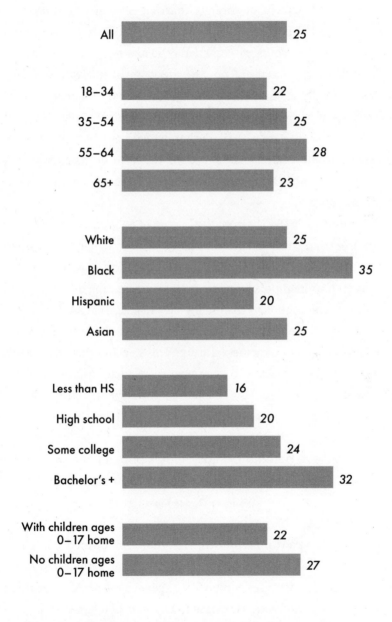

FIGURE 3.1 Demographics of Women Likely to Be Breadwinners[16]

It is interesting to note from the Institute for Family Studies survey results shown in Figure 3.1 that 28 percent of married middle-aged women in their midfifties to midsixties earn more than their spouses, compared to 22 percent of younger married women who are under twenty-five, and 25 percent of married women between thirty-five and fifty-four. Although younger women may be making greater economic gains, millennial women are not the group most likely to out-earn their partners. Racial and ethnic backgrounds also influence a woman's chances of being a primary breadwinner. Black women are most likely to make more than their husbands, with 35 percent of Black women achieving this status, compared to white or Asian women's probability, which is 10 percent lower, and Hispanic women, which is 20 percent lower.

According to 2018 data from the Bureau of Labor Statistics, 30 percent of American wives in heterosexual dual-income marriages earned more than their husbands.[17] In 1987, that number was 18 percent, so the percentage of women breadwinners is clearly increasing over time, and it is far more commonplace than many may realize. That said, there is a lot of hype out there that being the breadwinner is disastrous for women's relationships and happiness. Really? This negative narrative seems anachronistic and designed to keep women in their so-called place—unless we begin to embrace the absolute empowerment of being the primary breadwinner or a contributing earner in our relationship.

> "I believe being a breadwinner is one of the most empowering things a woman can be."
> —Vanessa Ogden Moss

As a female breadwinner myself, I feel more empowered, confident, free, and calm than I have ever been. But it is still a complicated equation, and it required a reset of my view of gender roles and a release of the idea that somebody was supposed to take care of me (i.e., I was supposed to have a partner who was my financial plan).

According to 2019 research from the Institute of Family Studies, "female breadwinners seem to face a 'happiness penalty' compared to women who earn less than their husbands."[18] The survey also found that men's happiness was marginally affected, regardless of whether they were breadwinners or not, as shown in Figure 3.2.

Family Life Satisfaction When It Comes to Who Earns More $
(%) who say "very satisfied" with their family life)

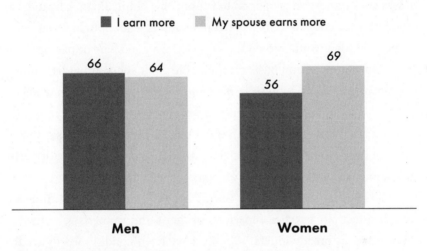

FIGURE 3.2 Family Life Satisfaction for Breadwinners[19]

Is this because we are still clinging to the centuries-old gender norms that say men should be the breadwinners and women should mind the home fires and care for the children?

A 2018 study by the Census Bureau found that when women do earn more, both husbands *and* wives are uncomfortable with it—to the point they actually lie about it![20] Women who earned more in heterosexual marriages said, on average, that they earned 1.5 percent less than they actually did; their husbands said they earned 2.9 percent more than they did. The census researchers, Marta Murray-Close and Misty L. Heggeness, concluded that people thought it was more socially desirable for men to earn more—so whether fudging the numbers was a conscious or unconscious choice, these social norms affected their answers. They called it "manning up and womaning down."

A 2017 Pew Research study also found that Americans continue to view men as the financial providers, even as women's contributions have grown over time.[21] Even though in a third of married or cohabiting couples in the United States, women bring in half or more of the earnings—a significant increase from the past—in most couples, men contribute more of the income. Approximately 71 percent of adults thought it was very important for a man to support his family financially to be a good partner, compared to 32 percent of adults who thought it was very important for a woman to do the same to be a good wife or partner.

Men put more emphasis on their role as financial providers; however, *nearly an equal number of men and women agree that a man needs to be able to provide for his family to be a good husband or partner* (72 percent and 71 percent, respectively). Only 25 percent of men say that a woman needs to be a good financial provider to be a good wife or partner, compared with 39 percent of women.

Clearly, traditional gender norms are very sticky and continue to deeply affect our psyches and views of men's and women's roles in the family and as breadwinners. Women have been conditioned by traditional narratives that have existed since the beginning of time to see the world through men's eyes. But it is time to see the world through our own lens. Money is usually considered a masculine thing, but it should be a gender-neutral thing. It is a means to an end, regardless of whether you are a woman or a man.

Whether women choose to be single or in a partnership, we need to lead the shift toward accepting women as engaged economic actors and recognizing our participation as the norm. I am not saying we need to act like men, give up the particular joys of womanhood, or totally abdicate our family responsibilities. We can both want a man to open the door for us out of politeness *and* embrace being a breadwinner. It isn't an all-or-nothing proposition, and yet traditionally it has been characterized as such. And we need to communicate this to young women and girls so that they aren't uncomfortable if they make more money than their partner. No more "womaning down."

My take is that we need to take action to empower ourselves to have financial independence and knowledge, and we need to sometimes put our financial well-being first for our own long-term survival and security; in turn, this will benefit not only ourselves but our families. We need to give ourselves permission to be successful in our own right and embrace and enjoy the freedom that comes from that. If you are in a partnership with a man who may have a fragile ego, be sure to communicate and discuss how you make the relationship work; reassess each person's roles and responsibilities in the relationship; and discuss how balance can be achieved by *each person's* contributions to the household responsibilities, both financial and otherwise. Communication is the key to changing social norms and beliefs. Starting at ground zero in your relationship is the first step.

Doing It All

What further distorts our view of women's roles and decreases our happiness as breadwinners is the fact that women still do 75 percent of all household chores and childcare. This phenomenon of expecting women to continue taking the lead on child-rearing and household duties while also earning more is the classic example of the "second shift" described by Arlie Russell Hochschild in her book aptly called *The Second Shift: Working Families and the Revolution at Home.* There is still the assumption that women need to do it all, which, quite frankly, makes no sense— all women, whether single or married or in a partnership, need to give themselves permission *not* to be Superwoman.

> "I Like Hugs. I Like Kisses. But What I Really Love
> Is Help with the Dishes."
> **—Pew Research**

According to American Sociological Association research conducted in 2020, equal sharing of household chores is directly linked to relationship satisfaction.[22] A 2007 Pew Research Center survey also found that "sharing household chores" now ranks third in importance on a list of things that contribute to successful marriages—well ahead of adequate income, good housing, common interests, and shared religious beliefs.

What Makes a Marriage Work?

(Percent saying each is very important for a successful marriage)

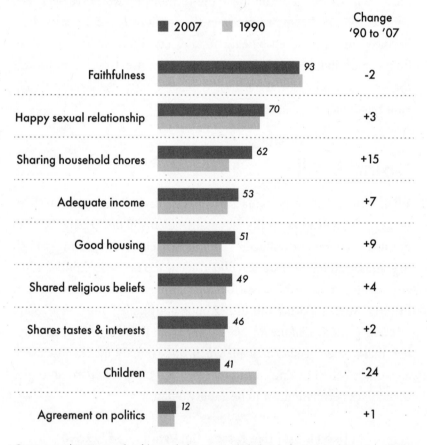

Question wording: Here is a list of things which some people think make for a successful marriage. Please tell me, for each one, whether you think it is very important, rather important, or not very important.

FIGURE 3.3 Ranking of Factors for a Successful Marriage[23]

These statistics are a cause for celebration; they indicate that we are clearly learning to value the intangibles in our relationships. That should encourage women to embrace their own economic self-realization and not worry about what people will think if they are a breadwinner. We don't need to be held back by these anachronistic notions. With open, direct, ongoing communication, we can still have flourishing relationships.

The Complexity of Financial Abuse

What Exactly Is Financial Abuse?

Financial abuse may not be as obvious as physical abuse; in fact, many women may not even be aware that it is an actual type of abuse. It is also not as black-and-white an issue as most of us may think. In most instances, we think of financial abuse in the context of a relationship with a romantic partner, such as a husband, domestic partner, or boyfriend, and often it is exactly that. But financial abuse can also occur in circumstances where parents financially abuse their children, or elderly parents are financially abused by their children, or employers and bosses prevent an employee from questioning their salary and financial rights in the workplace.

Financial abuse is essentially a form of manipulation in which money is used as a weapon to maintain power and control over another person.

What Does It Look Like?

Financial abuse is a common tactic used by people who choose to abuse through the control and isolation of their partner. Blending financial resources is frequently a tricky endeavor, and can often result in abuse by one of the parties.

Financial abuse can have many different looks. The abuser may try to control money by withholding or hiding it; giving the victim an allowance and closely watching how it is spent or demanding receipts for purchases; placing the victim's paycheck in their bank account and denying access to it; and preventing the victim from viewing or having access to bank accounts. Another tactic is to take actions that will ruin the victim's credit score, such as maxing out their credit cards without permission and not paying the credit card bills. They may keep the family in debt, even when they have resources, so that the victim thinks that there is little money available to live on.

An abuser's actions can often cross the line of legality. They may force you to file fraudulent legal financial documents, such as tax returns; or force you to give them your tax returns or confiscate joint tax returns, preventing you from having access. They may steal money, credit, property, or identity from you or your family and friends, or use funds from children's savings accounts without your permission.

Abusers may try to control your work life by forbidding you to work or limiting the hours you can work, forcing you to miss, leave, or be late to work, and persuading you to have a career that earns less than theirs. They may try to also ruin your home life by refusing to give you money to pay for necessities and shared expenses like food, clothing, transportation, or medical care and medicine. They may also be living in your home but refusing to work or contribute to the household.

—

The consequences of financial abuse are wide-ranging for women and their families. Ruined credit scores; lack of access to financial accounts; the inability to open new accounts solely in your name; sporadic employment histories that make it difficult to reenter the workforce (due to large gaps in employment history and outdated skills); and legal issues and culpability due to holdings in joint names, fraudulent tax returns, or tax liabilities incurred without your knowledge are just a few of the deleterious consequences that financial abuse can cause.

Many financial abuse victims continue to endure this treatment due to a lack of economic stability, viable options, or financial resources. Financial dependency is also a common reason that women often stay in physically abusive relationships; they believe they have no viable financial means to leave and survive.

Finding Freedom from Financial Abuse

If you are experiencing financial abuse (or any type of abuse) in your relationship, there are steps you can take immediately to extricate yourself from the situation. Create a goal to become and stay financially independent, and persistently work toward it.

GATHER AS MUCH FINANCIAL INFORMATION AS POSSIBLE.

Make sure you have copies of:

- Legal and financial documents
- Birth certificates
- Credit card statements
- Social Security numbers, and
- Health records.

SEEK HELP.

Create a network of people who can help you—and do not be afraid to ask for help. Talk to people about your situation and inquire if anyone might be able to help. If immediate family or friends are not a possibility, reach out to local domestic abuse support groups or other counselors. Most states have assistance programs to help survivors of domestic violence (financial abuse falls within this category). Find the resources offered in your state at the National Coalition Against Domestic Violence.

TALK TO A QUALIFIED FINANCIAL ADVISOR.

You can get free financial education and advice about dealing with debt, a mortgage, or credit issues from the nonprofit National Foundation for Credit Counseling (NFCC). This advisor can help you make a step-by-step plan to repair your credit and rebuild your finances.

BUILD AND MAINTAIN A SAFETY NET.

Build savings in your name only, without the knowledge of the abusive partner. Work on restoring and protecting your credit score. By freezing your credit accounts or having a credit bureau issue a fraud alert, you can make it harder for someone to open accounts in your name.

ESTABLISH YOUR OWN INCOME.

Retrain and seek employment, even if it is different from what you were doing when you left the workforce. Do not deposit your paycheck into your partner's account or a joint account.

How Can We Prevent Financial Abuse?

In an ideal world, we would never find ourselves having to take the steps listed above. Here are some proactive steps you can take to prevent financial abuse from having an impact on your relationship:

- Don't cosign with a partner who has a history of reckless financial behavior or late payments.
- Be aware and in control of household debt.
- Do not deposit your paychecks into your partner's sole account.
- Save your money (money you earn or inherit) in accounts in your name only. Contribute to and use joint accounts for joint activities and purchases only.
- Regardless of whether one spouse is employed or not, both should be knowledgeable of household finances.
- Stay employable. Even if you choose to be a stay-at-home partner, always be engaged in a manner that maintains desirable professional skills. For example, you could volunteer in the nonprofit world in some capacity that uses your professional skills.
- Do not allow a partner to convince you to take a lesser professional position with lower pay so that you make less than your partner.

- Set clear boundaries, and do not allow your partner to manipulate you into becoming totally financially dependent on them, or allow your partner to become totally financially dependent on you. Financial abuse and manipulation can work both ways.

Financial abuse may not always be obvious to the outside world, but it does exist. It can prevent the abused party from acting freely and independently, and can cause *mayhem* in their life. Hence, it is IMPERATIVE that we take responsibility for knowing the financial facts of our lives; and keep a watchful eye over financial transactions, affiliations, and relationships.

Money is power. Don't give up your power!

THE UPSHOT

Achieving financial independence becomes even more difficult when you have to negotiate your money decisions with others whose opinions might differ from yours. Knowing your money personality and your money language, and being willing to discuss them openly, will be a huge step forward. In every situation, make sure you have full and equal access to your financial life, and if you suspect that abuse may be happening—get help, immediately!

CHAPTER 4

The Blessing and the Curse: Technology

"Technology is a useful servant but
a dangerous master."

—Christian Lous Lange

WHEN I WAS a teenager in the seventies, we didn't have an answering machine. There were no VCRs, we listened to the radio and vinyl records for music, and the only catalog I ever heard about was Sears. If somebody wanted to get in touch with you, they had to call a landline and hope somebody answered. It was a simpler time, with slower communication and photo albums filled with Polaroid and Kodak pictures. Sometimes, looking back at that time, I wonder how anyone got anything done!

I will admit straight-up that I am now thoroughly attached to my cellphone; I am always checking my emails and alerts, and responding to messages. As a wealth manager, I am constantly communicating with my clients, and having a smartphone allows me to be prompt in my responses if I am not at my desk. I appreciate the ease of communication that is possible with these devices. However, my cellphone is also a distraction, and the apps, social media, and incessant advertising that target me make my phone a danger, too. In this chapter, we will discuss how technology can both help and harm women particularly, and what you can do to keep your money safe, using technology for greater financial freedom. It's important to have an understanding of the pros and cons of technology because, as you'll see in chapters 5 through 11, technology can help us take control over every aspect of our financial lives.

How Technology Affects Our Finances: The Good and the Bad

Technology is a tool, and just like any tool, it can have both positive and negative effects depending on how it's used. Let's try to get the best from technology and eliminate the bad things when it comes to our financial behavior.

The Good

Here are some of the ways that technology makes it easier for us to safely manage our financial lives:

FINANCIAL APPS

There is a plethora of apps that can help you with everything from budgeting, monitoring spending, and categorizing expenses to paying down debt, clipping coupons, and tracking receipts. These apps often have educational elements to teach you about their topic, which can make engagement less burdensome. In chapter 5, I discuss some apps that assist with budgeting. Do your research and find the right app for what you are trying to accomplish, whether it is budgeting, debt reduction, or increasing savings.

AUTOMATION

This is my favorite technological development. Technology can help us save time and set ourselves up for success in saving through automation. One of my favorite suggestions for building savings is to set up a monthly automated deposit into your savings or investment account; this takes away any possibility of procrastination, lack of commitment to savings, or competing uses for the money. It is a seamless and disciplined way to save. You can also set up auto-pay for credit cards and bills to ensure there are no late payments that will destroy your credit rating or incur penalties. Use automation to keep your finances on track, but please remember to monitor your online activity. Check your monthly statements to make sure everything is working according to plan and that there are no charges on your credit cards that don't look familiar.

PAYING BILLS

Financial institutions today offer many online banking tools that can reduce the time you spend paying bills. Take advantage of the options to pay bills or rent online to avoid mailing checks. Also, look into automatic overdraft protection that will move money from your savings to your checking account to cover potential overdrafts; this will save you the cost of fees and penalties.

INFORMATION AND EDUCATION

The internet is a great source of information and educational tools that can be used to improve your financial awareness. Take time to research issues and concepts, and to find the tools that can help you achieve financial organization and awareness so that you can make more informed decisions. This is worth your time. Remember, ignorance is not bliss!

INVESTMENT OPTIONS

Financial technology (also known as fintech) has made it easier for people to invest. There are several apps that allow you to get started with small initial investments. Platforms such as Acorns, Robinhood, and Stash allow you to set up accounts quickly and invest as little as one dollar. Fintech may level the playing field and provide greater access to investing; however, you should be cautious with these platforms (see "The Bad," below, for more on why). There are also robo-advisors that focus specifically on serving women, such as Ellevest. Ellevest is an online investment platform designed specifically for women. They work hard to educate women and help them achieve the same financial independence as men. According to their website, founder Sallie Krawcheck "realized that because the investing industry had been built and was primarily run by men, it had been built *for* men. And not for women. That's why the industry has historically kept women from fully achieving their financial goals. Sallie made it her life's mission to unleash women's financial power and help them take control of their financial futures."[1]

The Bad

Technology itself is neutral; it's not inherently good or inherently bad, but it can be used either way. Let's get into some of the risks associated with technology, so that you can become a smarter user.

OVERSPENDING

We talked about money personalities in chapter 3, and learned that some of us are disciplined with finances, while others tend to be more free-wheeling in our financial decision-making. Technology doesn't change our inherent traits, but it can make spending very easy, instant, and seductive—even for the most disciplined among us. Although technology has provided us with more convenient and automated ways to buy things, this same convenience and automation makes it more likely that we won't keep track of what we are spending. Think about all the times you shop online while watching television or speaking to someone . . . it's so easy to buy something that you don't need, and you'll most likely forget you did it until your package arrives!

Technology can provide us with access to more discounts and deals, which is a great thing; hopefully it makes us smarter shoppers. But beware of impulsive behavior and the influence of social media. CNBC reported that social media can make us spend more and save less.[2] The article cites an Allianz Life Insurance Company study that examined social media's impact on American spending habits; it found that nearly 90 percent of millennials who responded said social media created a tendency to compare their own wealth or lifestyle to that of their peers, while 71 percent of those in Generation X and 54 percent of baby boomers said the same. Sixty percent of millennials felt "inadequate" about their own life because of something they saw on social media, like flashy clothing or vacations, the study notes. As a result, 57 percent said they parted with money they hadn't planned to spend.[3]

MARKETING AUTOMATION

Then there are the ads on social media. When I am on Instagram or Facebook, it is very difficult not to be drawn in by the advertisements and promotions . . . we are only human. And as the 2020 docudrama *The Social Dilemma* pointed out, social media ads are specifically designed to draw us in; social networks make money when you click on their ads. They're designed to know your preferences and see your browsing history so that the item you had your eye on follows you around, creating a constant temptation and battle of willpower. The only way to avoid these temptations is to limit your time on social media, and limit the amount of access these apps have to your data through the settings. Educate yourself on how marketing automation works so that you can recognize when it's happening. Don't be drawn in by "limited time offers" and time-sensitive deals; these are sales ploys to make you feel a sense of urgency.

POOR INVESTMENTS

Although financial technology makes it easier to invest, the major downside is that it can lead to uninformed investment decision-making and the loss of some money, permanently. These platforms do not provide abundant research or guidance to their investors, nor do they provide sufficient diversification options. This is due to limited selections of investment choices focused primarily on equities, with no choices offered for other types of investments such as bonds, preferred stocks, or mutual funds. It is important to understand the fundamentals of what you are investing in so you understand why you are investing in it. Platforms such as Robinhood encourage day trading behavior, which, as I discuss in chapter 7, is not a recommended form of investing. Very few people make money day trading, as it is not a long-term strategy that builds consistent growth and minimizes loss of capital. Investing should not be a gamble; this is your hard-earned money, and experiencing a permanent loss isn't fun. You will never get ahead that way. With the quick movement of the financial markets and the constant influx of news, personal financial advice still makes the most sense, and you can find low-cost financial advisory services that put your interests first and can provide some financial planning. For long-term investors, an individual retirement account (IRA) or investment accounts with a mainstream financial advisor and brokerage may be a better alternative to Robinhood or an investing app. In many cases, you can open a no-minimum account and get commission-free trades on many if not most exchange-traded funds (ETFs) while still having access to all the data, charts, tools, and educational resources you need to make informed decisions.

My take is that personal advisory services are better than technological platforms that make investing almost too easy and consequently dangerous, due to often quick and uninformed decision-making.

Understanding Cybersecurity

Identity Theft and Fraud

The Federal Trade Commission (FTC) reported that it received more than 2.1 million fraud reports from consumers in 2020, with consumers losing more than $3.3 billion to fraud that year—up from the $1.8 billion that they lost in 2019. Thirty-four percent of consumers lost money due to fraud in 2020, up from 23 percent in 2019. Impostor scams, internet services, prizes, and telephone and mobile services were some of the most common ways the fraud was perpetrated.[4]

To add to that, a 2021 report by GIACT, titled "U.S. Identity Theft: The Stark Reality," revealed that in 2019 and 2020, almost of half of U.S. consumers (47 percent) experienced identity theft; one-third (37 percent) experienced "application fraud," which is the unauthorized use of one's identity to apply for an account; and one-third (38 percent) experienced "account takeover," which is unauthorized access to a consumer's existing accounts.[5] Malicious software, known as malware, is now not only affecting laptops and desktop computers but also mobile devices. New malware variants for mobile devices increased by 65 percent in 2017, with many malicious apps found in the "lifestyle" category, followed by music and audio apps, and books and reference apps. Hence, use of third-party apps (apps that are made by someone other than the manufacturer of a mobile device or its operating system—which are the majority of apps used) can infect your smartphone or tablet with malicious software.

That, coupled with all the information we share with various entities—which usually includes your name, address, phone number, credit card information, birthday, or Social Security number—put our information in harm's way due to data breaches. If *any* organization has your information, a cybercriminal may be able to access it. The United States is the number-one target for attacks, and according to a study from Juniper Research, cybercriminals will steal approximately 33 billion records in 2023! Data breaches in the United States were up 38 percent in the second quarter of 2021, compared to the first quarter of 2021![6] This is a rapidly growing problem with no end in sight. Unfortunately, I learned this lesson too late—way too late. Let me tell you about my cybersecurity nightmare.

A Personal Encounter with Fraud

On a Tuesday in April 2019, my cellphone suddenly had no service. My bill was fully paid and up-to-date, of course; I am the Fiscal Feminist, so I endeavor to be financially organized! I had a doctor's appointment in the early afternoon, and prior to walking into the office, my phone was working fine. I came out of the doctor's office a half hour later, and nothing, zilch, no phone service. I was wondering if there was a national emergency, as I knew my bill was in good standing. What to do?

I couldn't call Verizon because I had no service, so I dialed 611, hoping that would work. Luckily, I got a customer service representative, who told me that Verizon had no record of me or my phone number. How could that be? I'd had that phone number and account since 2009. Two hours later, after a long, frustrating phone call, Verizon determined that my phone number had been "ported." *What did that mean?*

Essentially, when a phone number has been "ported," a fraudster has taken over your mobile phone account and number. This allows them to use your phone number to seize control of many of your other accounts, including financial accounts. And that is exactly what happened to me.

The next thing I knew, my bank had emailed me, confirming that I had changed all my online banking log-in details, which I categorically had not done. When I tried to log in to my bank account, I was locked out! The fraudsters had taken control of my bank accounts, as though they were me, and were wiring money to outside accounts. I was unable to see what was going on and had to rely on the bank to inform me. Further, the bank questioned if I was somehow involved with the fraudsters, if I had provided them inadvertently, or intentionally, with my details. From there, it continued to spiral, with the fraudsters using my American Express card. When I discovered this at 5:30 a.m. the next morning, I swung into action to protect myself (see how in "What to Do If Your Data Is Breached," p. 97).

Why Did This Happen to ME?

This is the question most victims of fraud ask. During this very terrifying and nerve-wracking experience, I tried to figure out how someone could have gotten access to my usernames, passwords, and PINs. I felt violated, and I ultimately discovered that my personal email account had been hacked and my private information was being sold on the dark web, repeatedly. So how did I get to this point?

This debacle appears to be the result of a confluence of factors, including my own lack of caution in my cyber behavior:

- The breach could have been related to my debit card being compromised earlier in the year, in January 2019. A series of charges that far exceeded all limits appeared on my debit card within a thirty-six-hour period. My bank's fraud department did not notify me; however, I did get a call that *looked* like it was from my bank (their phone number and name popped up on my phone screen). It was not actually my bank calling—a fraudster had "spoofed" their phone number. "Spoofing" is a common method hackers use to impersonate another user on a network in order to steal data, spread malware, or bypass access controls. Although I did not give the fraudster impersonating a bank employee any personal information, they apparently already had it.
- I had a very easy password to my personal email address that did not include special symbols or capital letters, and I had been using this password for approximately nine years. To compound the problem, I used that same password for many accounts.
- I used the same PIN for multiple accounts, including my Verizon account and my bank account (just writing this I feel like a dolt!).
- I did not routinely update my personal computer at home when I got notifications to do so. I put it off and then ultimately forgot.
- I routinely used internet networks in hotels and in airports— which are totally unsecured and a hacker's delight!
- I didn't use two-step authentication when available.

How to Prevent Cybersecurity Fraud

I wish now that I had known how to prevent this breach of my data—because it's easier than we think. It only requires a little foresight and diligence to protect our assets. The punchline is this: *Don't be lazy like I was and keep everything too simple!*

- **Utilize password management tools.** I now use LastPass as my password manager generator for a low monthly fee (you can sign up for a free trial period). Most consumers have access to other helpful tools through their phones: iCloud Keychain and Samsung Pass are examples.

- **Set up two-factor authorization and alerts for as many services as possible.** The more complicated the security systems we have in place, the harder our accounts are to access.

- **Be very wary of online auto-fill settings.** If a hacker gains access to your credentials/computer, they will have the keys to the kingdom—that is what happened to me! You can prevent your browser or other applications from doing this by adjusting the settings.

- **Do not use the same email address for all things.** Create different email addresses for different activities. For example, create an email address dedicated to online shopping, one for bill payment, and one for personal emails. Do not use personal identifiers in the email address; use aliases. Consider using a "throwaway" email for subscriptions and memberships.

- **Limit the value of the information you give away to nonessential institutions.** Give as little information as possible when ordering online. For example, don't fill in your phone number and address if it is not required.

- **Limit the information that you make publicly available.** Social engineering is an ongoing concern, and people make it too easy to become familiar with their habits, movements, hobbies, and personal lives.

- **Trust but verify.** Most of us are too smart to send money to a stranger, but the moment we see a familiar number or email we forget about common sense. For example, if an email from a family member is received asking for money, give them a call or use another means to verify the request. Verify through multiple sources before taking any action when sending money or divulging information.

- **Do NOT use the Wi-Fi in a hotel or at the airport without a VPN!** These are unsecured networks, and hackers have a field day wandering around them. Pretty much any public network is unsecured, but hotel networks are particularly sketchy. A VPN is a "virtual private network." It encrypts your internet traffic in real time by disguising your online identity and hiding your location. It hides your IP address by letting the VPN network redirect it through a remote server configured by the VPN host. Do some research on the best VPNs and purchase one—it is well worth it in the long run. The cost runs about $12 per month.

What to Do If Your Data Is Breached

During this upheaval in my life, I learned that there are several things that should be done immediately once your identity has been breached:

- **Freeze your accounts.** Immediately reach out to all credit agencies, banking institutions, investment accounts, and credit card accounts, and freeze or close your accounts. I immediately closed my bank account, changed banks altogether, and froze my credit agency accounts. When you freeze your credit agency accounts, the freeze can be lifted when needed.

- **Research the scope of the problem.** Try to find out how hackers might have gained access.

- **Protect other online accounts.** Change passwords on all accounts. If your email account has been hacked, delete it and set up a new one (even if it is inconvenient!). Place fraud alerts on your existing institutions and accounts. Set up/add alerts at your financial institutions for activity like "card not present" transactions, online transactions, and transactions over a certain limit.

- **File reports with the FTC and your local police station.** Banks and credit card companies may place the burden of proof on the consumer in relation to fraud investigations. I was instructed to file a police report at my local police station, and the bank requested a copy of this report in relation to their own fraud investigation.

- **Monitor activity with vigilance.** Sign up for credit/online activity monitoring. Frequently monitor your account history. Access your detailed credit reports (free from each of the three major bureaus once a year), and reconcile information. I now pay a monthly fee to have access to all three credit bureaus' reports and activities, so I can monitor my status regularly.

I also took one further step and hired a cybersecurity company for proactive protection. They came to my home to evaluate my system. They discovered that it had been compromised, even though I had just purchased a new router. Through the email hack, my home systems had been totally infected. The company helped me to set up a new system and shared with me best practices regarding all things cybersecurity. I retain them now to essentially encrypt my home computer system, my laptop, and my phone, along with monthly monitoring of all traffic and blocking of suspicious activity before it enters my system.

There are several identity theft protection services available that are worth exploring. These services offer multilevel protection for your personal information and can add an extra layer of protection. A few to check out are Identity Guard, Aura, Identity Defense, LifeLock, Experian, IDShield, IdentityForce, and myFICO.

THE UPSHOT

Be vigilant! Cybersecurity breaches are going to continue to affect an increasing number of people. It is worth the extra time it takes to set up precautions. Please learn from my mistakes.

Technology will be with us forever, so let's give it the respect it's due and use it wisely and securely. We need to be proactive, sensible, and vigilant with it. It's a powerful source of options, information, and danger, so take it seriously! In the following chapters, technology will feature as a helpful tool for improving our financial health and wellness in many areas of our lives.

CHAPTER 5

Five Steps to Financial Freedom

"It takes as much energy to wish as it does to plan."

—Eleanor Roosevelt

PERSONAL FINANCIAL MANAGEMENT is inextricably linked to intentional self-care, all the things we do to remain holistically (physically, psychologically, emotionally, and spiritually) healthy. If we don't have a handle on our personal finances, the stress from a disorganized financial life will negatively impact us, both psychologically and physically. If we really care about ourselves, financial organization is as important as regular physical and mental health checkups. It is essential to our long-term survival and well-being!

My mantras are: "Ignorance is not bliss" and "Knowledge is power." Living in denial of your financial circumstances, hoping that somehow it will all work out, will cause recurring problems in all facets of your life. I know this for a fact. Earlier in my life, I was guilty of not having a handle on the integral facts of my financial situation, and this frequently led to fear, panic, and irresponsible financial decisions. It was easier for me to hope it would all work out in the end, which it didn't. I suffered some rough financial times by incurring debt without thinking too much about it, not budgeting because I thought I had better things to do with my time, and allowing others to control my financial destiny.

I want women to give themselves permission to be financially strategic so they can achieve a solid financial footing in both calm and turbulent times. Essentially, that is financial independence. I am encouraging you to get uncomfortable in the short term by asking the right questions to secure future calm financial waters, however life unfolds.

Let me clarify that I do not define financial independence as being able to retire at forty. I am a realist. Rather, I would like to define "financial independence" as the ability to live without financial fear during the roller-coaster ride of life because you are prepared enough to deal with life's ups and downs without going into debt, sacrificing, or skimping on necessities. Financial independence is something that you can achieve regardless of whether you're in a relationship. It is the ability to live your life as you desire within reasonable parameters, to be able to breathe. It doesn't mean you never have to work another day in your life, but it does mean you have the freedom to pivot by quitting a job you don't like, going back to school, starting a new business, or pursuing a new course in life without major upheaval. Freedom to choose, to have options. Freedom to live your best life without financial fear or liability.

The Fiscal Feminist
Top Ten Fundamentals

There are ten fundamental ideas that characterize a life of financial independence. If you embrace these mindset shifts, financial independence will always be within your grasp!

1. **Live in reality, not in denial.** Know and embrace the facts, financial and otherwise. Ignorance is NOT bliss. Don't make excuses!

2. **Remember that there's no time like the present to make a change.** You are the CEO of your life. Lead with purpose and make adjustments when the situation requires it.

3. **Be resilient.** Life is a twisted journey that requires perseverance, endurance, and patience. Stay strong in hard times—you will come out the other end victorious with commitment.

4. **Live without fear.** Worry and fear create stress and can make a bad situation worse.

5. **Practice gratitude.** Count your blessings daily; it will keep things in perspective.

6. **Set realistic goals and be consistent.** Set realistic, specific, and achievable financial goals, taking one step at a time so that you can stay committed and maintain good habits for the long term.

7. **Eliminate credit card debt.** Pay off lingering and mounting credit card debt in totality, and then pay your balance off monthly in full. Credit card debt is not your friend!

8. **Keep an emergency fund.** Make sure you have four to six months' worth of cash to cover expenses, if need be. Knowing you have funds if there is a job loss or unexpected emergency will give you peace of mind.

9. **Live within your means.** Having no credit card debt, saving for extraordinary expenses so you can pay them off immediately, and budgeting will allow you to increase your assets and have greater means.

10. **Practice intentional self-care.** It is so important that you have good nutrition, get regular sleep, have regular physical exercise, have some downtime, nurture your spirit, and have fun with the positive people in your life. Intentional self-care will reap many benefits, increase your energy, and sharpen your financial focus, too.

The Five-Step Program to Financial Freedom

Changing your mindset is the first, foundational step—but *how* do you actually achieve financial independence? This is the key question we're answering in this chapter. Not to be an alarmist, but there is an urgency to laying the foundation of your financial organization. Do not put it off another day! You wouldn't put off a lifesaving treatment, would you?

When thinking about your financial independence, you should consider both the here and now (the short term) and your retirement (the long term). The goal is to have independence in both stages. The first question you need to ask is: What do I want my lifestyle to look like? Obviously, the more minimalistic your lifestyle, the less money you need to accomplish independence. But be realistic and honest with yourself in your analysis.

In the next sections, we'll cover the Five-Step Program to Financial Freedom, my process for helping women recover and maintain their financial independence. The five steps are:

1. Create a Badass Budget
2. Eliminate Credit Card Debt
3. Maintain a Good Credit Score
4. Establish an Emergency Fund
5. Have Fun Saving

These five steps will help you take control of your financial life and establish the groundwork for financial flourishing.

Step 1: Create a Badass Budget

A budget is the bedrock of financial organization and will supply the information you need to create an organic and fluid financial strategy. Think of it as your very own mission control center that generates real-time information about your income and spending patterns.

LOVE YOURSELF!

Right about now, you might be thinking that budgeting sounds tedious and boring, and you have much better things to do with your time—things that will be much more enjoyable. WRONG! Creating a budget is a form of self-love, since it is the first step to eliminating financial stress. A budget is a leading indicator of your future financial health, and it is your road map to financial independence now and in the future. A budget provides you with a Zen state of mind so you can enjoy your life more; it is not meant to eliminate all fun from your life.

I read some inspiring stories on the YNAB website (youneedabudget.com) about real people who took the plunge and budgeted. Sometimes we need a little inspiration from another's success to take the first step. We are human, and nobody likes to take the medicine. But as Krys said in the title of her blog for the YNAB support forum, "It Hurt to Look at Our Finances: But I'm Doing It Anyway."[1] She describes her feeling of being "pursued by debt" and how her credit card float, a line of credit, and medical bills landed her and her family $20,000 in debt. They were overspending every month, and she said she "buried" her head in the sand and didn't confront the situation. This is not unusual! We all do this sometimes. I have done it—it is a human reaction. But Krys took action because she said that when she reviewed her family's finances it "Hurt. Physically," and her pain got her to budget and educate herself on how to do so. She got off the credit card float, paid off the cards, started separate funds for expenses, and is working toward contributing to an emergency fund. Krys was able to pay her debts off over a year and a half, save $18,000, and check off seven of her eight budgeting goals! Budgeting has to be intentional, and if you stick to it, it will be a game changer in your life. Budgeting can help you have a life of abundance; if you can use your resources wisely, you can create the life you want to live.

KNOW YOUR FINANCES

The first step in creating a budget is to get a picture of what your current income is and what your spending looks like now. If you don't know how you are spending your money, you won't be able to strategize about how to marshal your resources to achieve financial freedom. You need to get a clear picture of your income and a breakdown of your expenditures, both short- and long-term.

> **Tip:** A good rule of thumb is to follow the 50/30/20 Rule. Devote 50 percent of income to necessities (needs), 30 percent to discretionary items (wants), and 20 percent to paying down debt. Once you've paid down your debt, you can devote this 20 percent to saving and investing.

By doing the following, you can create the picture:

- **Determine your after-tax income.** If you receive a paycheck, you may have deductions for health/life insurance and 401(k) contributions. Add these back into your income so you can track them as expenses and savings. If you have other income from side-gigs, rental properties, or any other types of income, include the amounts after taxes and expenses.

- **Create a list of all your fixed and variable monthly expenses** (use your best estimation on the variable costs). Keep in mind that separating wants from needs can be difficult, because each person has a different definition of a "need." A gym membership may be a want for some but a need for others.

  » **Fixed costs** (ideally no more than 50 percent of income) for necessities include:
    - housing (rent, mortgage, property taxes)
    - basic utilities such as gas, electric, water, internet, and cellphone

- transportation and fuel
- groceries
- insurance (e.g., health, life, mortgage, auto)
- minimum loan payments
- childcare or other expenses that enable you to be employed

» **Variable costs** (ideally no more than 30 percent of income) for your "wants" include:
- clothing
- entertainment
- restaurants and food delivery services
- memberships to gyms, clubs, etc.
- online subscriptions
- travel and vacations
- all other costs that are not essential to your basic living needs.

» If you find it difficult collecting all variable costs, simply get a firm number on your fixed expenses and subtract that from the average of your total monthly expenses over the last couple of months. The figure that remains is an approximation of what your average variable expenses are on any given month. For example, if your fixed expenses equal $2,000/month and your average total expenses for the past few months has been $3,500, then your variable expenses account would be about $1,500.

- **Total your monthly expenses and compare them to your monthly income.** This will give you a quick snapshot of where you are. If your monthly expenses exceed your income, you are clearly living beyond your means. First, focus on reducing variable costs to save more. If that alone doesn't correct the expense overage, evaluate fixed costs and cut where you can. You may have to make some difficult decisions in the short term to align your income and expenses. This could include eating out less; reducing shopping for clothes, shoes, and beauty products and services; taking on part-time employment or picking up seasonal work; downsizing your living space; and getting more resourceful all the way around.

Tip: Your budget is an organic monitoring tool and, hence, it should be reviewed monthly to stay on track. It is not a one-and-done exercise.

MAKE BUDGETING EASY WITH APPS

There are many apps available that can make budgeting less labor-intensive; however, you can also create your own spreadsheet with several available tools. A real benefit to budgeting apps, though, is that they can track your expenditures in real time and often have alerts to keep you from overspending.

A few highly rated budgeting and saving apps (as of 2021) to consider are:

- **Mint** has been around for over a decade and is always ranked highly as a budget app. It is free, too! It automatically updates and categorizes all transactions, which gives you a real-time picture of money coming in and going out. You sync up your bank accounts, credit cards, savings, and loan accounts. It allows you to track bills, split transactions, set budgets that alert you when you are exceeding your maximum spending limit, customize categories, and set goals. It also provides free credit scores and monitoring.

- **You Need a Budget (YNAB)** is an app for very committed and detailed budgeters. It does come with a cost after a thirty-four-day free trial (either $84 a year or $11.99 per month). YNAB allows you to link accounts, but if users are uncomfortable doing this, they also have the option to manually add trans-actions. It uses the zero-based budgeting system, which is a method that "gives every dollar a job," with the goal being that your income minus your expenditures (including investments and savings) equals zero at every month's end. You allocate all your money to expenses, savings, and debt payments. If you have leftover money at the end of the month, you add it to the next month's budget or allocate it to emergency sav-ings, retirement savings, or a discretionary expense such as a vacation. Unlike other apps, YNAB only allows you to budget for the money you have and does not allow for forecasting of future dollars. Included in the cost of the app are free daily workshops on budgeting, debt, and building savings, and a library of educational resources.

- **PocketGuard** is a free app that always lets you know what is in your pocket. It will crunch the numbers to know how much "spendable" money you have after setting aside money for necessities, bills, and goals. It can help you monitor which expenses are eating up too much of the pie, and you can per-sonalize your reports with custom categories. It is user-friendly: you can see all accounts in one place after you have linked your banks, credit cards, loans, and investments. It keeps tracks of balances and your overall net worth. You can set goals to lower bills or increase savings; and it allows you to browse other financial products to discover if you can negotiate better rates on your cable, cellphone, mortgage payments, insurance, and other loans. It also has an "autosave" function that allows you to grow your savings automatically once you tell the app how much you want to save.

- **Goodbudget** is based on the envelope system, which essentially creates spending categories for each virtual envelope. This app is best for budgeters who like a simple manual style because, unlike other apps, Goodbudget does not sync bank accounts and other accounts. You manually enter account balances, cash amounts, debts, paychecks, and the financial details of every transaction you engage in. Once that is entered, you assign money toward envelopes (spending categories) and set a dollar amount. The free version limits you to ten envelopes, and one other person can be synced to it. There is also a paid Plus version with unlimited envelopes, up to five synced devices, and other features.

- **Mvelopes** is another app based on classic envelope budgeting. Although it does have a cost, it allows you to sync unlimited accounts in the basic version, and with the Premier and Plus versions, you can design a debt-reduction plan for your personal situation and receive expert guidance and feedback every three months from a finance trainer.

- **Personal Capital** is a robust free app that is a culmination of budgeting, investment monitoring, and retirement goal-tracking. You can connect checking, savings, credit cards, 401(k)s, IRAs, mortgages, and loans. You will get a general overview of where your money is going and if you're on track to meet your retirement and other long-term goals.

- **Simplifi by Quicken** answers the question: How much do you have to spend each month? It produces a personalized spending plan that will give you a real-time dollar figure showing what you have left to spend for the remainder of the month. Simplifi uses the three components of income, bills, and goals to tell you how much you can safely spend, and then monitors what you have left so you can adjust on the fly. It also sets up watchlists to monitor what you are spending in particular categories so you can limit spending by setting up targets. It is priced from $40 per year.

If you are not an app person, there are several browser-based tools for creating a budget. Check out the following resources for budgeting tools you can use immediately to get financially organized:

- **The Federal Trade Commission's budget worksheet:** The FTC offers a website to educate consumers about their money, including budgeting, credit, loans, debt, and identity theft. You can download the budgeting PDF from Consumer.gov and complete the fields.[2] This straightforward template is a good starting point for beginners.

- **Excel spreadsheet from Microsoft Office Templates:** Through Excel, Microsoft offers templates for a plethora of budgets, including a household expense budget, holiday budget planner, and event budgets. They offer templates for simple to complex budgets. Download an Excel file from Office templates.

- **Google Drive spreadsheets:** Google Drive allows you to create, upload, and share files. The Sheets app includes various budget templates, including monthly and annual. You can log in to your Google Drive account from your phone, tablet, or computer and share access with other members of your family. Sign in to Google Drive and browse all the available budgeting templates. It's that easy!

- **Mint free budgeting templates:** In addition to offering a budget app, Mint offers free budget templates. They have a general template and many templates for specific needs, including a daycare budget template, a student budget template, a college budget template, and many more options to match different lifestyles.

With all the available resources to help you jump-start budgeting, no excuses are allowed! Now is the time to take control of your money, rather than allowing your money to control you. Take the first step by creating a budget and reviewing it monthly. It will be absolutely empowering.

"It's not your salary that makes you rich;
it's your spending habits!"
—Charles A. Jaffe

Step 2: Eliminate the Enemy—Credit Card Debt

Living within your means and eliminating credit card debt have a cause-and-effect relationship. If you are consistently spending more than you make, and your expenses are greater than your income every month, you probably are using credit cards to make up the difference. Lingering credit card debt is insidious; it is the enemy of financial health and peace of mind. Credit card debt will cause you to ultimately experience anxiety, fear, and stress, as it often spirals out of control, sinking you deeper and deeper and deeper into the hole of debt. However, maintaining good credit is key to being able to thrive financially, with or without a partner. Do not rob yourself of future stability and security by not addressing lingering credit card debt immediately. After creating your badass budget and understanding how you spend your money, the most important next step is to pay down all credit card debt and make sure you are building a good credit history!

I understand that this may be a BIG ask. Being no stranger to credit card debt throughout certain periods of my life, I get that when you are struggling because you have lost a job or encountered some unexpected financial upheaval, it is very easy to rely on your credit cards and pile on the debt to get through. During my divorce proceedings, which lasted for years while I had three children in college and high school, I was often on the ropes financially as my ex-husband and I slugged it out in court. I made some difficult decisions to reduce expenses, but only after having incurred lingering debt that took years to pay down, and which negatively affected my credit score due to occasional late payments. That experience taught me that if I hadn't incurred so much debt, I would have been spared a lot of aggravation down the road. I needed to make the tough decisions to live within my means, downsize, and cut back on expenditures for my children long before I actually did so.

And then there is impulse buying! It is very easy to equate impulse purchases made with a credit card with happiness. Research has shown that "retail therapy" is a real thing—it restores a sense of control, distracts us from anxiety and sadness, and releases dopamine in the brain. But that doesn't mean it's good for you! Often, these purchases are made in the pursuit of the immediate gratification of that dopamine hit, instead of waiting for the delayed gratification of a balanced budget and a padded bank account. The ease of making the purchase is seductive, and because you are spending future money, it is less painful.

CASH VS. CREDIT

Many studies suggest that we are likely to spend more with a credit card than we would with cash. When you spend cash, you see the money leave your wallet; it is a tangible experience. But with credit card purchases, it may seem like you are not spending real money—and you are actually correct. When you use your credit card, you are not spending money but borrowing money that doesn't need to be paid back immediately.

A study conducted by Dun & Bradstreet found that people spend 12 to 18 percent more when using their credit cards rather than using cash.[3] According to a 2016 report from the Federal Reserve Bank of Boston, an average cash transaction was $22, compared to $112 for noncash transactions.[4] That is a 409 percent increase!

"Payment coupling" refers to the time difference between when you purchase an item and when you actually pay for it. According to a recent study, when you pay for something with credit cards, it is psychologically less painful because you are spending future money rather than present money—sounds like Monopoly money! A 2016 study published in the *Journal of Consumer Research* concluded that when we pay for purchases with cash, it is more "painful," but it increases the emotional attachment to the product purchased because paying with cold, hard cash was a real-time experience.[5]

CASH IS NO LONGER KING

It is true that most transactions in today's world are not made with cash. In 2018, the number of Automated Clearing House debit transactions exceeded the number of payments made by check.[6] In addition to debit and credit card usage, there are now peer-to-peer payment systems such as Venmo, which processed $31 billion in payments in the first quarter of 2020, a 48 percent increase in a year.[7] And, of course, there are mobile wallets, too. All these methods disassociate making a purchase from the feeling of actually spending your hard-earned cash. That said, there are responsible ways to use credit cards and digital payments, which I will address in this chapter.

> **Tip:** Paying down credit card debt is the first order of business. Ideally, try to pay off your entire credit card bill each month. Only making minimum payments on all credit card balances is VERY expensive and will take years and years to pay off.

NextAdvisor reported on the story of thirty-two-year-old A'Shira Nelson, founder of the Savvy Girl Money website.[8] Nelson had been carrying a $7,000 credit card balance for years. She got her first credit card in college and reliably made the minimum card payments monthly. She would max her card out and then pay it all off when she got her tax refund; then she would max out the card again. After college she incurred more debt. At twenty-eight, Nelson made the intentional decision to pay off her student loan debt and then her $7,000 credit card balance. How did she do it? She created a budget, of course, and realized she was spending money on the "craziest things." She made sacrifices. She also decided to use the debt avalanche method and paid off the credit card with the highest interest rate first, as explained below. And guess what? She paid off the $7,000 credit card debt in seven months!

Your Plan for Eliminating Credit Card Debt:

- First, take a very deep breath. This is doable with a strategy!
- Per Step 1, you have created your budget. If you still have not created a budget, go back to Step 1!
- Determine the outstanding balance and interest rate on each credit card you own.
- Consider the two popular strategies for tackling credit card debt and determine which suits your personality better and which you will be motivated to stick with. The "debt avalanche" method and the "debt snowball" method will be discussed later in this chapter. With both methods, you will continue to make minimum payments on all but one debt. The debt avalanche method focuses on the numbers, whereas the debt snowball method relies on behavior and psychology as a motivator.
- Consolidate credit card debt with consolidating loans or balance transfers.
- Seek debt counseling and debt relief.

REALLY IMPORTANT TIP: Do NOT continue to use credit cards while you are implementing this plan! Do not incur more debt. Shred them if you have to. Stop the madness!

THE DEBT AVALANCHE METHOD

The focus of the debt avalanche method is paying off the debt with the highest interest rate. You make minimum payments on all debt, and then use any remaining money to pay off the debt with the highest interest rate. Once that debt is fully paid, you use the money remaining after minimum payments to pay the *next* highest interest rate card, and so on until all balances are paid.

The debt avalanche method will save you the most money in interest payments because you get out of debt paying the least amount of interest. That said, it may take a longer time to completely pay down the first debt, and if you don't see fast progress, you may give up. This method requires discipline and tenacity. Although the progress isn't always easy to see, it will save you the most money on interest if you are consistent.

THE DEBT SNOWBALL

The debt snowball method focuses on paying off the smallest balances first. You pay all minimum payments on all credit card balances, and with the remaining funds you pay off the smallest credit card balance first. You do not focus on the interest rate but the size of the balance. Once you pay off the smallest debt, you move on to the next smallest debt and pay that off. You continue this process until all debts are paid in full.

Why use the debt snowball method if the debt avalanche method saves money? Because we humans need to be motivated to tackle something difficult and stick with it! The debt snowball method is a good way to work with your brain's dopamine reward system, using it to your advantage to help you pay off your debt instead of increasing your debt with impulse buys.

With the debt snowball method, you see quicker progress in paying debts off in full. The theory is that these quick wins will keep you motivated to stay in the strategy and to pay down all the debt. If you're lucky, your biggest debt will have the lowest interest rate, making this method a win-win!

> **Tip:** Check out the free Debt Snowball & Avalanche Payoff Calculator on the DoughRoller website.[9] You can enter all your debts and compare the payoff scenarios between the two methods.

CONSOLIDATE CREDIT CARD DEBT

Another method for eradicating credit card debt is through a credit card consolidation loan or a personal loan. A personal loan is an unsecured loan typically from $1,000 to $100,000. An unsecured loan doesn't require the borrower to use collateral as security for the lender. With an unsecured loan, the lender will approve or deny a loan by looking at the borrower's creditworthiness—their credit rating. Because an unsecured loan isn't backed by collateral, it is riskier for the lender; hence, lenders will require higher credit scores to approve the loan. Alternatively, a secured loan does require collateral to back up the loan. This can be physical property, such as a house or a car, or liquid assets such as cash. Examples of secured loans are a mortgage on a house or your car loan.

If you are overwhelmed by multiple monthly balances and payments, debt consolidation will combine these multiple payments into a single monthly payment. This will help you reorganize and perhaps pay off the debt faster. Ideally, the loan will have a lower annual percentage interest rate than your credit cards.

If you have a manageable amount of debt and your credit score is good enough to qualify for a low-interest loan, this option makes sense. For example, if you have three credit cards with interest rates ranging from 16 percent to 24 percent, you make your monthly minimum payments on time, and your credit is good, you may qualify for an unsecured loan at 7 percent. Currently, personal loan rates range from 6 percent to 36 percent. To find the best personal consolidation loans, shop around and compares rates from multiple lenders, keeping in mind that the loan with the lowest interest rate is the least expensive option and usually the best option.

> **Tip:** Check out the Make Lemonade credit card payoff calculator[10] to determine your savings from loan consolidation. Also check out Bankrate.com for personal loan calculators that can give you an idea of what your monthly payments would be with a personal loan.[11]

Pros and Cons of Credit Card Consolidation Loans

Pros:

- Fixed interest rate, monthly payments won't change
- One monthly payment
- Low interest rates for good to excellent credit
- Loan is a fixed term—a light at the end of the tunnel!

Cons:

- If you have bad credit, it may be difficult to get a lower rate.
- Some online loans may have an origination fee just to process your application.
- If you don't have a plan to prevent running up debt again in the future while you are paying the personal loan off, you are negating most of the benefit of the strategy.

Please remember that a consolidation loan isn't a panacea for all your debt problems. It doesn't address the underlying excessive spending habits that created the debt to begin with. It is imperative that your spending habits be addressed and curtailed to be within your budget. Look in the mirror, be honest with yourself, and promise you will love yourself more by not incurring further credit card debt!

BALANCE TRANSFER CARD

Another option to help eliminate credit card debt is to transfer credit card balances to a balance transfer card with 0 percent interest for a fixed period, usually between six and twenty-one months. You can transfer your high-interest credit card balance to this card, eliminating the interest rate burden.

When choosing a balance transfer card, be aware there most likely will be a balance transfer fee of 3 to 5 percent; some cards charge no transfer fee, but these are getting more difficult to find. Look for the length of the annual percentage rate (or APR) period—you want a long period of 0 percent interest, fifteen months or more if possible. Once the introductory 0 percent period is finished, the interest rate will shoot up and you will start paying interest again on the balance.

You will need good to excellent credit to qualify for a balance transfer card with an introductory 0 percent interest rate. Depending on the credit bureau, good credit scores start at 670.

CREDIT CARD DELINQUENCY—LATE PAYMENTS

Credit card delinquency is measured by how many days late your payments are. This dictates when credit card companies report to the credit bureaus how late your payments are, and how damaging it is to your credit score.

Some months you may feel financially overwhelmed and either forget to make your minimum payment or just decide not to because you don't want to spend your scarce money on the payment. According to a 2019 CNBC personal finance feature, a LendingTree study found that women were more likely to say that they didn't pay their credit card bills in full at least one time in six months, whereas men were found to usually pay their bills in full monthly.[12] When you are carrying credit card debt and are overwhelmed, it is easy to be late on payments—because you may be juggling too many payments. I know this from personal experience. The detrimental effects of late payments linger for years on your credit report. According to Experian, a major credit bureau, late payments stay on your credit report for up to seven years and will impact your credit score during that entire period.[13] One late credit card payment can cause seven years of hassle. I know because I had late payments, and they did stay on my credit report for seven years!

Any late payments over sixty days will hit your credit score very hard, and if payments are 120 days late or more, your account may be turned over to collections. Those incessant collections calls will increase over time, and your credit score will continue to tank. Getting those relentless calls is beyond stressful. Once your credit card account becomes 180 days delinquent, the credit card company is required to declare your account as charged-off. This is a big hit to your credit score and very detrimental to your creditworthiness.

Let's explore some solutions to serious delinquency.

First, reach out to your credit card companies and ask what they can do for you; many are prepared to work with you on individual solutions. Many credit card issuers have off-menu solutions for those who are struggling financially. Ask direct questions about short-term hardship programs, and be honest about your circumstances.

If your accounts are already seriously delinquent, reach out to a nonprofit credit counseling agency, such as the National Foundation for Credit Counseling. The NFCC is the largest nonprofit financial counseling organization in the United States, and its mission is to educate consumers about being financially responsible and help them climb out of debt when things are bleak and hope is lost. The NFCC offers low-cost debt counseling, so there is a fee, but no fees are payable until services are rendered. Typical charges include a setup fee of $50 or less, and possible monthly fees of $25, with fees being waived in some cases of extreme financial hardship. Debt counseling can be very effective in clearing intractable debt.

The U.S. Trustee Program is another option, offered through the U.S. Department of Justice, and features a search tool to help consumers find a credit counselor. Your state's attorney general's office or local consumer protection agency may also have recommendations for credit counseling.

THE BENEFITS OF RESPONSIBLE CREDIT CARD USE

It may come as a surprise, but responsible credit card spending can be a very good thing! Although overspending is a danger, if you can stick to your budget and pay your card off in *full* every month, then using a credit card has many benefits.

The biggest benefit to responsible credit card use is increasing your credit score, which can help you later when you want to get a loan for a new car or house. That is a big perk!

Credit cards have a number of other benefits, too. For example, credit cards offer fraud protections, and with the 0 percent liability that most cards offer, they are safer to use than cash and debit cards. If you have an issue with a purchase or somebody fraudulently uses your card, credit card companies will provide consumer protections. With some businesses not accepting cash anymore, credit card use may be a good option. Credit cards also have point reward systems, which you can use for purchases or paying off your card later, as well as for perks like travel insurance, cellphone insurance, discounts, and more. They can be a powerful tool if used wisely.

> **Tip:** Think of your credit card as cash, and only use it when you know you can pay it back in full every month. PERIOD. If you can do that, then you are good to go.

Step 3: Maintain a Good Credit Rating

Why is your credit score so very important? Because you get many financial rewards for having a good one! Your credit score follows you and affects many financial decisions and outcomes. It will impact buying a house or a car, and getting insurance. Keeping your eye on the prize of a good credit rating is essential to sound financial health and organization.

Some of the benefits of good credit are:

- You will qualify for better interest rates and pay lower finance charges, which means you will be able to pay the debt off faster.
- You will have more negotiating power when qualifying for a new loan (personal loans, car loans, and mortgages, to name a few), which may allow you to take advantage of cost-saving offers; if you have a low credit score, you are at the mercy of lenders on loan terms.

- Your borrowing capacity is based on your income and credit score. Banks will lend you more if you have a solid history of timely payments.
- If you rent, you will have an easier approval process with your landlord. A bad credit score, outstanding rent balances, or a previous eviction can seriously hinder your ability to rent an apartment or house.
- You will pay less for car insurance. Auto insurers review your credit report and insurance history to establish your insurance risk score. If you have a low credit score, they will charge you higher premiums.
- You may be able to get a cellphone contract without paying a security deposit. If you have a low credit rating, cellphone providers may not give you a contract and you will have to use the pay-as-you go route, which is more expensive.
- You may not have to pay utility security deposits when you establish utility services in your name.
- You get to be really proud of yourself for working diligently to maintain a good credit score!

This is an effort worth making! Paying all debts on time is the primary way to maintain a good credit rating.

Reminder: Commingling debt with a spouse or another person can affect your credit rating!

COMMINGLING DEBT

Once you commingle debt with a spouse, it is almost impossible to de-mingle it! Even if you get divorced, a creditor will not recognize the court's assignment of debt responsibility because lenders are not bound by your divorce agreement, since they are not a party to it. This means that just because you and your soon-to-be ex-spouse agree that one of you will pay the Visa while the other pays the Mastercard, it means nothing to the lender. If credit cards are held jointly, then whether you are divorced or not, the lender can come after you for repayment.

Maintaining separate credit when you're married has nothing to do with trust, whether you love the person, whether you think the marriage will last, or whether you are coldhearted; it is just practical. Beware, though, that in the few community property states (Alaska, Arizona, California, Idaho, Louisiana, Nevada, New Mexico, Washington, Wisconsin, and Texas), you will both be liable for credit card debt even if only one of you applied for the card. Community property states believe that you both probably benefited from the debt, hence you should both be liable. If you live in a community property state, my recommendation is to review credit card bills monthly and monitor charges incurred by both parties so at least you know where you stand debt-wise. Don't delegate payment to your partner and have no knowledge of balances.

Bad credit will follow you and have many detrimental ripple effects in your life, so do not feel uncomfortable having separate credit from your spouse or monitoring credit closely if you live in a community property state.

HOW CAN I MONITOR MY CREDIT RATING?

Your credit report is a summary of your borrowing and repayment history and all activity, such as new accounts, closed accounts, unpaid bills, late bills, collections, and bankruptcies. Negative facts on your credit report remain there for seven years before falling away.

The three main credit bureaus are Equifax, Experian, and TransUnion. By law, you are entitled to one free credit report every year from each of the three bureaus. A good practice is to order a report from a different credit bureau every four months, so that you can review your score throughout the year. You can also order your free reports through annualcreditreport.com. In addition, there are several credit monitoring services that allow you to keep an eye on your credit score and credit report. Some of them have fees, and some are free. Credit Karma is free, and you can check it to get your credit score.

Checking your credit score does not lower your credit score; this is called a soft inquiry. A soft inquiry occurs when you check your own credit score or when a lender checks your score for preapproval of an offer. A hard inquiry occurs when a lender pulls your credit when you apply for a loan or credit card, and it can reduce your credit score. Each hard inquiry stays on your credit report for up to two years, but it shouldn't affect your score for more than a few months.

Keeping a watchful eye on your credit score should be an ongoing exercise, just like monitoring your budget and your spending. It is critical that you ascertain credit reports are correct, identify any potentially fraudulent activity, and respond before it damages your credit. Dispute all inaccurate information.

Step 4: Establish an Emergency Fund

According to a 2019 report from the AARP Public Policy Institute, despite a prolonged period of economic growth and record low unemployment in the United States, a significant percentage of American households are one unexpected event away from financial distress.[14] Shortly after this study was released, we experienced the COVID-19 pandemic, which wreaked economic havoc and caused high unemployment. Having an emergency savings fund would have helped many people ride out the upheaval of the pandemic.

The report states that:

- 53 percent of U.S. households have no emergency savings account.
- The emergency savings challenge is widespread and includes 51 percent of people over the age of fifty and people at every income level.
- Household income alone does not determine whether someone has an emergency savings account.

In May 2020, the Federal Reserve reported that approximately 40 percent of American households would struggle to cope with an unexpected $400 expense.[15] And according to research from the Pew Charitable Trusts, 33 percent of American families say they have no money that they would call savings, including 10 percent who have incomes of $100,000 a year. "Americans have very little saved in preparation for financial shocks, putting many families at risk," said Clinton Key, a researcher for Pew's financial security and mobility project. "Our analysis shows that most families will be faced with a significant and possibly destabilizing unexpected expense at some point. It's critical for families to build emergency savings."[16]

The hard-core reality is that a car repair, a medical bill, a loss of a job, or a reduction in hours could disrupt many households' finances and well-being.

WHY IS AN EMERGENCY FUND SO IMPORTANT?

The old saying that "cash is king" is meaningful in many ways, but it really resonates when we talk about the need for household liquidity.

The root of liquidity is the word *liquid,* which the Oxford Dictionary tells us means "a substance that flows freely but is of constant volume, having a consistency like that of water or oil." A liquid asset in financial terms is defined as "cash on hand, or an asset that can be readily converted to cash." Cash is the most liquid asset, while tangible assets such as real estate or fine art are considered illiquid. The Federal Reserve considers liquid savings to include balances in checking and savings accounts; cash; prepaid cards; and stocks, bonds, and mutual funds (because these can be readily sold and become cash quickly).

Emergency savings are a form of liquidity; that is, cash on hand. These funds give you the ability to quickly deploy funds to deal with an unexpected emergency or event. The rule of thumb is to have three to six months of living expenses in an emergency fund savings account, to stave off disaster in the case of an unforeseen circumstance. The three-month minimum is related to the average term of unemployment due to job loss. But clearly, a six-month fund is preferable, especially when you consider the possibility of long-term unexpected medical events and the fallout from the recent pandemic. My recommendation is to keep this money in cash. Some people may argue that, with low interest rates, having six months of cash to cover expenses parked in a savings account and not generating significant return is not optimal. But I disagree. If you have this emergency money invested in the market and there is a market dip at the time when you need it, you experience a permanent loss of capital, which defeats the purpose of the safety net. Yes, when the market is up, it sounds like a good option to invest in this fund, but as I explain in chapter 7, volatility in the market exists, which causes ups and downs. My recommendation is to keep the six months of emergency fund savings in cash in your savings account.

> **Tip:** Regardless of your income, it is essential to have six months of living expenses saved in an emergency savings fund. Think of it as your life raft!

Evidence suggests that having liquid savings and an emergency fund keeps household finances on track, even if there is an unforeseen event. Here's why:

- Having an emergency fund shows that you have a strategic mind-set, and that you aren't throwing caution to the wind and hoping it will all work out in the event something unexpectedly goes awry.
- In addition to being a buffer against financial hardship in the short term, emergency savings contribute to long-term financial security. Individuals with savings are less likely to incur unsecured debt and other high-cost financial bailouts that often result in long-term indebtedness or bankruptcy.
- Emergency savings protect the longevity of retirement assets. Frequently, when there is an emergency, people will rely on

their retirement accounts to fund the cost by borrowing from them or taking early withdrawals. According to a 2020 survey by the Transamerica Center for Retirement Studies, 49 percent of employees expect that they will use their retirement savings for a nonretirement expense, with 21 percent of loans from retirement accounts being taken to cover a financial emergency.[17] Using retirement savings for rainy-day expenses can result in high costs in the form of lost interest and earnings, taxes, and other financial penalties. Altogether, the effect of early withdrawals, and, to a lesser extent, loans from 401(k) plans and IRAs, is about 20 percent lower retirement savings overall.

Tip: Don't "borrow" from your retirement. Borrowing against retirement accounts to fund emergency situations is actually stealing from your future!

There is a great article on the HerMoney website that describes how having emergency funds saved seven women when emergencies arose in their lives.[18] Each has a compelling story about how their emergency funds helped them get through uncertain times, including caring for a disabled son, covering an unexpected tax bill, recovering financially from a divorce, and saving the family from an apartment crisis. Valerie, one of the women interviewed, said her emergency savings enabled her to be with her father when he passed away. These are real women who experienced compelling emergencies; their emergency funds helped them navigate situations that would have been much worse if they didn't have an emergency fund cushion.

EMERGENCY FUNDS ARE FOR EVERYONE

Regardless of income, an emergency fund is essential. We all have unexpected events!

Having an emergency savings account is not necessarily dependent on income. One in four Americans earning over $150,000 per year has no emergency savings, while many low-income families are able to save with budgeting and planning.[19]

There's an old adage that says the more money you make, the more money you spend. It's absolutely correct, and hence, although one would think people who have higher wages would save more, that is not often true because they spend more. According to a 2021 report by the Center on Budget and Policy Priorities, pre-pandemic, approximately one in four families (26 percent) at all income levels will have at least three disruptions in a year.[20] Annually, a significant drop in income affects 17.6 percent of families, 6.2 percent of families experience an involuntary job loss, and 5.1 percent have a health-related incident. A 2020 Pew Research study found that 43 percent of adults in the United States, or someone in their household, lost their job or experienced a pay cut due to the pandemic.[21] Among lower-income earners, 52 percent of adults or someone in their household lost jobs. Twenty-three percent of lower-income households said they have a rainy-day fund, compared to 48 percent of middle-income adults.

Fact: Low-income families with savings are more financially resilient than middle-income families without savings.

"Too many people spend money they earned . . .
to buy things they don't want . . . to impress
people that they don't like."
—Will Rogers

HOW TO MAKE YOUR EMERGENCY FUND A REALITY

- **Prioritize having an emergency fund!** Exercise discipline and make this a priority before spending on discretionary items. Ask yourself: Is buying something you don't actually need worth *not* having an emergency fund in the event something unanticipated occurs? Is putting yourself and your family at risk worthy of this discretionary purchase?

- **Automate your savings.** Set up an automated amount of money to be transferred to your savings account every week or month, or per paycheck, until you reach the goal of six months' coverage. This way, you don't have to do anything; the money is automatically transferred. Check out AmericaSaves.org for tips on how to make a plan for automated savings.

- **Start with small short-term goals.** Better to start with an achievable goal, such as $20 per week, than to set a goal you will find difficult to maintain, such as $500 per month, because it is too egregious. Get used to saving and feeling the benefits thereof. Once you reach your short-term goal of establishing your emergency fund, and you enjoy seeing your bank account grow, you can set a new goal for saving beyond the emergency fund.

- **Stay the course!** Do not give up on this goal, because it could very well save you from a ruinous situation. Families with more savings have financial health and experience less hardship than families with little or no savings.

Establishing an emergency fund is one of the most important things that you can do for yourself. It will give you peace of mind and a safety net. When you are experiencing an unexpected situation, it will give you space to think and deal with the problem at hand, rather than worrying about how you are going to keep a roof over your head and pay for necessities while navigating a challenging situation.

I promise you that once you have your emergency fund established, you will feel safer, calmer, and have more freedom of choice in reacting to unexpected turmoil.

Step 5: Have Fun Saving!

DON'T THINK OF IT AS SAVING. THINK OF IT AS FUN!

Saving doesn't mean not spending on anything; it means prioritizing your financial goals and making saving a top goal. Often saving money feels elusive. We wonder, *Where did all the money go? What did we spend it on, and how is it we have no savings?*

Stop living in denial, thinking that you will start saving one day when all the stars line up. You must put a plan in place now and get serious! There is no time like the present. Otherwise, time will pass, and you will continue not to save and fall farther and farther behind.

By now, if you've been following each step, you have determined your budget, paid down credit card debt, started paying bills in full every month, and established an emergency savings fund. Once you've done that, you can start saving and investing with excess funds.

To put money into savings or investments, start by using the same strategies you used when building your emergency fund. Once you get the ball rolling, try some of these daily, weekly, and monthly saving tips to accelerate your savings:

- **Keep an eye on interest.** The miles, points, and cash-back offers are only valuable if you're not falling into debt or paying interest.

- **Use the envelope budgeting system.** This has worked for me! If you have issues with overspending and control, set aside a certain amount of cash for a particular period (e.g., a week or a month). Once you spend the cash, it's gone, and that's it—you are done spending for that period.

- **Pay your bills with auto-pay.** This will ensure that your bills are paid in a timely manner and you do not incur late charges and penalties.

- **Implement the twenty-four-hour rule.** Do not buy discretionary items (large and small) impulsively and then suffer buyer's remorse! Have a self-imposed twenty-four-hour rule, and wait for that time to pass before you pull the trigger and buy the item(s). This rule is good for online shopping, too, which is designed to lure you into impulse buys.

- **Save what you spend.** Every time you treat yourself to a nonessential purchase, put the same amount in your savings account simultaneously. Whether you buy a latte or a pair of shoes, put the same amount in your savings account right away. Remember: small, seemingly insignificant contributions to savings add up!

- **Calculate the purchase cost of an item.** Figure out how many hours of work it will take you to pay for that purchase. Divide the cost of the item by your hourly wage. Reality check! Is that handbag worth ten hours of work?

- **Unsubscribe!** You know the stores that you like the most, so unsubscribe from their marketing emails to avoid temptation. Opt out!

- **Make a grocery shopping list.** Save money on groceries by making a list of the items you actually need, instead of wandering around the grocery store buying random items because you are hungry or just want to buy something.

- **Gently reduce your dining-out budget.** Commit to a certain number of times per month that you will dine out, and stick to it. Don't totally sacrifice your lifestyle, because you need to live and enjoy life, but don't dine out just because it's convenient. Also, when you do eat out, try to limit alcohol consumption—alcohol costs more than food!

- **Evaluate your utility bills quarterly.** Every quarter, review your electric bill, cable bill, and phone bill to determine if you can save money. This is also a good time to check if you have the optimal, most cost-effective plan. I do this religiously, and often I get a better plan that saves money after my review!

- **Plan and budget in advance for vacations.** Budget planning for extraordinary expenses, such as a vacation, should be included in your annual budget and never organized on a whim. Allot a certain amount of money for the vacation, save for it, and enjoy the vacation without worrying about the bills you will have to pay upon your return home.

- **Plan a gift-giving budget.** Give yourself plenty of time to plan for giving gifts. Set spending limits—expensive doesn't always mean thoughtful! Look for sales, and do your best to plan out all family and friend gift purchases annually so that you can set a gift expense budget.

- **Establish a monthly entertainment budget.** Whether you like the cinema, the theater, concerts, or extreme sports, set up an affordable, sensible monthly budget for these discretionary expenditures so you can have some fun while you are saving!

- **If you get a tax refund or a windfall, SAVE IT!** Every time you receive a refund, bonus, or windfall, save a portion of it before you start spending it all.

- **Start saving for retirement as early as you possibly can.** Although retirement may seem a long way off, it is never too early to start saving for it. Before you know it (take it from me), you are older than you think, and retirement is looming large. Retirement savings will compound and grow over your lifetime, which will ensure that you can live in dignity in your old age. If you start late with this, the consequences may be dire indeed. Living expenses in retirement will be greater than you expect, and your compounding savings need to grow to accommodate the effects of inflation over time. Living solely on Social Security payments in retirement will be very difficult. Max out on 401(k) contributions if you have a company 401(k) plan, and take advantage of your employer match if they offer it. If you don't have a 401(k) plan, contribute to a Roth IRA or traditional IRA instead. I will address retirement savings in more depth in chapter 6.

These are just a few tips to get you started. Once you start seeing your savings account grow, you will be motivated to do more. Give it a chance and have some fun!

THE UPSHOT

Getting financially organized takes time and effort—it isn't necessarily easy. To quote Theodore Roosevelt, "Nothing in this world is worth having or worth doing unless it means effort, pain, difficulty. No kind of life is worth leading if it is always an easy life."[22] If you follow the five steps, however, your sweet reward will be a financially sound long-term existence. You will have peace of mind knowing that you are able to deal with any unexpected situations without a complete implosion. Taking these steps will lay a solid infrastructure for your life; you will be in control, not the victim of random circumstances and poor planning and decision-making. We are all personally responsible for our own well-being, and taking these five steps are a good start to minimizing stress and tension in your life. Once you have completed the five steps to laying your financial foundation, you are poised to embark on funding your retirement savings and implementing an investment strategy.

CHAPTER 6

The Linchpin:
Funding Your Retirement
(Start Early!)

"You may delay, but time will not."

—Benjamin Franklin

THE VERY GOOD NEWS is that we are all living longer than ever before. Both of my maternal grandparents passed in their early sixties (which is sort of scary, as I am sixty-two as I write this). My parents, on the other hand, are ninety and ninety-two years of age. The average life expectancy in the last sixty-five years has surged due to advancements in modern medicine. Those who make it to sixty-five can be expected to live another twenty years, and if you make it to seventy-five, you can be expected to live approximately another twelve years. Researcher and *Forbes* contributor Wade Pfau estimates that life expectancy has risen by about one year per decade since the 1950s.[1] If these trends continue, it is probable you will outlive your parents and grandparents if you have a healthy lifestyle.

The further good news is that women tend to live longer than men. In 2020, average life expectancy at age 65 is 21.1 years for women and 18.6 years for men.[2] The gap between men and women is fairly consistent across racial and ethnic groups. So, what could be bad about living longer? Absolutely nothing, if you have the resources and savings to fund your life in retirement. If you don't have sufficient resources, it could be a very harrowing and challenging time, and that would be very sad. Retirement is supposed to be the time when we can pursue all the activities and interests that we couldn't when we were younger and overwhelmed with work and/or family responsibilities. Finally, you get some "me" time. But to enjoy it, you have to plan for it—well in advance.

Reality Check

It is well known that women have made progress in educational attainment, employment, and earnings over the last one hundred years, but we rarely discuss women's status in retirement. And this is an issue that we absolutely need to be discussing in LOUD voices.

Why? Because women are living longer, and therefore must draw down their retirement wealth over a longer period of time than men. As a result, women are more likely to run out of retirement savings. According to a report by the Brookings Institution, poverty rates for women increase with age, from 8.6 percent among women aged sixty-five to sixty-nine to 13.5 percent among women aged eighty or older. In 2017, among elderly women, the poverty rate was 4.3 percent for those who were married, 13.9 percent for widows, 15.8 percent for divorced women, and 21.5 percent for women who had never married.[3] An increasing number of women reaching retirement are divorced or unmarried, and in every marital status group, women with children had higher poverty rates than women without children, a pattern that does not hold for men. According to the National Institute on Retirement Security, women were 80 percent more likely than men to be impoverished at age sixty-five and older, while women ages seventy-five to seventy-nine were three times more likely to fall below the poverty level as compared to their male counterparts.[4]

I've already mentioned my own experience and the challenges I encountered with my divorce at age fifty-five. Due to my relentless persistence—fueled by a sudden, overwhelming fear of how I would survive in my old age, my previous Wall Street résumé, and divine intervention—I became a financial advisor in my fifties. Over the last eight years, I have been playing financial catch-up to build my resources and prepare for my ultimate retirement—which won't be for a long time. I have a lot of catching up to do; luckily, I enjoy my profession and finally have total control over my financial future. Like many women, I will work well into my seventies, because I want to ensure a retirement in dignity when I finally do take that step. My situation was a confluence of many unfortunate situations and expenses all occurring at once: a long, protracted divorce proceeding, because I had no premarital planning; no premarital financial discussions with my ex-husband (as mentioned in chapter 3); agreeing to life-changing decisions to support my ex-husband's career at the expense of my own career development and wealth accumulation; and paying for private educational institutions for my children without compromise or consideration of my own future needs.

I would be in a much better position today if all that hadn't transpired and I had made different decisions, but I am putting the pedal to the metal now and playing retirement funding catch-up.

The Retirement Deficit

Various factors influence how much wealth women have in retirement. Women earn less on average than men do over their lifetime; these lower lifetime earnings make it more difficult for women to save for retirement and result in lower Social Security payments as well. Women also live longer than men, have greater caregiving responsibilities for children and aging parents, and are often risk averse and less financially knowledgeable—all of which contribute to fewer resources in retirement. This situation is known as the retirement deficit.

Lower lifetime earnings have a ripple effect throughout women's lives and lead to decreased retirement wealth. The most important link is through Social Security, which provides more than half of family income to 52 percent of the elderly and at least 90 percent of income to 25 percent of the elderly. On average, women receive 80 percent of the Social Security benefits that men receive because women tend to experience more career disruptions. Benefits are based on a person's thirty-five highest-earning years. Women with long career interruptions risk not having thirty-five years with positive earnings, and the wage gaps due to inequality in pay further reduce women's benefits. The motherhood penalty applies here, too: having a first child reduces a woman's Social Security benefits (through reduced earnings) by an average of 16 percent. A 2017 study by the Center for Retirement Research at Boston College found that the lifetime earnings of mothers with one child are 28 percent less than the earnings of childless women, all else being equal, and that each additional child lowers lifetime earnings by another 3 percent. The per-child motherhood penalty is almost negligible among women receiving spousal benefits at full retirement age (sixty-six to sixty-seven years of age), but mothers who receive benefits on only their own earnings histories see significantly lower Social Security income than childless working women.[5] Essentially, if you have long or frequent gaps in your career, and you can't claim the spousal benefit (see below), you will have greatly reduced Social Security benefits in retirement.

Women who leave work to care for an elderly family member—a responsibility that predominantly falls on women over fifty—not only lose wages but also lose an average of $142,000 in lifetime Social Security benefits.[6] Spouses (or ex-spouses, if the marriage lasted more than ten years) can choose to receive benefits based on their own earnings history or to receive half of their spouse's benefit, whichever is higher. Given the trends in employment, earnings, and marriage, women are increasingly choosing to receive their own benefits.

A further ripple effect is that women's lower lifetime earnings also reduce the amount of wealth women can accumulate from employer-sponsored retirement plans.

Ending the Retirement Deficit

If these facts are a bit depressing, you can take heart in knowing that change is possible. We need government policy changes and labor market practice changes to fix a retirement system that was not designed to accommodate women's life experiences and demands. Accelerating these changes will help level the playing field for women in retirement.

Basically, we need to make it easier for women to work while managing all the other responsibilities that fall predominantly on their shoulders. Policy changes that would provide robust federal paid family and medical leave programs would allow women to save for retirement and earn Social Security credits while providing care to children and relatives. Caring for family members is work and should be viewed as such, with compensation. This caregiving work benefits society, strengthens families, and fosters stable homes and supportive environments. The Brookings Gender Equality Series outlined the following solutions:[7]

- Employers should be required to provide employees with a certain amount of paid time off for caregiving, parental leave, and periods of illness. Nine states (California, Colorado, Connecticut, Massachusetts, New Jersey, New York, Oregon, Rhode Island, and Washington) and the District of Columbia already have such programs.
- Under a Social Security caregiver credit, the government could assign a value to caregiving work that would be used as part of Social Security benefit calculations. This is being done in the United Kingdom, France, Germany, and Sweden, where caregiver credits are provided for public pensions.

- Subsidizing high-quality childcare would enable more mothers to remain in the workforce.

- Reforming the tax code either to provide a second-earner tax credit or to tax individuals rather than families would improve incentives for married women to work.

- Adoption of a nationwide automatic individual retirement account program could make many women eligible for a tax-advantaged workplace retirement platform. Women continue to comprise a majority of the 55 million workers who are not covered by an employer-sponsored retirement plan.

- Expanding Supplemental Security Income benefits to close the gap between Social Security income and the poverty threshold could benefit many elderly women who are living in poverty.

- Increasing support from Medicare and Medicaid for end-of-life care, which would be expanded to include palliative care (specialized care for people with serious illnesses). Most insurance plans only cover palliative care for people in hospice care with six months or less to live. Those who are not in hospice and are afflicted with cancer, heart disease, or Alzheimer's disease would benefit from an array of services delivered in their home. Changes along these lines would allow people who are not hospice-eligible to receive care, which would directly benefit women as they live longer.

- A reform of divorce laws that could help women adequately prepare for their long-term financial needs after divorce.

It is important that we push for changes in federal and state government policies and in labor practices in order to strengthen women's economic health in retirement. If we don't make noise about this to shift public opinion, it will take hundreds of years for women and children to benefit from economic progress. Tick tock—the clock is ticking and it is time for action.

Don't Delay—Start Saving Now

The most important advice I can give anyone is to save for retirement as early as you can. And if you haven't been focused on doing so, or had other demands on your money, start now *whatever your age*, even if you can only save a little bit. It sounds like common sense, since we all hope to have long and fruitful lives, yet too often we leave to chance how we will navigate old age. That is not a good or sensible game plan with much hope of success. Once you start saving and you see your accounts grow, you feel good and motivated to keep doing it. It is a habit—a good habit—and once you start, you will feel AMAZING!

Try to visualize what your life will look like in retirement if you have very little savings and must rely primarily on Social Security income to get by. Social Security is, on average, about $1,500 per month, or about $18,000 per year.[8] This is far less than most salaried positions in the United States, and, in most cases, not enough to cover monthly expenses like a mortgage, food, gas, car payments, clothing, entertainment, etc. This is not a pretty picture, so let that vision of the not-so-great future light a fire in you to begin saving whatever you can immediately. It is never too late to start; trust me, I know from my personal experience.

The magic of compounding interest in your retirement funds will grow your money exponentially. Essentially, your money will make more money for you through the power of compounding. The chart that follows provides a great visual to illustrate the power of compounding over time.

The New York Times "Your Money" columnist Ron Lieber put it this way: "If two people put the same amount of money away each year ($5,000), earn the same return on their investments (6 percent annually) and stop saving upon retirement at the same age (sixty-seven), one will end up with nearly twice as much money just by starting at twenty-two instead of thirty-two. Put another way: The investor who started saving ten years earlier would have about $500,000 more at retirement. It's that simple."[9]

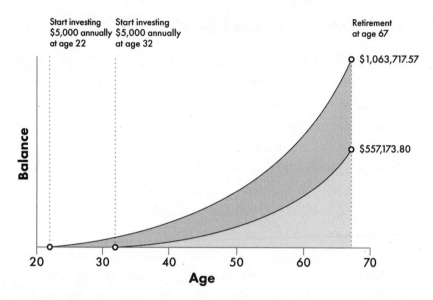

Start investing $5,000 annually at age 22
Start investing $5,000 annually at age 32
Retirement at age 67

$1,063,717.57

$557,173.80

Balance

Age

20 30 40 50 60 70

FIGURE 6.1 Compounding Interest[10]

It is easy to make excuses for putting retirement savings off because there always seems to be some other pressing need. Also, if we have family obligations, children we want to send to university, or other seemingly important demands, it is easy to prioritize those expenditures over saving for our own retirement. There is no correct amount to save; just save as much as you can, even if it is only $25 per paycheck. Start small if you must and keep increasing it over time. This is about self-love and self-care. You know the old adage: you have to take care of yourself before you take care of others. As they say in-flight, put your oxygen mask on first.

Your Retirement Options

Before we explore how to invest for retirement, let's get a picture of the potential income streams you can have at that time.

As discussed earlier, many women rely primarily on Social Security benefits to fund their retirement. But in this day and age, Social Security payments are often not enough to support a comfortable life (and I don't mean an extravagant lifestyle, but just a rather basic lifestyle). So, let's talk about Social Security, as it is the baseline for retirement income.

Basic Guide to Collecting Social Security

We know that women receive Social Security benefits that are, on average, 80 percent of those men receive. This is because women make less money over their working lives, have career interruptions, and are responsible for child- and eldercare. Social Security benefits are based on the amount of income you earned throughout your working life. If you never had a paid job, or if you earned less than the minimum qualifying amount over your lifetime, you may be able to claim a spousal benefit if you are, or have been, married. More about that later . . .

WHEN TO CLAIM YOUR SOCIAL SECURITY BENEFIT

Deciding at what age to claim your Social Security benefit can be a complicated question with economic implications. If you claim too early, you will be receiving smaller checks in perpetuity. If you postpone claiming, you will get larger checks for a shorter time, which will ultimately be affected by your longevity. Let's discuss calculating that all-important sweet spot between payments and longevity.

You can elect to receive your Social Security benefits at age sixty-two. This is the earliest you can claim, although you will not receive your full benefit at this age. Social Security establishes a table of "full retirement ages," which are dependent on the year you were born and are the ages at which people can receive full retirement benefits from Social Security. For example, if you were born in 1960 or later, your full retirement age is sixty-seven.

At full retirement age, you receive the full benefit based on the amount of Social Security tax paid into the system through your lifetime. If you choose to take your benefit early—for example, at sixty-two—your benefit will be reduced by 30 percent if you were born in 1960 or later. This is a permanent reduction. On the other hand, if you choose to delay taking your Social Security income until after full retirement age, you will receive a credit for each year past your full retirement age, up to the age of seventy, equal to an annual 8 percent increase for each year you delay. If you wait to claim until seventy, you get a higher monthly benefit, but fewer checks than you would if you claimed early or at full retirement age.

Let's look at an example of calculating your break-even age, shown in Figure 6.2. If you were born in 1962, your full retirement age is sixty-seven, and you choose to receive your Social Security benefit at sixty-two, your benefit will be reduced permanently by 30 percent. Assuming a full retirement benefit of $1,000 per month as an example, you would receive only $700 per month. If you wait until you are sixty-seven to claim, you will receive $3,600 more per year. Between sixty-two and sixty-seven, you would receive $42,000 ($8,400 per year) if you claim early, at sixty-two. However, if you claim at sixty-seven, it will take you 11.67 years ($42,000 ÷ $3,600) to break even with claiming early, at which time you will be seventy-eight years old. If you claim at sixty-seven, or full retirement age, and go on to live beyond seventy-eight years of age, every year longer you live, you will get 30 percent more in retirement funding than if you had claimed at sixty-two.

Age you claim Social Security if you are born in 1962, assuming $1,000 monthly full retirement benefit	Monthly Income	Annual Income	Break-even Age
62	$700	$8,400	n/a
67	$1,000	$12,000	78
70	$1,259	$15,108	82

FIGURE 6.2 Social Security Benefits

The upshot is: if you think it is probable that you will live past your break-even age, you should defer taking Social Security income early.

WHAT IF YOU NEVER WORKED?

If you have never worked or haven't worked enough to garner enough Social Security credits, you may be able to receive spousal benefits. To receive spousal benefits, you must be either sixty-two years old, or any age and caring for a child who is entitled to receive benefits on your spouse's record (either the child is younger than sixteen or disabled).

The spousal benefit is up to one-half of the amount that your spouse will receive at full retirement age. If you take it early at sixty-two or before you reach full retirement age, the benefit is permanently reduced (as discussed above). If you have worked and are eligible to receive your own benefits, you get the higher of the two.

IF YOU ARE DIVORCED AND HAVEN'T REMARRIED

If you have been divorced for two years and were married for at least ten years and have not remarried, you will be eligible for the spousal benefit of your ex-spouse, regardless of whether your ex-spouse has remarried. As long as your ex-spouse qualifies for receiving the Social Security benefit, you can claim on their record.

This is a welcome bit of good news for divorced women who haven't been able to work enough to receive their own benefit, or who would have a lesser benefit by claiming on their own record.

Investing in Yourself—Retirement Savings Options

Now that you are making the choice to get the retirement savings ball rolling, what are the best options for investing your money wisely? The first thing to know is that your retirement investment account options are dictated by where and how you work.

401(k)

Many employers offer a 401(k) retirement savings platform to their employees (although many smaller employers do not). It's easy to enroll by filling out the form and choosing the percentage of your paycheck you want to save each month. Your employer will automatically remove that amount from your pre-tax paycheck and deposit it with their 401(k) investment platform, for example, Vanguard or Fidelity.

If you have an awesome employer, they may match some of your savings in a 401(k). The match is usually up to 3 percent of your salary. It is like an instant raise, and with the power of compounding, will pay you even more over time. So, find out what the match is and make sure to take advantage of it—because who doesn't like free money, right?

The 401(k) plans are tax-advantaged plans. There are two types: a traditional 401(k) plan and a Roth 401(k) plan. The difference between the two is primarily when you are taxed. Here are some facts to know about the two plans.

TRADITIONAL 401(K)

- When you contribute to a traditional 401(k), your taxes are reduced the year you contribute because your contribution is made from your gross (pre-tax) income, which reduces your taxable income for that year.
- The maximum amount that an employee can contribute is adjusted periodically, As of 2022, employees under the age of fifty can contribute up to $20,500 per year, and employees over fifty can contribute $27,000.
- The earnings on a traditional 401(k) account are tax-deferred, which means they are not taxed until withdrawn. Distributions when withdrawn will be taxed as ordinary income.
- Owners of traditional 401(k)s must be fifty-nine-and-a-half or older to take withdrawals without penalties. If distributions are taken prior to that age, there is a 10 percent penalty on the

withdrawal. Depending on your plan, certain exceptions may apply, allowing for a waiver of the penalty. These exceptions are called hardship distributions and they must be due to "immediate and heavy" financial need and are limited to the amount necessary to satisfy the financial need.

- Traditional 401(k)s require mandatory withdrawals to commence at age seventy-two.

ROTH 401(K)

- Unlike a traditional 401(k), a Roth 401(k) is funded with after-tax dollars. There are no income limitations for Roth 401(k)s as there are with Roth IRAs that require you to make less than a certain amount of money per year in order to contribute.
- The contribution limits are the same as for a traditional 401(k).
- Withdrawals are tax-free because taxes were paid prior to your contribution.
- Like traditional 401(k)s, Roth 401(k)s require mandatory withdrawals to commence at age seventy-two.

WHICH TYPE OF 401(K) IS BEST FOR YOU?

If you are young and think you are going to be in a higher tax bracket later in life, then a Roth 401(k) makes sense. If you are in a higher tax bracket now and believe that you will be in a lower tax bracket in retirement, a traditional 401(k) makes sense; this is because you can reduce your taxable income with the pre-tax contribution now and pay taxes at a lower rate on the distribution in the future. If your employer offers both traditional and Roth 401(k)s, you don't have to choose; you can contribute to both, with the combined contributions not exceeding the limit, and hedge your bets!

If you work for a nonprofit or the government, you probably won't have a 401(k) plan available to you. Instead, you may either have a 457 plan, which is very similar to a 401(k), if you are a state or local government employee, or a 403(b) plan, if you work for a nonprofit such as a school, charity, or religious organization. A 403(b) can be expensive, with high fees and investment selections limited to annuities. It may be more prudent to skip the 403(b) plan and contribute to one of the IRAs discussed later in the chapter.

When you leave your job, you can roll over your 401(k) or 403(b), tax-free, to an individual retirement account, which will allow you to have more control over your account, and much more diverse and broad investment options. As you change jobs throughout your career, it is best to roll your 401(k)s into an IRA and have all your retirement assets in one account. Now let's talk about IRAs . . .

Individual Retirement Accounts

People who don't have access to 401(k)s, or who are self-employed, can open individual retirement accounts. In this section, I will outline the basics of the various IRA options that you can choose from. Most people have heard of traditional IRAs and Roth IRAs, which are for individuals. For self-employed people and small business owners, simplified employee pension (SEP) IRAs and Savings Incentive Match Plan for Employees (SIMPLE) IRAs are options; for nonworking spouses, there are spousal IRAs.

If it all sounds a bit confusing, don't stress too much: a few key factors will help you decide which IRA is right for you. Your choice will be based on your income, employment status, and tax benefit. Note that with the exception of a spousal IRA (which is for nonworking spouses), you can only contribute to any type of IRA if you have "earned income," or taxable compensation.

TRADITIONAL IRAS

As of January 2020, there is no maximum age to contribute to a traditional IRA, as long as you have taxable compensation (before 2020, you could only contribute until you were seventy-and-a-half). You can contribute up to $6,000 in 2021, or $7,000 if you happen to be fifty or older (often called a catch-up contribution for older folks). The contribution limits change from year to year, so check the IRS website for up-to-date information on contribution limits. The 2022 IRA contribution limits did not change from 2021.

Generally, with a traditional IRA, you can deduct your contribution on your tax return, thus lowering your taxable income for the year. If you don't have a retirement plan at work, such as a 401(k) or 403(b), generally you can take a full deduction for your traditional IRA contribution, up to your maximum contribution level. Deductibility of the contribution depends on whether you or your spouse have a workplace retirement plan and your current income.

The good news is that investment earnings are not taxed as long as the money remains in the IRA. Withdrawals are taxed when you withdraw in retirement at your tax rate at that time.

There are some withdrawal rules to be aware of for a traditional IRA. If you withdraw before the age of fifty-nine-and-a-half, you may incur a 10 percent penalty in addition to taxes on the withdrawal, unless you qualify for an exception. Exceptions include: unreimbursed medical expenses; health insurance premiums when you are unemployed; a permanent disability; higher-education expenses for you, your spouse, or your child; or buying a home for the first time.

As of 2021, at age seventy-two, holders of traditional IRAs must begin taking required minimum distributions, which are based on account size and life expectancy. Failure to take the required minimum distribution can result in a penalty. Again, check the most up-to-date government information as to the required age.

ROTH IRAS

The Roth IRA is a good option for people who don't pay a lot of taxes now. Unlike a traditional IRA, which has pre-tax contributions, with a Roth, you pay taxes on the money before you contribute. But the beauty of the Roth is that withdrawals during retirement are tax-free, and unlike with the traditional IRA, you don't have to take required minimum distributions at a certain age.

Roth IRAs have the same annual contribution limits as traditional IRAs (2022: $6,000 if you are under fifty, and $7,000 if you are over fifty. However, take note that with Roth IRAs, there are income limitations, which means you can't make over a certain amount of money if you want to contribute to a Roth. In 2022 single filers can't make more than $144,000, and married couples can't jointly make more than $214,000. You can contribute to a Roth IRA as long as you have eligible earned income, regardless of your age. You can contribute to both a Roth IRA and a workplace retirement plan as long as you are within the income limits. If income limits permit you to contribute to both a Roth 401(k) and a Roth IRA, you can contribute the maximum amount to the Roth 401(k), currently $19,500, and concurrently contribute the maximum to your Roth IRA, currently $6,000 (for a total contribution to both of $25,500). Contributing to both a Roth IRA and a 401(k) allows you to save as much as the law allows in tax-advantaged accounts.

You can also contribute to a Roth IRA and a traditional IRA at the same time, but only up to the contribution limit ($6,000) for IRAs; for example, $3,000 to each one for a total of $6,000, which is the current contribution limit for IRAs.

Another big difference between Roth and traditional IRAs is that you can withdraw contributions at any age from a Roth without owing income taxes or penalties, because you have already paid taxes on this money. "Contributions" are the money you deposited into your Roth account; they do not include any interest or dividends your account has earned (i.e., "earnings") since you invested the money. Those earnings grow tax-free within the Roth. You can withdraw both contributions and earnings penalty-free if you are at least fifty-nine-and-a-half and have had the account for at least five years; the IRS calls this a "qualified withdrawal." Once you've waited five years and you are at least fifty-nine-and-a-half, all withdrawals from a Roth IRA will be tax-free. The same exceptions apply to Roths as apply to traditional IRAs for early withdrawals without incurring a penalty.

CHOOSING THE RIGHT IRA

When it comes to choosing the right IRA for you, the pivotal question is whether you think your tax rate will be higher or lower during retirement. Roth IRAs are a good deal for younger people who may have lower incomes now and don't pay a lot of taxes, but who may be in a higher tax bracket later in life. They don't need the tax deduction from the traditional IRA contribution because they aren't paying a lot of taxes at this point in their lives. Most of us don't have crystal balls, but all things being equal, if you anticipate increasing your income over time, and hence being in a higher tax bracket later in life, a Roth makes sense, as long as you are within the income limits. Another option is to contribute to both. Just remember that your total contribution can't exceed the contribution limits for the year (e.g., in 2021, $6,000 or $7,000).

SIMPLIFIED EMPLOYEE PENSION IRAS

A simplified employee pension IRA, or SEP IRA, is a type of traditional IRA for self-employed people or small businesses. This is an attractive option for business owners because it doesn't incur the costs of setting up conventional employer-sponsored retirement plans, and contribution limits are higher than individual IRA levels. A SEP IRA allows employers to contribute to their employee's retirement accounts and their own.

The really big perk to SEP IRAs is that the annual contribution levels are much higher than other IRAs; in 2022, it is the lesser of 25 percent of employee compensation, or $61,000. For example, if you make $100,000 per year, 25 percent of your compensation is $25,000, and that is thus the maximum you can contribute to your SEP. If you make $250,000, however, 25 percent of your compensation would be $62,500, and the maximum contribution you can make to your SEP is $61,000. You can contribute the maximum allowed contribution to both a SEP IRA and a Roth IRA as long as you are within income limits for the Roth IRA, That allows for some turbo-charged retirement savings! The employer contributes on behalf of employees. Other notable highlights are:

- An employer must contribute equally (on a percentage basis of salary) to all employee accounts, including their own.
- Contribution size can vary yearly based on the business's cash flow, but must always be equal for all eligible workers. ·
- Employees are not allowed to contribute to the plan via salary deferral.
- Sole proprietors (a one-person business) can open a SEP IRA for themselves.
- Catch-up contributions for workers fifty and older are not allowed.

Like traditional IRAs, SEP IRAs require minimum distributions beginning at age seventy-two. Distributions before age fifty-nine-and-a-half are taxed as income and subject to a 10 percent penalty, unless the reason for the distribution satisfies one of the early withdrawal exceptions.

SAVINGS INCENTIVE MATCH PLAN FOR EMPLOYEES IRAS

A Savings Incentive Match Plan for Employees IRA, or SIMPLE IRA, is similar to an employer-sponsored 401(k). Like a SEP IRA, it is for self-employed people and small businesses with fewer than one hundred employees. The difference between a SIMPLE and a SEP IRA is that employees can contribute through salary deferral. For self-employed people, SEPs are usually better because they have higher contribution limits, which allows the contributor to save a lot more.

With SIMPLE IRAs, contributions by employees are pre-tax, meaning your employer doesn't withhold taxes on your contribution before it is deposited. So, employees don't get to deduct this contribution, because that would be claiming the contribution twice. A few other fun facts to know about SIMPLEs:

- Contribution limits are lower than for 401(k)s—$14,000 versus $20,500 in 2022
- Unlike the SEP, catch-up contributions are allowed for folks fifty or older, who can save an additional $3,000.

- Employers are generally required to make a 3 percent matching contribution or a fixed contribution of 2 percent of each eligible employee's compensation.
- To qualify to participate in a SIMPLE IRA, an employee must have earned at least $5,000 during any two years before the current calendar year and expect to receive at least that amount in the current year.
- Unlike with most workplace plans, participants can roll the money from a SIMPLE IRA into a traditional IRA after two years of participation—with a 401(k) you can't usually do that until you change jobs.
- Early withdrawals from a SIMPLE IRA (within the first two years of contributing to the account) may be subject to a whopping 25 percent penalty plus income taxes.

SPOUSAL IRAS

A spousal IRA is the exception to the earned income requirement for contributing to an IRA. If one person in the couple isn't working, that person can still have their own separate IRA. This is a great thing for women who are taking time out of the workforce to care for children; it ensures they don't lose out on retirement savings because of caregiving responsibilities.

What you need to know about spousal IRAs:

- Couples must file a joint tax return and have taxable income to be eligible.
- Contribution limits are the same as for traditional or Roth IRAs: the nonworking spouse can contribute up to $6,000, or $7,000 for those fifty or older, in 2020, 2021, and 2022. The working spouse can contribute the same amount to his or her own IRA.
- The total amount contributed to both IRAs must be the lesser of your joint taxable income or double the annual IRA contribution limit (e.g., $12,000 for those under fifty).

- The account must be opened in the nonworking spouse's name using his or her Social Security number, which means that the IRA is legally in the name of the nonworking spouse.

Investing Your Retirement Funds

Okay, now that you have a retirement savings plan, what are you supposed to invest in? Good question! Let's try to keep this simple so you can easily get the ball rolling.

Most 401(k) plans are on platforms that offer target-dated mutual funds (targeted to your year of retirement). Mutual funds are baskets of funds that contain stocks and bonds from companies of different sizes from all over the world. You can choose the fund based on the year you would like to retire; if that's 30 years from now, choose the fund with the target date of 30 years. As you get closer to the target date, the fund will automatically change the mix of investments to be less risky. Target funds eliminate the need for you to worry about what to invest in, as that is done for you by investment managers based on your goals and time horizon.

Another option is to invest in index funds, which allow people to directly invest in different asset classes (stocks, bonds, or alternative investments) and saves on fees. Index funds mirror the performance of a stock index, like the S&P 500, for example, or a bond index. Standard & Poor's (S&P) is a company that provides data for credit ratings and is the foremost index provider. The S&P 500 tracks the performance of the five hundred largest public companies in the United States. You will need to choose what index asset classes to invest in and how much of your portfolio to put into each index fund/asset class. Index funds include exchange-traded funds and mutual funds. An example of a stock index fund is the State Street SPDR S&P 500 ETF Trust, and an example of a bond index fund is the Fidelity US Bond Index Fund (FXNAX).

You should strive for a diversified portfolio (i.e., don't have all your eggs in one investment basket) and have a combination of an S&P index fund, an international stock index fund, and a bond index fund, which should provide enough variety to be the core of a diversified portfolio. Other possible additions to the mix of funds are small-cap stocks, mid-cap stocks, emerging market stocks. and real estate investment trusts (REITs). Remember that with index funds, you will have to change your asset allocations (i.e., the amount you have in each type of fund) by yourself if you want to react to market changes.

One of the best things about IRAs compared to 401(k) plans is that you can invest in a much larger selection of investment options. You can choose individual stocks, bonds, alternatives, mutual funds, or exchange-traded funds. That said, having more options can make your choice more difficult, and it's riskier if you aren't knowledgeable about what to consider when selecting investments. Here are a few pointers on how to choose investments for your IRA:

- **Understand asset allocation.** Asset allocation is how you divide up your money among different types of investments such as stocks, bonds, cash, and alternatives. Within each type of investment, there are specific classes. For example, stock choices can be large-cap stocks, or small- or mid-cap stocks; and areas of investment can be tech, energy, consumer staples, consumer discretionary, etc. Diversification is important to hedge your risk, but knowledgeable diversification is key.

- **What is your risk tolerance?** How comfortable do you feel with risk, and what is your time horizon? Risk and time horizon are linked because, in general, you want to take on more risk when you are younger and decrease risk as you get closer to retirement. You want to always take on enough risk that your money will grow, but not so much risk that you bail out of your investment strategy when the market is having a rocky patch.

- **Think about leaving it to a professional.** If you don't have the time or the interest to learn about asset allocation and investment selection, why not hire a professional investment advisor who can suggest an appropriate strategy and actively manage your investments over time during all sorts of market activity? Find a fiduciary advisor you click with and trust, and work with that person to achieve your long-term retirement goals. Another option is to use a robo-advisor that will build and manage an exchange-traded fund portfolio for you based on certain questions; this is usually done for a nominal management fee. Many popular IRA platforms offer these automatic services.

Check out chapter 7 for more on investment strategy.

Long-Term Care Insurance

Nobody wants to think about the fact that they might need long-term care when they are elderly, that we may need others to take care of us if we don't have the physical or mental capabilities to do so ourselves. Thinking about this is depressing and unsettling. But, according to a 2018 AARP report, by the time you reach sixty-five, your chances are 50/50 that you will need long-term care someday. If you do, you will spend an average of $140,000 for it.[11] This is a pretty sobering statistic, but we can't put our heads in the sand; we are all living longer and need to plan for it.

PAYING FOR LONG-TERM CARE

For many people, long-term care funding is an unsolved problem. You can self-fund long-term care expenses if you save enough money for retirement and you pull less than 4 percent out of your savings in retirement to fund your living expenses. This is another motivation to save for retirement and start early. You need to have a plan for this, so when thinking about retirement savings, consider that this could be an expense down the line.

Another option is to get a long-term care insurance policy. Long-term care insurance premiums are steep, and you may be in shock when you get a quote. That said, the cost of the premium may well be worth it, given that currently the median monthly cost for a home health aide is over $4,000, and a nursing home can cost anywhere from $8,000 to $12,000 per month (and that cost will grow in the years ahead!). To get a premium that is affordable, consider starting to look for long-term care insurance in your fifties or early sixties, before premiums rise sharply or worsening health rules out robust coverage. Typically, every year you delay, it will be more expensive, as initial premiums at age sixty-five, for example, are 8 to 10 percent higher than those for new customers who are sixty-four. Starting too early, however, can be counterproductive. You could get a policy with a lower premium in your forties, but you will likely be paying premiums for more than two decades before you file a claim.

Unlike the traditional long-term care policies of yesteryear, there are now "hybrid" policies that will return money to your heirs if you never use the policy and allow you to lock your premium in up front. Hybrid policies are more expensive than traditional policies. Work with an independent insurance agent who sells policies from several companies rather than one insurer, and who can sell long-term care partnership policies that require insurance professionals to engage in continuing education.

The Final Caveat: Don't Raid Your Retirement Savings!

Why would anyone want to do this? As we all know, life is far from linear, and sometimes things happen unexpectedly that totally disrupt our flow and require some creative thinking to address. You know the saying "Desperate times call for desperate measures"? Dipping into one's retirement savings qualifies as a "desperate measure," and sometimes we might think there is no alternative.

Historically, the aftermath of divorce and job loss have been the reasons most cited for making an early withdrawal from, or taking a loan against, a retirement plan. However, COVID-19 changed all that.

According to a MagnifyMoney survey, nearly 30 percent of Americans dipped into their retirement savings because of the pandemic. To add insult to injury, 21 percent said they lowered their contributions, and 26 percent stopped making contributions altogether.[12]

Before you take the step of dipping into your retirement savings, I implore you to consider other alternatives. The permanent loss of principal, not to mention the loss of the long-term benefits of compound growth, is extremely detrimental to your retirement outlook. Even worse is if you withdraw retirement savings during a market downturn. The worst time to withdraw investment assets is in the middle of a downturn and extreme volatility; investments will be worthless and, hence, you will have to withdraw a greater percentage of your account. This turns temporary paper losses into permanent realized losses. Even if you try to replenish later, you will have lost all the compounding of growth from the withdrawn principal. Compounding is one of the most powerful tools to boost retirement savings; and making a withdrawal, especially during the early stages of investing, reduces that effect.

THE UPSHOT

Make retirement savings a priority, treat the savings as sacrosanct, and enjoy the vision of a well-funded retirement in which you can enjoy the fruits of life. Retirement savings are a key building block to financial independence and freedom of choice. *You are worthy of both, so sacrificing some money now to save for your retirement is well worth the effort.*

CHAPTER 7

Investing: The Catalyst for Financial Independence

"Money is only a tool. It will take you wherever you wish, but it will not replace you as the driver."

—Ayn Rand

REMEMBER THAT FINANCIAL independence is the ability to live without financial fear during the roller-coaster ride of life because you are prepared enough to deal with ups and downs without going into debt, sacrificing, or skimping on necessities. It is the ability to live your life as you desire within reasonable parameters, to be able to breathe. It doesn't mean you never have to work another day in your life, but it does mean you have the freedom to pivot by quitting a job you don't like, going back to school, starting a new business, or pursuing a new course in life without major upheaval. It means freedom to choose, to have options.

Investing is a key tool when it comes to achieving financial independence so that you aren't merely surviving in your life. Investing is about thriving, both now and in the future. Investing and watching your balances grow is empowering, and it reduces the fear of the future.

As I discussed in chapter 6, women have to save a higher percentage of their salary just to achieve parity with men for retirement savings. This is due to the gender pay gap and the fact that women live longer than men. We have already discussed the need to budget, eliminate credit card debt, set up an emergency fund, and max out your annual contributions to retirement savings. Once you have done that, the next crucial step is to invest.

Overcoming Our Resistance to Investing

Fear, anxiety, inadequacy, and *dread* are words that 47 percent of women with at least $25,000 of investable assets associate with financial planning, according to the March 2020 Women and Wealth Insights Study from U.S. Bank.[1] Why is this the case? Largely, it's an issue of avoidance and fear of the unknown. Once we learn to take the reins of our finances, the fear we once felt dissolves!

According to the Federal Reserve, women are less comfortable managing their retirement investments and making investment decisions than men. Only a fraction of American women (26 percent) are investing in the stock market. A Transamerica Center for Retirement Studies report in September 2020 found that only 17 percent of women are very confident that they will be able to retire comfortably, and 21 percent of employed women say their confidence in retiring comfortably has decreased due to the pandemic. Further, more than half of women (55 percent) expect to retire after age sixty-five or don't plan on retiring at all![2] Wow—no rest for weary women!

To exacerbate the situation, women are generally more risk-averse than men. *Financial Advisor* magazine cites a Hearts & Wallets study that found that female investors hold more cash than male investors.[3] On average, they allocate 37 percent of their assets to bank savings, checking accounts, or CDs—compared to men, who allocate 25 percent.

Men also have double the allocation to individual stock holdings compared to women. Women overall invest 40 percent less money than men do, according to a survey by digital investment platform Wealthsimple.[4]

And yet, women actually outperform men when they do invest, and they earn consistently higher returns than men, according to Fidelity Investments. Women performed better than men by 0.4 percent and also consistently save a higher percentage of their salaries.[5] With a higher savings rate and earning a higher return, the impact can be significant over time.

A piece of good news on the women and investment front is that some women are forming and joining women investment clubs that provide a safe space to learn, ask questions, and invest. These groups offer a nonjudgmental environment that encourages women to learn more and grow confidence in the investing realm—and that spur women to actually invest! Meetup, a website that acts as a conduit for people to meet others with similar interests in their area, has more than 150 women's investment groups participating on the platform. According to *Real Simple* magazine, a few of the largest women and investing Meetup groups are: the Austin Women's Investing Group (Texas), with more than 2,100 members; Girls Just Want to Have Funds (Minneapolis, Minnesota), with 1,900 members; Smart Women Finish Rich in Atlanta (Georgia), with more than 1,600 members; and Lady Investors in Montreal (Quebec), with over 1,300 members.[6] Not all the groups are the same. Some are forums to talk about investments, some are learning forums where experts are invited to discuss relevant topics, and some are actual investment clubs where women pool their money to buy investments. Anything that creates an environment for women to actively engage in investing discussions and that fosters mentorship and confidence in investing sounds like a terrific idea to me! If you feel like some camaraderie, teaching, and support will inspire you to start investing, then check out the investment clubs in your area.

According to McKinsey & Company, women are the new face of wealth. In 2020, women controlled a third of total U.S. household financial assets, more than $10 trillion. By 2030, American women are expected to control a good portion of the $30 trillion in financial assets that baby boomers possess.[7] So now more than ever, women need to engage with investing. Figure 7.1 shows the percentage of women who control finances in different asset brackets.

Value of assets controlled by gender
($ trillion)

Share controlled by women (%)

Asset band	Women	Men		Share controlled by women (%)
$100,000–$249,999	1.1	1.4	2.5	43
$250,000–$499,999	1.5	2.9	4.4	33
$500,000–$999,999	2.9	4.9	7.8	37
$1,000,000–$2,499,999	2.6	7.9	10.5	25
$2,500,000–$4,999,999	1.3	4.4	5.7	23
$5,000,000 or more	1.5	2.4	4.0	39
Total	**10.9**	**24.0**	**34.9**	**31**

FIGURE 7.1 Women's Control of Assets[8]

Women need to have a greater sense of urgency with respect to saving for retirement and investing, and they need to confront their investment phobia to attain financial independence. Although holding cash has its place, if the preponderance of your investable money is in cash, it will not keep pace with inflation over time and grow enough to take you through retirement—especially in the current interest rate environment. Financial independence requires a lifetime commitment to prudent investing; it is not a one-and-done commitment. It needs to be informed and intentional.

Let's break down any phobias or fears we may still have by understanding some simple truths about investing. Oxford Languages defines *fear* as "an unpleasant emotion caused by the belief that someone or something is dangerous, likely to cause pain, or a threat."

"The investor's chief problem—and his worst enemy—
is likely to be himself. In the end, how your investments
behave is much less important than how you behave."

—Benjamin Graham

With proper knowledge and a holistic strategy, there is no reason to be fearful of investing—it can reap major benefits for you! It's not dangerous if it's done with knowledge, composure, and sense. It's not supposed to be a Las Vegas gambling experience; that isn't investing, it's just a fool's errand.

Most people believe that market movement is dictated primarily by traditional economic theories, but that theory is a fallacy. Behavioral economics reveals that stock price movement is frequently influenced by emotional decisions made by investors, not by rationality. During increased market volatility, such as that experienced during the COVID-19 pandemic, investors make more decisions based on bias and fear than on rational, cool-headed planning. The three key biases that become prevalent during market turbulence are affect bias, herd behavior, and loss aversion. What are these biases, and what should we look out for in our own decision-making?

Affect bias is when we shortcut decision-making by letting good or bad feelings influence us, instead of logical responses to information. During market turbulence, one of the most prevalent emotions to surface in investors is fear! During a sudden drop in the markets (remember March 9 and March 12, 2020?), panic triggers overwhelming fear in many investors; in turn, they overestimate the risk of losing their money permanently. If they have a diversified portfolio (discussed later in this chapter) and a long-term strategy, this fear is irrational, and could cause permanent capital loss if they liquidate (sell) their investments at lows.

Herd behavior is when we do what everybody else seems to be doing rather than making decisions based on knowledge, information, and rationality. With incessant media coverage and fearmongering, investors stay glued to their televisions and think they should do what everybody else seems to be doing, or at least what the media says everybody else is doing. Collective pessimism can lead to stock prices crashing, regardless of their fundamental values. We might as well be sheep, with behavior like that.

Finally, *loss aversion* is the result of people not feeling gains and losses equally. We experience losses twice as strongly as gains—if we lose $100, it hurts exponentially more compared to the good feeling we experience if we gain $100. Loss aversion makes us want to avoid risk and will cause us to make conservative changes that may not actually be aligned with our long-term goals. By definition, investing involves risk, and as the historical facts reveal, even with dips, long-term investing is the most efficient route to growing one's capital and achieving financial independence.

The Facts about Investing

There is a plethora of opinions and theories about how to invest, and with incessant coverage of the markets in the media and pundits of all types weighing in on what every market movement means, it can be difficult for us to make sound investment decisions. Let's define the core concepts of investing, cut through the noise of speculation and hyperbole in the media, and focus on fundamental investing strategy for the long term.

Fact: There is no reward without risk. Period.

This does not mean we should throw caution to the wind; treat the stock market like Las Vegas; and take on outsized, irrational risks. Risk involves uncertainty, but with unemotional decision-making based on fundamental analysis, risk can be managed and used to create opportunity.

Often, we hear the words *risk* and *volatility* used when people talk about investments. They are not the same, but the volatility of an investment helps to frame the risk of an investment. Volatility is the prediction of future price movement, which can encompass both gains and losses. But risk is solely the prediction of *permanent loss.*

As investors, we must learn to stomach volatility. COVID-19 initially caused a very short and intense drop in the market, with a quick recovery. That said, there continued to be intra-day volatility in 2020. For example, on June 15, 2020, the market was up approximately 750 points at opening, up 250 points midday, turned negative, and then rallied to close positive at 157 points. Clearly, focusing on intraday movements is exhausting and really is not indicative of long-term results.

Fact: We need to think long-term.

The Standard and Poor's 500 (also known as the S&P 500 Index—a tool that shows the stock growth of five hundred large companies) had an average annual return of 11.81 percent from 1980 through the end of 2019. Wow! That sounds like a great annual return, right? Yes, it does, but let's put it in context. During that time, there were up years and down years, and the index returned between 9 percent and 12 percent annually only three times during that time period. Usually, it was above or below the average annual return of 11.81 percent, and sometimes significantly.

We need to be long-term players so returns that fluctuate yearly are given the time to grow and produce solid "annual returns" over time.

What is the definition of *annual return*? According to Investopedia, "an annualized total return is the geometric average amount of money earned by an investment each year over a given time period."[9] The operative words to focus on are "over a given time period." Many investors don't remember that volatility—whether a week, a day, or a year—is historically very short-term. Patience is your friend in the stock market, and if you reframe your point of view to look at short-term volatility from a long-term perspective, it will totally change its significance. Say you invested $10,000 in 1980 at an 11.81 percent average annual return. By 2019, that $10,000 would have grown to $870,281, even though, as you can see from the chart that follows, there was occasional volatility along the way. Clearly, having patience and not reacting emotionally paid off if you stayed the course with your investment.

Long-Term Growth: Growth of $10,000 Invested in S&P 500 Index (1980–2019)

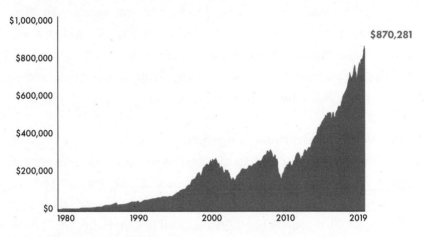

FIGURE 7.2 Long-Term Growth[10]

Fact: Volatility is our friend.

Volatility can provide great gains for opportunistic investors with a solid strategy driven by fundamentals. Staying with the example above, let's say we have two investors who both invested $10,000 on December 31, 1979. The opportunistic investor invested during a market drop of 8 percent, and the apprehensive investor shifted assets to cash or safer investments. By 2019, the opportunistic investor had an investment valued at approximately $1.3 million, while the apprehensive investor's investment was valued at approximately $408,000.[11] The path chosen definitely had consequences for the long-term outlook and future retirement prospects of these two investors. The point is that selling at market lows out of emotion can be very destructive to your long-term gain. Staying the course, or adding to a solid position during market drops, will increase your gain exponentially.

The upshot is that volatility is our friend. I am not saying that it doesn't cause trepidation, but the historical facts support the idea that having a solid long-term investment strategy and riding out short-term dips along the way bears fruit that one cannot achieve with cash or conservative investments. Volatility simply is the price movement of an investment, and the facts show that it is not permanent. Since 1949, there have been nine periods of 20 percent-or-greater declines in the S&P 500. The average 33 percent decline of these cycles can be painful to endure, but missing out on the average bull market's 268 percent return is even more painful. Most bear markets have had a relatively short duration (fourteen months on average), which also makes trying to time the market in the short term a fool's errand full of unpredictable outcomes.

Strategies for Investing

Enough said. So, what is the strategy for enduring volatility and not losing money permanently? Diversification, fundamentals, and a disciplined long-term strategy, of course!

Diversification

Diversification is a technique that reduces risk by distributing investments among various financial instruments, industries, and other categories. It aims to maximize returns by investing in a variety of areas that would each react differently to the same event. But please note that it may come with lower rewards in the short term because the risk is reduced by the diversification. Although it does not guarantee against loss, diversification is the most important component of reaching long-range financial goals while minimizing risk and volatility within your portfolio; that said, there will always be some level of price volatility.

When you as an investor are thinking about your ideal return, think about "risk-adjusted return." Basically, how much risk are you willing to assume to get a certain return? This concept allows you to compare the performance of high-risk, high-return investments to less risky, lower-return investments. Generally speaking, the higher the potential return of an investment, the higher the associated risk, and there is no guarantee that you will achieve that return. As an investor, your long-term goal should be to preserve capital (your investment) while achieving growth of the investment without taking outsized risks that could result in large losses.

A simple rule of thumb is that younger investors have more time and generally can handle more risk (e.g., higher allocation to equities), as the longtime horizon of their investment portfolio can withstand market volatility (there's time to make up losses and truly benefit from the powers of compounding). Older investors or investors with less time (e.g., money needed within five years to send kids to college or retire) should invest more conservatively to ensure money is there when it is needed. Realizing losses to fund liquidity or cash needs in the middle of a market downturn is something that can have lasting and serious implications for an investor's goals and objectives.

The goal of diversification is not really to boost outsized performance, but it does have the potential to improve returns, whatever risk level you choose. If one portion of your portfolio is declining, it may ensure that other portions are not declining, or not declining as much. It is best to have a mix of stocks, bonds, funds, real estate, and alternatives in your portfolio. These investment options are called assets.

A BRIEF PRIMER ON ASSET TYPES

Each type of asset performs differently as the economy grows and shrinks, and each offers varying potential for gain and loss.

- **Stocks** offer the potential for the highest return over time, but keep in mind that their prices can fluctuate over shorter periods. Focus on the fundamentals of companies when stock investing. Remember that buying stocks is buying ownership in a company. Does the company have cash flow, too much debt, good management? Are they allocating funds for capital expenditures and shareholder return and dividends? Also, be mindful of overconcentration in one stock; it's probably prudent not to have one stock make up more than 5 percent of your portfolio.

- **Bonds** can offer steadier returns with fixed interest payments. A bond is essentially a loan made by the investor to the borrower, and the owner of the bond (you, the investor) is a creditor to the issuer of the bond (either a corporation or a government entity). Bonds are generally considered "safer" investments than stocks and offer a lower return.

- **Funds** tend to already be diversified because they usually hold many investments in one basket. But be aware that some funds may hold only one type of investment; for example, stocks in consumer goods companies. A fund can be broadly diversified, with investments in many different industries or different types of assets, or narrowly diversified. Types of investment funds include mutual funds, exchange-traded funds, and money market funds.

- **CDs (certificates of deposits)** and savings accounts will not fluctuate in value but will grow steadily based on the interest rate or other contractual terms. These are basically cash accounts and, given the current low-interest-rate environment, they don't produce much interest income. It depends on the interest rate at any given time. Generally, cash can't keep pace with inflation over time, so it is not the most effective investment for growth of investment and retirement savings.

- **Real estate** can appreciate slowly over time and offers the potential for income if it is a rental property investment. But physical real estate can be expensive to maintain and is illiquid, which means it may take time to sell.

- **Alternative investments** are investments that aren't correlated to the stock market and can't be categorized as a stock, bond, or cash. They do not generally move in the same direction as the stock market and can include liquid hedge funds, real estate investment trusts, private equity, hedge funds, and other options.

Once you have your mix of stocks, bonds, and alternatives, check the weightings of each allocation on a regular basis to make sure that they still make sense given current market conditions. From time to time, you should rebalance your allocations.

> "Invest for the long haul. Don't get too greedy and don't get too scared."
> —Shelby M.C. Davis

Long-Term Strategy vs. Short-Term Strategy

It is human nature to want instant gratification and an immediate upside—that's just how we are wired. But it really is not a prudent investment strategy. People like to talk about "day trading" and often act like it is easy to make a lot of money doing it. This is just not true, and in my opinion, day trading is not a prudent investment strategy for the average gal. Day trading involves rapidly buying and selling securities to take advantage of small movements in price. This type of trading is a serious commitment of both time and money, and if you don't have enough money, you will get destroyed by the rough cycles; it's a risky business indeed.

Research shows that 80 percent of day traders lose their capital and are out within one year. Instead of getting rich, you are more likely to go broke quick. The U.S. Securities and Exchange Commission (SEC) points out that "day traders typically suffer severe financial losses in their first months of trading, and many never graduate to profit-making status."[12] I don't like those odds for my hard-earned money, so I believe in a long-term, fundamentals strategy.

Having a long-term investment strategy based on fundamentals, research, and a holistic approach is the real deal that will produce solid returns over the years. With long-term investments, investors can ride out the highs and lows of market movement and generate a better long-term return. One of the advantages associated with long-term investing is the potential for compounding. When your investments produce income such as dividends, those earnings get reinvested and can earn even more. The longer your money stays invested, the greater the opportunity for compounding and growth. Keep in mind that while compounding has a beneficial long-term outcome, there may be periods when your money won't grow. Although there are no guarantees, the value of compounded investment earnings often are greater over many years than your contributions alone.

Reminders:

- Panic and fear are not your friends.
- The benefits of long-term, disciplined investing speak for themselves.
- Be intentional in your strategy, and diversify your allocations.
- Do your research, and don't act like a sheep.
- Don't make emotional investment moves.

How to Invest

Hopefully at this point you're convinced that it's time to start investing. You may be thinking that this all sounds complicated and confusing. How do you actually get started with investing? Fear not; there are simple ways to get started on your investing journey. Remember that the sooner you begin investing, the longer your money can grow. Let that motivate you to get started as soon as possible. My advice is to not invest in anything you don't understand and to be proactive and take charge of your own investment education. Time spent doing so can reap rewards that will give you the financial independence you deserve.

A common misconception is that you need a lot of money to begin investing. But that isn't true. There are now many options available that allow you to open accounts with a nominal investment. Many mutual funds, for example, allow you to open an account with as little as a $50 investment.

Different types of funds to consider are:

- **Equity funds.** These funds invest in stocks. You can choose from growth stock funds (these stocks generally don't pay dividends and are about appreciation of the stock price); income stock funds (which hold stocks that pay dividends); value stocks (a stock where the price is low relative to the company's performance); and large-cap stocks, mid-cap stocks, small cap-stocks, or a combination of various types of stocks.

- **Fixed-income funds.** These funds invest in investments that pay a fixed rate of return, such as bonds. They can include government bonds, corporate bonds, and high-yield bonds.

- **Balanced funds.** These funds invest in a mix of equities and fixed income, and provide ready-made diversification by balancing the achievement of solid returns against the risk of losing money. Aggressive balanced funds will hold more equities and fewer bonds, and conservative balanced funds will hold more fixed income.

- **Index funds.** These funds track various indexes or benchmarks. The Standard and Poor's 500 index is one of the most popular because it tracks the five hundred companies listed on the S&P 500 and includes large, well-known U.S.-based companies in a diverse range of businesses. But there are many more index fund options to consider, too. Index funds can track small, medium, or large companies, sectors or industries (such as technology or healthcare, for example), market opportunities such as emerging markets, or stocks on international exchanges.

- **Specialty funds.** These funds might invest in real estate, socially responsible investments, or commodities, to name a few examples.

Active Investing or Passive Investing?

We all have different lifestyles, interests, and time constraints that may determine the answer to the above question.

Active investing means you take a hands-on approach to investing, research your investments yourself, and construct and maintain your portfolio on your own, or you use an investment advisor who will construct and manage your portfolio by choosing investment positions and deciding when to trade them. If you are going to select your own investments and buy and sell through an online broker, you can consider yourself an active investor. Just keep in mind that you will need time to conduct your research on investment opportunities, have the knowledge to conduct analysis on your potential investments, and actually have a desire to spend time doing this. Passive investing is putting your money into investment funds where the fund's portfolio manager is selecting investments and managing the fund.

This distinction also applies to the management of mutual funds and exchange-traded funds. Actively managed funds have investment managers or management teams that pick stocks or securities that they expect to outperform their benchmark or otherwise add value to the overall portfolio. Passively managed funds track an index and don't have managers making investment decisions.

Investment Management Options

There are a variety of options on offer that will assist you with investing and investment strategy. If you are just starting out and don't want to choose funds or stocks on your own, there are low-fee, computer-based options (robo-advisors) that choose and manage a portfolio for you after you answer some simple questions. Some offer access to financial advisors for questions, and some are specifically for women investors, such as Ellevest. Other robo-advisors to check out are Vanguard, Betterment, SoFi, and Stash.

If you want personalized advice and holistic planning, do your research and work with a financial advisor. Not only can many financial advisors help you with a long-term investment strategy based on your time horizon, personal goals, and risk tolerance, but they can also prepare a financial plan, which can illustrate how long your money will last throughout your lifetime based on defined assumptions.

But take note, not all financial advisors are created equal, and you should ask certain questions to the prospective advisor:

1. **Are you a fiduciary?** Fiduciaries are legally required to work in the "best" interest of their clients. Non-fiduciaries are held to the lesser standard of "suitability," which means they may recommend investments that are not the most ideal for you. Fiduciary advisors are legally bound to eliminate all conflicts of interest.

2. **How do you get paid?** Focus on **fee-only** advisors. Fee-only advisors usually charge a percentage of assets under management, which means that they have skin in the game (if your assets decrease, they get paid less). Again, this eliminates conflicts of interest and should be a totally transparent arrangement. A fee-based financial advisor is not the same as a fee-only financial advisor. A fee-based advisor may earn a fee for developing a financial plan for you, while also earning a commission for selling you a certain insurance product or investment. A fee-only financial advisor earns no commissions.

3. **What are your qualifications?** The term *investment advisor* is not regulated, which means it can be used by people who are primarily selling investment products but not formulating investment strategy and curating investment selections. Research the person's designations (are they accredited?), educational background, and use Form ADV to check their record. Investment advisors use Form ADV to register with the Securities and Exchange Commission and the state securities authorities. It is available to the public on the SEC's Investment Advisor Public Disclosure website.

4. **What is your investment philosophy?** It is important that the advisor explain their strategy to you and that you understand it. Don't be afraid to ask questions and delve deep into why they have the strategy they do. You need to be confident in how your long-term financial goals are going to be achieved. If they can't explain this to you clearly and logically, then they probably don't know, either.

5. **Who is your custodian?** It is best if your financial advisor has an independent custodian to hold your investments (rather than act as their own custodian) and from which you will receive monthly statements.

6. **How often will we meet?** How much access do you have to the advisor? How regularly will you meet? Is the advisor available for phone calls and emails outside scheduled meetings?

Finally, there's one question you have to ask yourself: Does it feel like a good fit?

A Word about Impact Investing, or Socially Conscious Investments

There are many terms floating around for this type of investing. It can be called socially responsible investing, socially conscious investing, social-impact investing, impact investing, or ESG (environmental, social, and governance) investing. I am going to call it social-impact investing, for simplicity's sake.

Social-impact investing is investing in companies and funds that have positive social impact and provide some monetary return to you, which is different from community investing, where the return is measured on community impact and not monetary return to the investor. The Global Impact Investing Network defines social impact investments as "investments made with the intention to generate positive, measurable social and environmental impact alongside a financial return.

Impact investments can be made in both emerging and developed markets, and target a range of returns from below market to market rate, depending on investors' strategic goals."[13]

If you are interested in social impact investing, my advice is to keep in mind that these are still investments contributing to your wealth creation. Take time to review the fundamentals of the investment to ensure some potential return. Focus on a company's management practices and whether they are a sustainable enterprise that will enhance community improvement over the long term while generating solid investment returns for you. When investing in a social-impact fund, check fees and historical returns. Even socially responsible investors are constrained by the returns they can afford to sacrifice without jeopardizing their financial security.

If you are passionate about social-impact investing, evaluate the investments performance and impact as you would any other investment that contributes to the growth of your wealth and long-term financial security.

THE UPSHOT

It takes discipline and consistent investing to build wealth, as well as patience and unemotional decision-making. Make regular saving and investing a priority by setting up automated, regular deposits to your investment accounts. Automated, regular deposits, no matter how small, set you up for success. With automated deposits, you don't have to remember to make monthly deposits to your investment account; it just happens automatically and takes all the stress out of it.

Another thing to remember is that reviewing and stress-testing your investment strategy shouldn't be done only in times of crisis. It is helpful during bull markets and periods of personal and professional success as well. Make time to regularly review your investment strategy in the context of your holistic financial picture to keep on track with goals and given time horizons.

Take a deep breath, do your research, and empower yourself by having your money make money for you!

"The future depends on what you do today."

—Mahatma Gandhi

CHAPTER 8

Your Home:
Should You Buy or Rent?

"Home is where the heart is."

—Proverb

IS A HOME A PHYSICAL PLACE—essentially a house—or a state of mind in which you feel at peace and secure? I have pondered this question over the years, as I have been both a homeowner and a renter, depending on my life situation. Homeownership is often associated with the American Dream as a symbol of wealth and independence. It's an ideal that has permeated our psyche as almost an obligatory building block of achieving financial independence. However, I believe this is a somewhat antiquated view, and that there are pros and cons to both renting and buying, depending on your circumstances. If you are contemplating purchasing a home, you should view it like any other financial decision and make sure it is a sensible investment given your overall financial situation and personal circumstances.

There is no correct answer to the "buy or rent" question, and the decision depends on your preferences, plans, and finances. According to iPropertyManagement, as of January 2021, homeownership was nearing

179

a ten-year high, with homeowners outnumbering renters two to one (with 67.4 percent of American adults owning their home and 32.6 percent renting).[1] However, industry experts predict that rental demand will increase over the subsequent five years due to the rental housing shortages already being experienced. The 2008 Great Recession turned the tide on renting, which skyrocketed in popularity while ownership numbers remained flat.

The choice to rent or buy will probably come up several times over the course of your life. When I started out in my career, I rented an apartment in New York City. Next, I bought a house in Westchester County when I was newly married; then we moved to London and rented a house there for several years. Once we knew we were going to remain in London indefinitely, we bought a house there, and when I got divorced and moved back to the United States, I rented for ten years while I figured out my life and built up my financial assets, and then bought a house again! Life circumstances change, and that often affects where and how you live.

The metrics for deciding to rent or buy are different, with the costs of buying being more complicated and varied. Let's break it down.

Buying

The Factors to Consider

If you think you are going to be living in your home for several years, you have enough for a down payment, and you don't have short-term liquidity needs, homeownership may be a good option for you. It doesn't always make sense to buy a home, even though traditional thinking may say it should be your number-one priority. Make a reasoned evaluation of your situation, and consider the following questions when deciding.

WHERE DO YOU WANT TO LIVE?

Every housing market and buyer is different. The housing markets in New York, San Francisco, and Los Angeles are more expensive than cities such as Phoenix, Las Vegas, or Detroit. Also, every buyer has different preferences; for example, you might weigh location factors like good schools, jobs, safety, and proximity to public transportation and recreation over the size and condition of the home. Evaluate the factors that are most important to you, and determine whether you can get the things you want in the area you would like to live within your budget.

HOW MUCH CAN YOU AFFORD FOR THE PRICE OF THE HOME?

Determining how much you can afford to spend on a home purchase depends on several factors, including your income, credit score, and lifestyle. It is best to figure this out before you go house hunting and get caught up in the excitement, which might result in you falling in love with a house out of reach.

You can find home affordability calculators online that will give you a frame of reference for what you can afford and how much of a mortgage you can qualify for. The calculation will be based on your location, yearly income, monthly debt, and how much money you have for a down payment and closing costs. You can use these calculators to figure out how much cash you need on hand for the down payment and closing costs based on the price you are targeting.

Lenders will evaluate your debt-to-income ratio when reviewing your mortgage application. As a rule, lenders don't like to lend to borrowers who are laden with debt. Generally, you want to make sure that your mortgage payment, which includes principal, interest, property taxes, home, and mortgage insurance and homeowner's association dues, is not more than 29 percent of your gross monthly income. Also, it is important that your total monthly debt (mortgage, car loans, student debt, credit card debt, etc.) is not more than 41 percent of your total monthly income.

THE DOWN PAYMENT: HOW MUCH CAN YOU AFFORD, AND HOW MUCH DO YOU HAVE TO PUT DOWN?

Most people think you have to put down 20 percent on a house purchase. But the good news is that few lenders require 20 percent at closing on conventional mortgages. That said, it can still be prudent to put that amount down if you can. Down payments help take the risk off the lender by building trust between you and them, and they reciprocate by giving you better credit terms. So, if you put more money down, there's a better chance of your monthly payments being lower; other perks include avoiding the cost of mortgage insurance and having more equity in your new home.

WHAT IS THE TERM OF THE MORTGAGE?

A thirty-year mortgage term is probably the most common, and the length of time that you will be paying the loan matters. The rule of thumb is that the shorter the term of the loan, the lower the interest rate. But even with a lower interest rate, paying the same amount of money over a shorter period usually means higher monthly payments.

HOW LONG DO YOU PLAN TO STAY?

Buying makes more sense if you are planning on staying in a home for a while. If you'll only be living in that location for a few years, renting will almost always be your best choice. In that scenario, if you're planning to pack up and leave in the short term, you probably don't want to spend the time and money necessary to buy a house (with a down payment, closing costs, loan charges, appraisal fees, and so on) and then deal with the possibility of not being able to sell your home on your timetable when you want to move on. This applies if you are in personal transition, too. If you are expecting a career relocation, or you plan on getting married and combining finances in a couple of years, buying a house might not make sense. After my divorce, I needed time to get my personal infrastructure laid down before I made any permanent financial commitments.

WHAT IS THE COST OF RENTING A SIMILAR HOME?

In many cases, renting can be cheaper than buying a home because of the up-front costs, the maintenance costs, and the possible renovation costs involved with owning a home; renters don't have to contend with all of that. Keep in mind that the monthly principal and interest on your mortgage isn't all you have to pay; you'll also have property taxes, homeowner's insurance, and (in many cases) mortgage insurance as well as homeowners' association fees.

The Pros and Cons of Buying

THE PROS

- Stability—you decide if and when you want to move, not the landlord.
- Financial predictability—a fixed-rate mortgage payment doesn't change.
- Freedom to renovate and customize your living space to your taste.
- Pride of ownership—it's your asset.
- Building home equity over time as you pay your mortgage and as the market price of your home appreciates.
- Paying down your mortgage reduces how much you owe, and as your home value appreciates, you are essentially saving and building wealth.
- Tax deductions on your mortgage interest expense.

THE CONS

- High up-front costs.
- Property taxes can and will increase over time.
- Ongoing maintenance and repair costs.
- Home and possibly mortgage insurance expenses.

- The value of the home can decrease due to market conditions.
- Less flexibility to relocate. A house is an illiquid asset, and you may not be able to sell it on the timetable you would like.

Renting

The Factors to Consider

Many people prefer renting because they enjoy the flexibility of being able to change neighborhoods, cities, or states at the end of their lease. If you don't like where you live or you relocate for your job, renting makes life much simpler. Also, you don't have to come up with a significant down payment, and the whole process is quicker.

HOW MUCH SHOULD YOU SPEND ON YOUR RENT?

A popular guideline for how much to spend on rent is the 30 percent rule, which states that you should spend approximately 30 percent of your gross income on rent. So, if you earn $3,000 per month before taxes, your rent should be about $900 per month. This is a good guideline, but not a hard-and-fast rule. If you live in an area where you can get an amazing rental for less than 30 percent of your gross monthly income, then definitely go for it! You will be able to save more money and grow your wealth with the difference. On the other hand, if you live in a very expensive city, such as San Francisco, where median rents are over $2,500 per month for a one-bedroom apartment, it may not be feasible to stick to the 30 percent rule.

CAN YOU STICK TO THE 50/30/20 RULE?

Remember the 50/30/20 Rule covered in chapter 5, when we discussed the Badass Budget? It's important to factor that into your rent affordability analysis. Let's refresh our memory: the 50/30/20 budget rule simply says that you allocate 50 percent of your after-tax income (take-home pay) to necessities, 30 percent to wants, and 20 percent to paying down debt and saving.

Let's say you earn $2,500 per month after taxes. You would allocate $1,250 (50 percent) for needs such as rent, utilities, groceries, car payments, and minimal debt payments; $750 to wants like shopping, going out to dinner, concerts, etc.; and $500 to paying debt and savings. Your rent expense figures into the 50 percent part of the rule, and if you have high fixed costs, that will mean your rent affordability will be decreased. For example, if you spend monthly $200 on your car payment, $120 on car insurance, $200 on a student loan payment, $100 on groceries, and $90 on utilities, that totals $710, which leaves you with $540 (out of $1,250) per month for rent. You could spend less on wants if you want to spend more on rent, but then you must be disciplined in not overspending and incurring credit card debt to do so. You can also look for savings in other ways: by scaling back on your cable package, for example, or looking for the best deal on car insurance, reducing grocery bills by planning meals, or getting a roommate.

CAN YOU STILL PRIORITIZE SAVINGS?

Remember that you still need to have an emergency fund and contribute to retirement savings, so blowing all your hard-earned money on outsized rent and not thinking of your future self is very shortsighted. Homeowners are building up equity, and hence wealth, through their house purchase, but renters are not. However, there is less cost involved in renting, and with the reduced costs, renters should be saving more.

WHAT ARE THE COSTS OF RENTING?

The initial costs to renting include the security deposit and possibly a real estate broker's fee. Recurring costs include monthly rent and the cost of renter's insurance.

The Pros and Cons of Renting

THE PROS

- Flexibility—renters are free to move at the end of their lease term.
- Don't have to pay for home maintenance and repairs.
- Fewer up-front costs—no down payment or closing costs.
- Fewer ongoing costs, such as property taxes, homeowner association dues, and property insurance.
- Easier to find accommodations that suit your preferences.
- Potentially available community amenities.

THE CONS

- Rent prices can increase annually.
- Landlords may not be responsive to requested repairs and problems and may defer attending to them.
- You may be at the mercy of the landlord and be required to move out.
- You are limited in your ability to make it your own style or aesthetic.
- Rent payments do not build up equity or wealth.

THE UPSHOT

Deciding whether to rent or buy your home is not just about money. It's about your personal current circumstances, your vision for your life, and your overall comfort. Follow your own preferences and ignore people who insist that owning always makes sense in the long run, or if your monthly mortgage payment would be the same or less than your rent payment. These blanket statements don't take into account housing markets' volatility or your life circumstances. Also, once you add up all the costs of buying a house, you may decide that you would be better off renting and investing the money you would have put into a home that you purchased.

There are no right answers, and answers may change over time. Do what is right for you and enjoy your living space!

"Home isn't a place, it's a feeling."

—Cecelia Ahern

CHAPTER 9

Hidden Financial Risks and How to Protect Yourself: Cohabitation, Marriage, and Roommates

WITH OUR BUSY SCHEDULES and so many responsibilities to juggle, we sometimes make significant personal decisions without careful consideration, which can have significant financial consequences. In the tapestry of life, we regularly make decisions as to who we live with (whether it is a significant other or a roommate); whether we commingle our assets with our spouses; and how we establish our credit, either jointly or independently. These decisions are wrapped up in personal relationships, and the hidden risks, though not patently obvious, should be considered. As always, an honest, open, and practical approach to these matters is the best strategy when it comes to being fulfilled personally and protecting your individual financial status. With some forethought and planning, we can protect ourselves from unanticipated twists and turns in situations.

Whether we are single, young, and just beginning a career, or divorced or widowed, we may have found that special someone we love and are considering living with or marrying. This is a wonderful development, and a time of joy! We want to have sustained happiness in this relationship and allow all the things that money can't buy to flourish. Whether these decisions are made after periods of contemplation or impulsively, they will alter the course of our life, and with a bit of preparation and planning prior to taking the leap, we can secure certain financially advantageous outcomes for both parties if things change down the line. The preventive advice in this chapter applies to both women and men—all people! As the old adage states: "Plan for what is difficult while it is easy."

It is time to establish a new tradition and change the paradigm. With the ever-changing roles of women at home and at work, more women are in the workforce, increasingly the primary breadwinners; and often have significant assets from employment, divorce, death of a spouse, or inheritance. If you are considering cohabiting or marrying, protecting your assets and future financial security should be paramount in your mind, and not an afterthought. It is about nurturing and protecting your estate while you are living.

We need to be proactive because we cannot possibly envision all the twists and turns of life, some of which can cause serious problems and put our and our family's future at risk. I encourage everyone to have these conversations before calling the moving company or walking down the aisle. Let's change the love narrative to include preparation and prevention; it doesn't mean you love your partner any less!

My unfortunate divorce experience enlightened me as to what steps I could and should have taken to avoid putting myself at such risk. I got married in 1987, and back then, nobody really talked about prenups, or separate property trusts, or the financial ramifications to me specifically if I decided to be a full-time stay-at-home mother. Honestly, I didn't really think about any of these decisions; I just proceeded without caution and assumed all would turn out just fine. The thought of a future divorce or valuing my homemaking responsibilities never crossed my mind. But things are different now, and we are all wiser and hopefully more careful with our future self's life and security.

There are a few things each of us can do to put some protections in place for our long-term financial security. Let's explore ways we can protect ourselves during each stage of our lives.

The First Step: Create a Separate Property Trust

A separate property trust is a revocable living trust created to hold property acquired outside of the marital estate, regardless of whether it is acquired before, during, or after marriage, or by inheritance either before, during, or after marriage. Examples of separate property include: a savings or investment account held in your name only that you fund with money that you earn; a house that you purchased with your own money that is in your name only; or an inheritance you received for you only.

A single or divorced woman should create a separate property trust before cohabitation/marriage and fund it with her assets to set up her game plan. This will avoid probate (in the event of death) and clarify and delineate the ownership status and separate property character of the total assets that she owned prior to marriage or cohabitation (even if currently she doesn't have substantial assets; it affects the status of future asset acquisition, too). Even if you are not considering cohabitation or marriage at this time, if you are a single woman with assets or on the path to accumulating assets, you should establish a separate property trust. If you do cohabit or get married at some point, the existence of your separate property trust will allow you to create a prominent line in the sand as to what is your separate property, so that it does not get commingled with marital or joint property.

Also, keep in mind that having a separate property trust does not preclude the ability to have a community property trust with a spouse—which would hold any community property acquired by a couple during marriage. One type of trust does not preclude having the other type.

You can retain a lawyer to create the trust, or you can do it yourself with online services such as LegalZoom. I created a separate property trust and, even though I recently got married, the trust clearly delin-eates what property I hold separately from any community property with my husband. I created it when I had just begun my journey of self-realization in re-creating my career and rebuilding my assets, and before I even thought I would marry again.

I want to reiterate that if you are a woman who is working and accumulating assets, even if you are young and starting out, you should create a separate property trust. This is especially important for asset protection in a second or third marriage, because the separate prop-erty trust will ring-fence any assets that you had prior to that marriage and keep them separate. You can name your children as beneficiaries to the trust so that your assets pass to your kids upon your death and are not automatically passed to your second/third spouse. In most second and third marriages, it is likely that each partner will bring more wealth to the relationship, and children and grandchildren can cause further emotional complications, especially with respect to inheritance.

A Word about Cohabitation

What if we want to live together and not get formally married? It is quite common today for couples of all ages to choose to live together before marriage or to have no intention of marriage—and they will often pur-chase property and build a financial house together.

Over the years, marriage rates have declined, and the percentage of U.S. adults who cohabitate with an unmarried partner has risen, according to a Pew Research Center Study.[1] In 2019, the U.S. Census Bureau cited that the number of unmarried partners living together in the United States had nearly tripled in two decades, from 6 million to 17 million, which is 7 percent of the total adult population.[2] The demo-graphics of cohabiters has also evolved, with a significant increase in cohabitation among older adults as divorce rates have risen, as you can see in Figure 9.1.

Partners in Cohabitating Households by Age Group: 1996–2017 *(in percent)*

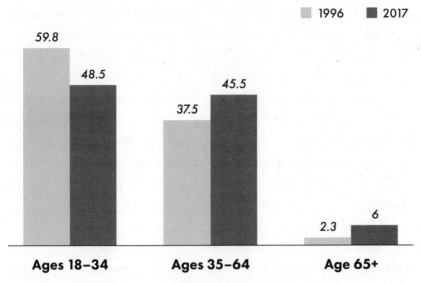

FIGURE 9.1 Partners in Cohabitating Households by Age Group: 1996–2017[3]

Currently, a larger share of adults has cohabited than has been married. Pew Research reports that among adults eighteen to forty-four, 59 percent have lived with an unmarried partner at some point, while only 50 percent have ever been married, and 38 percent of the cohabiters have had two or more partners over the course of their life. Further, according to Pew, more than half of cohabiting adults have children living in the household with them.[4]

Whether it's you, your daughter or son, a brother or sister, a parent, or a friend, it is likely that somebody in your orbit is living with, or has lived with, a significant other without being married. This is no longer just an issue for younger people.

So What's the Big Deal?

Plain and simple, whether you choose to cohabitate because of love, as a step toward marriage, for convenience, or for financial reasons, it is probable that over time, assets and money may be commingled, intentionally or unintentionally, and individuals may unintentionally acquire or relinquish certain rights because of cohabitation with their partner.

Unmarried couples are not afforded the same legal protections when it comes to property rights as married couples. Currently, only a small number of states permit couples to get married through common-law marriage, and the requirements for doing so are much more stringent than just living together. Hence, most couples living together are not deemed to be common-law married and don't have the legal protections of a married couple.

Given that, if you are intending to live with someone for more than a short time, it is in your best interest to have a cohabitation agreement that spells out who owns what and how it would be distributed, as well as support payments and estate planning issues, if the couple parts company. The agreement can also address issues while living together, such as who is responsible for which monthly expenses, how much you will each contribute to monthly expenses, etc. Basically, a cohabitation agreement is a written contract between two people who are not married; it is designed to address the variety of personal, financial, and family issues you and your partner may face in the event of an emergency or a breakup. If couples do get married after living together, the cohabitation agreement can serve as a basis for a prenuptial agreement, which is always recommended.

Right about now, you might be saying, "This is the most unromantic thing to do; why upset the apple cart and discuss this with my partner?" Because even with the best of intentions, things can change in a relationship, and it is better to create a fair agreement at the outset, without pressure, to address what happens if the relationship breaks down. It will save you a lot of emotional and financial heartache if something does come to pass. Being practical doesn't mean you aren't romantic—in fact, I would argue that addressing issues early on shows you have greater confidence and trust in your relationship. If you are afraid to discuss this with your partner, it could mean that your relationship isn't as solid as you think.

Cohabitation Agreements

In addition to creating a separate property trust, single women who intend to cohabit or are cohabiting should consider entering into a cohabitation agreement to confirm their arrangement with their significant other with respect to their legal rights to individually and jointly acquired property.

For example, a couple may purchase a home together with one party providing the full down payment. It is important to have clarity regarding the ownership of the house in the event of a breakup to obviate any alleged side arrangements later. If you don't have this clearly delineated, the other party may refuse to move out, which could create havoc.

The cohabitation agreement can set forth what exactly will occur concerning a division of assets (furniture, real estate, cars, etc.) acquired during the cohabitation, which will reduce acrimony and confusion.

The further good news is that the cohabitation agreement can be drafted as a combo cohabitation agreement/prenuptial agreement. Even if you haven't discussed marriage, the cohabitation agreement can have all the provisions that you and your partner agree will take effect if and when the next step occurs. All the hard work is done before engagement and marriage, and it provides the perfect transition because it converts into the prenuptial agreement and takes away the need to have that conversation immediately before tying the knot.

Most agreements include:

- How specific assets are owned.
- Whether or not, and how, income and expenses are shared.
- How newly acquired assets are owned.
- How bank accounts, credit cards, insurance policies, etc. will be managed.

- How specific assets will be distributed in the event of a separation, or what process will be used for resolving disputes of property rights.
- If you buy a house together, address "how" the ownership is listed on the deed (whether as joint tenants or tenants-in-common), how much of the house each partner owns, buyout rights, how the house will be appraised, and who stays in the house if there is a breakup.
- Liability for debts: unmarried partners are not responsible for each other's debt unless they have a joint account or are a cosigner or guarantor, which is different from the situation with married couples, where partners can be held liable for marital debts.
- Support payments after the breakup for one of the partners.
- Surviving partners: If one of the partners dies, the surviving partner has no rights to the deceased partner's individual property unless left to the surviving partner by a will or trust of the deceased partner (this is because you are not considered a legal spouse). You can also include medical directives and powers of attorney.

Preparing for Marriage

You said yes! The arrangements are now in motion, and there is so much to plan, and, it seems, so little time.

Engagement and marriage are significant steps and will change your life emotionally and financially, without a doubt. It is a time of joy, love, and planning. It is normal and natural to get caught up in the flurry of romantic excitement and not want to discuss money and what happens if it doesn't work out as we expect. Who in their right mind wants to talk about money and division of property before you even walk down the aisle?

You do! Our relationship with money is in many ways a reflection of our relationship with ourselves. Whether we like it or not, we all need money to live, and if we don't have control over our financial security, it will have a direct deleterious effect on our happiness and well-being.

Having a premarital discussion about finances and property reflects a strong sense of self-esteem, preparation, and good sense. Women are often the bedrock of their families; if we do not prepare for unexpected events, it may prevent us, at a later date, from taking care of ourselves and the ones we love—our children—and subject the family to extreme disruption.

My call to action is for you to have the courage to have these discussions while love is in full force, and not to be fearful that you are hurting your partner in some way by doing so. My goal is for you to enter this new, wonderful stage of your life on equal footing, with eyes wide open, and with the belief that you are the key to your own happiness, both now and in the future. Are you willing to risk future turmoil because you can't bring yourself to have this conversation and are instead throwing caution to the wind?

Prenuptial Agreements

If you have not been cohabiting and/or have no cohabitation agreement prior to marriage, you and your partner should create a prenuptial agreement.

A prenuptial agreement is entered into before marriage to document the nature of property acquired before and during marriage; and the division of property and income (including support/alimony) in the unfortunate event of divorce, separation, or death. The idea is for separate property to remain separate—to prevent application of the community property or equitable distribution laws to your separate property.

Although spouses are always free to enter into a binding agreement regarding their marital property rights during the marriage (via a postnuptial agreement, which we'll cover next), *agreements regarding spousal support—that is, alimony—must be entered into before marriage (via prenuptial agreement) to be enforceable.* With more women being the primary breadwinners, women paying spousal support is not an unusual occurrence.

The Tax Cuts and Jobs Act of 2017 has increased the "cost" of spousal support by repealing the deduction for alimony paid after 2019. Hence, in the event of divorces occurring after 2018, the high-income earning spouse will pay tax on all their income, even that portion of their income that is paid over to their ex-spouse (their ex-spouse will no longer pay income tax on alimony received). To limit the potentially devastating effects of this new law to the person who pays alimony, high-income earners can instead enter into a prenuptial agreement that limits the amount and duration of spousal support or eliminates the obligation to pay spousal support altogether.

Alternatively, if you think you might choose to stay at home with your children in lieu of climbing the corporate ladder, you may wish to enter into a prenuptial agreement setting forth the right to receive a certain amount of spousal support in the event of divorce, as an added layer of security.

If, before you get married, you think you might want to be a stay-at-home mom, or SAHM, take some time to create a future monetary value for your contribution to raising children and the running of the household and incorporate it as part of your prenuptial agreement. That is a settlement amount to compensate you for:

- Lost professional development
- The fact that you cannot contribute to 401(k)s or Social Security during your time out of the workforce
- The transition time it might take you to be financially independent

In the event of a divorce, splitting everything down the middle probably isn't fair to a SAHM, who gave up a salary to take care of the spouse, the house, and the children. She should most certainly be compensated by an agreed valuation for loss of career development (in fact, a step backward), wages, and benefits over the time of not working outside the home. This should be clearly stated in the prenuptial agreement. If only I had known to do this, it would have saved me so much stress, discomfort, and fear. But nobody talked about this when I got married in the eighties and decided to stay home. I gave up my career and ultimately suffered because of it when I got divorced. I want to make sure that doesn't happen to you! (Later in this chapter, I discuss factors to consider when deciding whether you want to be a SAHM.)

Prenuptial agreements are also protective in situations where one spouse has children from a former marriage. Such an agreement helps to ensure that a spouse's separate property goes to their own children. A prenuptial agreement provides added protection against separate property claims brought by the children against the trust and/or estate. Further, prenuptial agreements can be amended later if the landscape changes and both parties agree to change the terms.

Without a prenuptial agreement, you subject yourself to the default rules and guidelines of the court, and the judge has discretion and jurisdiction to determine what is community property and separate property. If you have agreed as a couple up front as to property division and the manner in which to calculate a lump-sum settlement and/or alimony prior to marriage, you have seized control of a potentially volatile situation that could result in a deterioration of lifestyle and a period fraught with financial uncertainty; you have agreed not to leave that decision to a judge who doesn't know anything about you or your life.

During Marriage

Oh no! I don't have a prenuptial agreement! What can I do now that I am already hitched?

Postnuptial Agreements

So maybe it didn't ever occur to you to have a prenuptial agreement, and you are already married. You can accomplish almost everything a prenuptial agreement does with a postnuptial agreement, with the exception of spousal support terms (i.e., alimony), as discussed previously.

Once you are married, you may think you are too far down the path to bring this up. However, the same uncertainty and possible unfortunate outcomes can still occur if you do not come to an agreement with respect to property division in the event of an unanticipated breakup. In the interest of protecting your future mental, physical, and financial health, a candid conversation, when all is copacetic, about money and future unanticipated occurrences will benefit both parties and can strengthen the relationship.

The Process

The recommendation for establishing any of these agreements (cohabitation, prenup, or postnup) is for one party to retain a lawyer to draft the agreement and submit it to the other party for review with their own independent counsel. If both parties have their own separate counsel, it strengthens the agreement and mitigates against one party stating later that they weren't represented and didn't understand. If both parties are in general agreement and there is minimal negotiation, the cost should be minimal, and it will be well worth it in the long run.

There are DIY versions of prenups/postnups online, which, of course, will be cheaper to prepare than hiring a lawyer. That said, it is worth it in my opinion to hire a lawyer. Courts are more likely to enforce these agreements when lawyers have represented both spouses, as courts believe the parties will have a greater understanding of what they agreed to and full knowledge of the parameters of the contract. It may be an up-front expense, but an enforceable prenuptial or postnuptial agreement will save you an abundance of potential cost and suffering.

A Word about Second and Third Marriages

More and more people are getting married for second and third times—40 percent of brides and grooms have been previously married. Unfortunately, the divorce rate for second marriages is a whopping 67 percent, so the possibility of divorce is present.[5] Even if you do stay married, eventually one of you will pass, and a prenuptial agreement can eliminate confusion and aggravation for you and your heirs.

Most people in second/third marriages come into the marriage with assets, liabilities, and obligations. Before tying the knot, mention to your partner your outstanding debts, loans, prior bankruptcy filings, income sources, investments, retirement assets, and any other financial assets or obligations. This is an essential exercise; it will set the tone for relationship openness, and it will give you peace of mind that you won't be saddled with an unforeseen obligation of your future spouse's debt.

If you have alimony or child support payments, or even if you expect to provide financial support to aging parents or adult children in the future, address this as early as possible. Depending on the terms of a prior divorce settlement and the law in your state, a new marriage or even cohabitation can affect alimony, child support, and even custody of the children; hence, it is best to plan for these contingencies before the second marriage.

Prior to my second marriage, we had full disclosure of our financial assets, debts, and obligations. I have aging parents, and I contribute financially to their care, and I have adult children whom I occasionally help out financially. Our discussions made it crystal clear where we both were and what our respective expectations were about our commingled finances. I was also very transparent about the legacy I intend to leave to my children. These talks truly strengthened our relationship.

You should also update your will, trust, and beneficiary information to reflect your new marital status and what property you want to pass to your children, spouse, or stepchildren. If you do not specify this, property that is deemed marital property could be distributed after you pass in a manner that you may not have intended to a recipient you might not want to receive it.

Long-Term Care Insurance

If there is a large age gap between spouses, a discussion about long-term care is essential. It is possible that the older spouse may need long-term care in a nursing home or facility down the road, and the couple's assets will have to pay for that care, which is very expensive and can lead to financial difficulties or even bankruptcy. The couple should discuss the possibility of long-term care insurance as a form of asset protection for the younger spouse.

Commingling Assets

This concept applies to marital property and can be a complex topic. That said, it can be managed with some planning and strategy, which will benefit each spouse in the event of divorce. It is best to discuss and plan for this before you get married. It will pave the way for future harmony and, if you were to get divorced, it will save you both time, money, and lots of stress.

Before you get married, the property you own is considered separate property. If you had $20,000 before you got married, that amount qualifies as separate property unless you commingle it with marital property later (for example, by putting that money in a joint account with your spouse). Another example: If you owned a home before you got married, moved into it with your new spouse, and then both of you paid the mortgage moving forward, the house would no longer be separate property. Your new spouse would have an interest in it if the two of you were to divorce, and your house would now be considered commingled property.

Here are a few examples of how funds get commingled:

- If you inherit money and deposit the inheritance into a joint account with your spouse, those funds become marital property.
- If you owned a home before your marriage and following the marriage the mortgage is paid for using funds from a joint bank account, the home will become marital property.
- If you and your spouse combine your resources during your marriage to buy a car, television, home, or any other type of property, that property will become marital property.
- If you have an investment account or start one that both you and your spouse's incomes contribute to, the funds in the account will be considered marital property.
- If you have a checking or savings account that both you and your spouse are depositing funds into, those funds will be considered marital property.
- If you borrowed money from family and used it to benefit you and your spouse, those funds would become marital property. In cases where money is owed at the time of the divorce, it would be the responsibility of both spouses to repay it.

To avoid the hassle of dividing marital property during a divorce, it is optimal to keep property separate that you would like to continue being legally yours, and yours alone.

How can you do this? Here are a few suggestions to avoid commingling:

- One of the easiest ways to go about keeping separate property from commingling and becoming marital property is to set up a prenuptial agreement in which it is plainly stated which property will be considered marital property and which will remain separate.

- Never use your separate property to pay off marital debts. If your parents were to give you a large sum of money as a gift, for example, do not use it to pay off your home that is held in joint names or to pay for credit card debt. When a marriage benefits from funds, those funds become marital property.

- If you own property prior to your marriage, keep your name alone on the deed, and, if that separate property requires maintenance, only use your income to fund it. You should also keep strict records to prove that your spouse did not contribute to its maintenance.

- Before making a large purchase, such as a home or a car, consider discussing if it should be marital property or separate property. If you want to have an equal interest in it, use marital funds to purchase it.

- If you want any property purchases to remain separate, only use funds that are considered separate property to buy them, and keep records about the funds used to make the purchases.

You get the picture. Keep the money and assets you don't want to be considered marital property separate by owning them in a separate property trust and/or separate accounts in your name only and having a prenuptial or postnuptial agreement that clearly specifies the delineations.

A quick note about filing tax returns: Holding separate property in your name does not mean that you should file your tax return separately from your spouse. You can still file jointly with your spouse. The two reasons to file separately would be a separation or pending divorce, or, in a childless marriage, if one spouse makes significantly more money than the other spouse and the lower-paid spouse would be eligible for substantial itemizable deductions if they file separately. Generally, joint filing is more advantageous, especially for couples with children.

Credit: Being Credit-Wise

Once you commingle debt with a spouse, it is almost impossible to de-mingle it! Even if you get divorced, a creditor will not recognize the court's assignment of debt responsibility because lenders are not bound by your divorce agreement because they are not a party to it. That means just because you and your soon-to-be ex-spouse agree that one of you will pay the Visa while the other pays the Mastercard, it means nothing to the lender. If credit cards are held jointly, then whether you are divorced or not, the lender can come after you for repayment.

Maintaining separate credit when you're married has nothing to do with trust, whether you love the person, whether you think the marriage will last, or whether you are coldhearted; it is just practical. Beware, though, that in the few community property states (Alaska, Arizona, California, Idaho, Louisiana, Nevada, New Mexico, Washington, Wisconsin, and Texas), you will both be liable for credit card debt even if only one of you applied for the card. Community property states believe that you both probably benefited from the debt, hence you should both be liable. If you live in a community property state, my recommendation is to review credit card bills monthly and monitor charges incurred by both parties so at least you know where you stand, debt-wise. Don't delegate payment to your partner and have no knowledge of balances.

Bad credit will follow you and have many detrimental ripple effects in your life, so do not feel uncomfortable having separate credit from your spouse, or monitoring credit closely if you live in a community property state.

Factors to Consider for Stay-at-Home Moms

Having children is one of the greatest blessings in life. Childcare decisions are extremely personal and involve a host of considerations for each parent. Suddenly, you are responsible for a little being who needs you to do everything for them. It is a big change, and there can often be competing emotions when it comes to childcare. Some women want to stay at home because they don't want to leave their child with someone else; others believe it will save money for the family if one parent stays home.

As with all life-altering decisions with financial implications, communication between partners is paramount. Jessica Sayers of Moms.com recommends several things to consider before you make the decision:[6]

- **Are you comfortable leaving your career?** Prior to pregnancy, you may have been very focused on your career and working hard to climb the ladder of success. It is okay not to want to give up your career; wanting to have a career *and* be a mom does not make you a bad mother. As discussed earlier, by staying at home full-time, you will disrupt your career trajectory and lose the ability to contribute to a 401(k) and Social Security. Be honest with yourself and your partner about this so you do not feel regret about any choice you make. There should be no judgments about this from anyone.

- **Will you actually be saving money if you stay at home?** Many people stay at home because they want to save money. Do a deep-dive analysis that incorporates the effect of the loss of your salary on satisfying ongoing expenses, and determine whether, in fact, your family would be more financially sound if you remained working, even with the additional childcare expense. Examine your budget to determine if one income can cover all expenses or if there needs to be some cutting of extra expenses if you decide to stay home.

- **Determine an estimated time frame for how long you will be a SAHM.** The decision about when it is best to return to work is different for each of us. Whether you want to stay at home until your child is in preschool, high school, or until after your children graduate from high school, communicate with your partner about the time frame so all expectations are in line and the budgetary ramifications to the household are understood.

- **Consider all the options.** Before you make the decision, make sure that you know all your options and that you have spoken to your employer about what options you have postpregnancy. Perhaps you can work different shifts, part-time, or remotely. Be thorough in your investigation before making any decisions.

- **Talk to other SAHMs about their experience.** Hearing firsthand from SAHMs about their daily experiences, responsibilities, and thoughts about their decision to stay at home can be very effective in helping you make up your mind.

- **Communicate with your partner about clear and delineated responsibilities.** If you are considering staying at home, be sure to have a discussion with your partner about what your responsibilities will be in your new role and what their responsibilities will be. A clear understanding of each person's responsibilities will reduce resentment and allow you to determine how to structure your time, including time just for you.

- **Do YOU want to do it?** Before deciding, ponder what your true desires are for your family, your career, and your finances. Also, think about how you will be spending your time and the difference to your current situation. Being a stay-at-home parent will mean a lot of time spent at home, with less social interaction than you had while working. When I stayed at home after my first daughter was born, it took some real adjustment on my part. I had a career as a lawyer and then a banker, and suddenly,

I was knee-deep in household chores, feeling a bit isolated, and questioning the point of my career. I don't think I would have made the same decision now, but with that said, I enjoyed the time I had with my children. There are no right answers. Follow your gut feeling after considering all the options.

Do whatever you feel you need to do for your family, and whatever brings you the most joy. But go into it with your eyes wide open.

Living with Roommates

For those not cohabiting with a partner but living with roommates, here are a few words of advice. When you rent an apartment or a home, you will be required to have renter's insurance. Unlike immediate family members living together, roommates are not automatically covered on renter's insurance policies unless they are actually listed on the policy. The following are a few pointers about renter's insurance:

- A roommate does not have to be on the lease to be added to the policy.
- A maximum of two unrelated people can be on a single policy, so additional roommates will need to buy a separate policy.
- There's no extra charge to add a roommate, and it won't change your premium either. You may want to increase your coverage if you have a lot of valuables, but you'll still probably pay less than you would alone since you get to split the cost.
- Theft by a roommate—or intentional damage—is not covered by insurance, whether they're on the policy or not. Be judicious in your choice of roommates.
- Since you are sharing the coverage with your roommate, all claim checks will be payable to both of you, and either person can change or cancel the policy. Again, sharing coverage is something you do only with someone you know and trust.

THE UPSHOT

As we traverse the journey of life, we choose a career, live with people, marry, divorce, and decide whether we want to have children. The choices we make have lasting and often permanent effects on our lives, both emotional and financial. Relationships can be joyous, and they can be fraught with tension. Either way, our relationship decisions can have hidden financial risks. We should be aware of these risks and strategically plan around them to protect our financial futures, come what may. Don't make significant personal decisions without pondering the consequences to your future stability so you can address them and enjoy your life.

CHAPTER 10

Divorce: Breaking Up Is Hard to Do

"And so rock bottom became the solid foundation on which I rebuilt my life."

—J.K. Rowling

AMEN TO THAT, sister! I have been married, divorced, and now married again. This is a difficult chapter to write. Even though ten years have passed since my initial divorce decree, and even though I remarried last year, I still have unresolved feelings and thoughts about my divorce. It was, in both good and bad ways, one of the most defining moments of my life. After twenty-three years of marriage and three beautiful daughters, my ex-husband and I pulled the plug, and the divorce was an emotional roller coaster. Given that we were both ex-lawyers, I suppose it was inevitable that our divorce would end up in litigation in a courtroom. If you've been through divorce, then you have an idea of what the pain and emotional trauma can be like.

Although divorce is a gnarly topic and usually just a downright unpleasant experience, I must address it, simply because divorce is prevalent and happens to many of us. We cannot risk being uninformed, confused, or indecisive during the divorce experience; otherwise, we may suffer some irreversible, damaging consequences.

The strange thing is that although I hit rock bottom financially and emotionally, the experience propelled me to redefine myself, claim my option to self-realize, chase *my* dreams, and become financially and emotionally independent. I am stronger, better, and at peace now. I have reclaimed my self-esteem, pondered the experience, and learned from it to evolve into a better version of myself. I don't linger in the space of failure, a victim mentality, bitterness, and anger anymore. In retrospect, and with 20/20 hindsight, I understand why it happened, and that sometimes for the long-term happiness of both individuals, it *needs* to happen. If I hadn't gotten divorced, I wouldn't be writing this book right now and trying to raise women's consciousness to get financially organized and knowledgeable, and I wouldn't be a wealth manager with a career that I love and am passionate about.

There are many complicated and esoteric aspects to divorce, and my goal in this chapter is to give you an overview of what you can do before, during, and after divorce to reduce clouded judgment and emotional drain while safeguarding your finances. It is very difficult to think clearly during the divorce experience. Emotions are elevated; and the traumas of divorce can cause even lawyers, bankers, and accountants—people who "know" how to get divorced—to lose focus during their divorce experiences. I was a corporate lawyer and then a banker, and yet, I totally lost the plot because I was careless in my attention to our finances during our marriage. I was fearful, angry, uninformed, and frequently bewildered by the developments of our long and contentious divorce.

It would take a separate book to address the many things to consider during a divorce. This chapter, however, will give you a general road map. Specifically, it will highlight actions you should take to prepare for divorce so that you will have a strategy and can make decisions with your emotions in check.

The Pregame: Five Things to Do Before You Get Divorced

Whether you are deciding to leave the person you're married to or your partner has asked for a divorce, this time can be fraught with emotional turmoil. Although this uncertain time is overwhelming, it is essential that you also focus on the logistical aspects of the decision before you make any moves to file for divorce. It may be hard to see far into the future, but the decisions you make now will lay the foundation for the next period of your life. You want to do some forensic research into your finances so you have the lay of the land and the facts at hand.

1. Organize Your Finances and Gather Financial Documents

You need to have a clear picture of your joint and individual finances *before* you get divorced. The purpose of divorce is to equitably distribute the marital assets and debts to each person. For this to happen, and for you to negotiate effectively, you need to understand clearly your total joint financial picture. Prepare a marital balance sheet that includes all assets (real estate, cars, retirement accounts, bank accounts, investment accounts, etc.) and liabilities (mortgages, credit card debt, loans, notes, etc.).

Divorces depend heavily on documentation, and if you wait to try to accumulate documents until after you file for divorce, you take the risk that your spouse may make it difficult for you to access the needed documents. Not all spouses react well to being served with divorce papers, and they may set up roadblocks to prevent you getting the necessary documents after you have filed. To the extent possible, gather all documents that you need *before* filing for divorce. Make copies of all relevant financial documents, including:

- Bank account statements (checking, savings, money markets)
- Brokerage account statements

- Mortgage documentation
- Deeds
- Pay stubs and/or W2s
- Federal and state tax returns
- Credit card statements
- Loan documents for any outstanding loans
- Insurance policies
- Retirement account (401[k]s, IRAs, pensions) statements
- Car loan statements

Keep these documents in a safe place, either electronically or physically.

2. Check Your Credit Report

It is likely that you have joint credit cards with your spouse and that your credit is linked. Get a copy of your credit report to evaluate what your credit rating is currently and the components of your score, then monitor it monthly during the divorce process. Often one spouse or the other will run up charges prior to divorce. Before you separate, if possible, it is advisable to pay off and close all joint credit accounts. Try to come up with an agreement to pay these debts off and, if you are unable to do so, explore getting the accounts frozen. Once the divorce is final, the balances owed can be transferred to the party the court holds responsible for the debt. Make sure all credit card bills are being paid during the divorce process, even if you believe it is your spouse's responsibility. Pay the minimum. Divorce proceedings can be protracted, and it only takes one late payment to hurt your credit.

3. Establish Credit in Your Own Name, and Open New Accounts in Your Name

If you have shared credit with your spouse for many years, it may be difficult after a divorce to establish credit in your own name and purchase a car or a home. It is very, very important that you establish your own credit and build up a good credit score before divorce. It is best to open new accounts and credit cards in your own name while you are still married. Go to a bank where you do not have joint accounts with your spouse, and open a checking and savings account in your name only.

4. Make the Decision about Your Living Situation

Moving out of the family home can affect your interest in the property and, if your spouse pays the mortgage during the divorce proceedings, it is possible that a judge could factor that into any decision made about property distribution. Although you may be ready to live a separate life, speak to an attorney before you make any decisions concerning your living arrangements during the divorce process.

5. Understand the Different Divorce Alternatives

There are four different types of divorce routes: mediation, collaborative, litigation, and do-it-yourself. Each option involves a different process and different professionals. It is obviously easier and less expensive if you and your spouse can settle your issues without litigation, but that doesn't always happen. Make sure you choose an attorney who knows the value of settling but who can be an effective advocate for you should you need to litigate. Interview three divorce lawyers who have at least five years of experience in family and divorce law matters, and determine who is a good fit for you. These proceedings are very personal, and you need to feel at ease with your counsel.

If your spouse controls access to all the family funds, it is possible you could have difficulty coming up with the resources necessary to hire an attorney, so again, be proactive and make sure that you have funds secure and available only to you!

Consider Your Social Security Benefits of the Future

This may make you want to wait for formal divorce if you haven't been married for ten years.

A divorced spouse who was married for at least ten years and who has not remarried will be entitled to the spousal benefit of the ex-spouse even if the ex-spouse has remarried. A divorced spouse who is sixty-two is eligible for Social Security benefits equal to the greater of those based on their earnings, or 50 percent of their ex-spouse's benefit. If you haven't worked throughout your marriage, remaining married for at least ten years could be beneficial for your future retirement benefits. Waiting to divorce until you have been married for ten years may be very important to your lifestyle in retirement.

During Divorce

The type of divorce you decide to proceed with could also have an impact on the outcome for you. If you believe that you and your soon-to-be ex-spouse can reasonably negotiate and agree as to how to divide up the marital assets without deception or acrimony, then a mediated or collaborative divorce proceeding may be options. If you believe that there may not be transparency or the ability to reasonably negotiate, then a litigated divorce is probably the route you should take.

The Four Divorce Options

MEDIATION

In a divorce mediation, the divorcing couple retains a neutral, specially trained third-party mediator to mediate a settlement and come to agreement on all aspects of the divorce. It is critical that the mediator is neutral and does not advocate for either party. The mediator can't make decisions, force either spouse to accept a term, or insist that either spouse sign a contract. They can make suggestions to help resolve lingering issues, but they cannot make any decisions. Divorce mediators should be trained in conflict resolution and have extensive knowledge of the state's divorce laws. In my opinion, both parties should consult their own individual divorce attorneys *during* the mediation process and *before* signing the final divorce settlement agreement. Once the couple agrees on all the outstanding issues, the mediator will draft a divorce settlement agreement for both spouses (and their attorneys) to review, sign, and present to the judge.

Why do people choose divorce mediation? Because it is usually less expensive than divorce litigation, and it can proceed much faster. It allows couples to maintain power and control over their divorce, as opposed to having a judge decide their individual fates. In most states, mediation is voluntary, so if either spouse disagrees and prefers to follow the traditional divorce route, a court won't force your spouse to engage in mediation. In some states, the court can require couples to demonstrate a good-faith effort in mediation before scheduling additional court hearings.

In order for divorce mediation to be successful, it is essential that both spouses are willing to provide the other spouse and the mediator with sensitive information, including documentation relating to bank accounts, retirement, pensions, stocks, and all other assets and debts. Since provision of all financial information is voluntary in mediation, you wouldn't have the option to subpoena records if one party doesn't cooperate in providing information.

What are the pros and cons of divorce mediation?

The pros are:

- It may result in a better long-term relationship with your soon-to-be ex because you don't fight in court.
- It may be better for the children, as it is usually less confrontational.

- It has a quicker resolution.
- It reduces expenses.
- You—and not a judge—are in control of your divorce.
- It is a more discreet and private process.

The cons are:

- If it fails, it is a waste of time and money.
- It could be unfavorable to one spouse or not thorough because the mediator is inexperienced or biased toward one party.
- Any legal complication or issue of law will still need to be ruled on by a judge.
- It may be unenforceable if it is lopsided and hence can be challenged.
- It may fail to uncover assets of one of the spouses.
- It may reinforce unhealthy behavioral patterns that have been established in the relationship, with one spouse dominating the negotiations.

One final note concerning divorces where there is a history of domestic violence: If the parties have a history of domestic abuse, most mediators won't take the case because it's difficult to keep both spouses on track, and it's challenging for the mediator to determine if the victim agrees to the settlement due to fear of or intimidation by the abuser. In states that require mediation, if a history of physical violence can be demonstrated, the court will not require mandatory sessions.

COLLABORATIVE DIVORCE

Collaborative divorce is a team approach. The divorcing couple obtains professional help from experts in the legal, financial, and mental health fields. Each party hires an attorney specially trained in the collaborative divorce process. You will meet with your attorney separately, and you and your attorney will meet with your spouse and their attorney regularly. Often the collaborative process may involve bringing in other neutral professionals, such as divorce financial analysts/advisors to work through financial issues, or child custody specialists such as a therapist to help resolve emotionally charged issues. Essentially, each team member assists the family in their area of expertise, and then all recommendations are integrated to help formulate the divorce settlement.

Collaborative divorce is different from mediation because all parties are committed to settlement as the sole agenda, and each side has legal advice and advocacy built into the process. In the collaborative process, both spouses and their respective attorneys sign an agreement requiring both attorneys to withdraw from the case if a settlement is not reached and the couple ends up going to court. If this happens, each party must get a new attorney.

As with mediation, both parties must voluntarily provide information for negotiations to be fruitful, such as tax returns, salary, and employment information; business valuation information; and all information regarding assets and liabilities. There is no subpoena power in this process. If you suspect that your spouse will try and hide information from you, collaborative divorce may not be right for you. If a couple has a complex financial situation, or businesses or professional practices are involved, it can be relatively easy to hide assets and income, and that may skew the fairness of the settlement.

Again, if you and your spouse have a history of domestic violence or you're unable to communicate, it's likely that you'll need to file for a contested divorce, which typically focuses on what each spouse is entitled to by state law.

LITIGATED DIVORCE

In a litigated divorce process, each spouse will hire their own attorney to act as an advocate, protecting their interests and advising on issues so the client achieves the best possible result. A "litigated divorce" does not mean that a divorce ends up in court. In fact, the divorce litigation process involves multiple steps, and begins with gathering evidence during the discovery process and the crafting of settlement proposals and counterproposals. The attorney is a negotiator at this stage. The goal is to negotiate an out-of-court settlement with the assistance of an attorney advocate and full disclosure of all pertinent information. In this process, information from the other spouse can be subpoenaed if they are not cooperating with providing documentation. The primary topics for negotiation are division of marital debts and assets, child custody and child support, and spousal support.

If the couple has tried everything and still can't come to an agreement, then the attorney changes from "negotiator" to "litigator," and the case will go to trial. The attorneys present their case and enter all documents into evidence. After reviewing the evidence and any testimony, the judge will make the final decisions as to how all assets and liabilities will be divided, if there will be alimony and for how long, and on issues relating to child custody and child support. This decision can be appealed.

This option is the most expensive of the four, and it puts your future in the hands of a judge who knows little about you and your family. In 2019, Business Insider reported that the average cost of a divorce is about $15,000.[1] That said, a litigated divorce does provide for advocacy and greater ability to achieve transparency. If everyone involved refrains from taking an overly contentious approach, it will save on legal fees and reduce emotional damage, so the goal should be to strive toward a settlement before going to trial.

My divorce was a fully litigated divorce. It was highly contentious and, quite frankly, emotionally draining. However, I wanted complete disclosure and a fair outcome, and after many proposals and counterproposals, it became clear that we would never come to an agreement without going to trial. After the first divorce decree, my ex-husband initiated another action a year later to revise the decree, and he succeeded in his quest to change the terms of the original decree. This process involved great expense and forced me to go back and forth to London to be present at the proceedings. The second decree was extremely disadvantageous to me financially; and I literally had no more resources, financially or emotionally, to continue fighting.

My recommendation is to try to agree on a negotiated settlement to save yourself the turmoil of trial—but only if you believe the settlement is fair. Would I do it again? Yes, I think I would, because we had such an adversarial relationship that trial was the only possible way to resolve the conflict. If we'd had a prenuptial agreement, then the tumultuous mayhem would have been eliminated; many of the issues would have been decided before we got to the point of not being able to communicate on any topic.

DO-IT-YOURSELF DIVORCE

The same principles that apply to all do-it-yourself projects apply to a DIY divorce. The pros when it comes to DIY divorce are that it is cheaper, because you don't hire attorneys; and it can be quicker if you and your spouse agree on everything from property division, child parenting time, and legal decision-making authority for children to child and spousal support. That said, divorce is very complicated, and irreversible mistakes can easily be made, so before agreeing to this, be very sure that you have the ability to navigate these tricky waters and protect your long-term financial and emotional security. If you have only been married for a few years, there are no children, few assets and debts to divide, comparable incomes, and no alimony, this is a quick and inexpensive solution.

Freelance editor and writer Ariel Curry experienced a DIY divorce when her first marriage ended after three years. Ariel said, "We had only been married a few years, we didn't have a house, we didn't have children, and nearly all of our debts were paid off. We realized relatively quickly in our relationship that it wasn't going to work, and we chose a DIY divorce because we wanted to keep things amicable. Neither of us had any desire to hurt the other; we just wanted it to end as peacefully as possible. While I don't believe there's ever such a thing as an 'easy' divorce, this was the easiest option available. We were able to part ways by splitting everything down the middle and carry on with our lives."[2]

DIY divorce is valid and legal, as long as the divorce paperwork and filing fees are submitted correctly, with the approval of both spouses. To be eligible for a DIY divorce, both spouses must apply for an uncontested divorce, and both spouses must be in agreement about the decision to divorce, with neither party contesting the dissolution of the marriage. A family law judge will need to approve the marital settlement and issue a divorce decree for the dissolution to be finalized. If the judge determines that the agreement is fair and does not blatantly favor one spouse over the other, the marital settlement is likely to be approved by the court.

Some things to consider if you are contemplating a DIY divorce:

- If you and your spouse own significant real estate, assets, and/or debts, it is advisable to work with a financial advisor or accountant to calculate the tax impact.
- Before finalizing your marital settlement agreement, you and your spouse should understand the short- and long-term tax consequences of the proposed final agreement. Working with an accountant or financial advisor will ensure that you have accurate information about taxes you may have to pay in the near or long-term future.
- DIY divorce requires that you and your spouse have a basic understanding of the required family law forms that will be submitted in your divorce package.
- While the DIY divorce mediation process may seem simple, it involves hours of time in completing dozens of legal forms, formalizing and documenting mutually agreed negotiations between spouses, and serving and filing legal papers in court. Also keep in mind that paperwork is often rejected by the court because the forms are not completed in the correct way.
- Even though a DIY divorce service allows couples to avoid using attorneys, issues may arise that necessitate seeking legal advice on specific issues.

Who Do You Want on Your Divorce Team?

Divorce is a tapestry of legal, financial, and emotional issues—a real super-duper trifecta of stressors. One advisor doesn't cut it to address each stressor. Build a team that can help you legally, financially, and emotionally. Your attorney is the point person for legal strategy and is not a therapist. It is also a good idea to consult a certified divorce financial analyst who can delve deep into the financial landscape of your marital situation and assist you with developing a plan that protects you and your children's short- and long-term financial well-being. And certainly, last but not least, you need emotional and psychological support—a therapist who can listen, guide, and support you and/or your support system of family and friends. This is a time where you will need emotional support, plain and simple.

Different States, Different Rules, as to How Assets are Divided

Divorce laws are different in different states, so where you live will determine how your assets and debts are divided.

EQUITABLE DISTRIBUTION OR COMMUNITY PROPERTY

There are two types of property division: community property and equitable distribution. First, determine whether you live in a community property state or an equitable distribution state. There are eight community property states: Arizona, California, Idaho, Louisiana, Nevada, New Mexico, Texas, and Washington. Alaska has an optional community property act, and Wisconsin is essentially a community property state, but it has exceptions to the typical community property laws. The remaining states are equitable distribution states.

What's the difference? In community property states, both spouses are considered equal owners of marital property. Remember when we discussed "separate property" in chapter 9? Marital property does not include assets you owned before the marriage, or that you received individually before or during the marriage or hold in a separate property trust or property designated as such in a prenuptial or postnuptial agreement. Whatever you earn or acquire during the marriage that is not "separate property" is considered co-owned by both parties, regardless of whose name is on the title or who earned the money. This property (any commingled property) will be split down the middle, 50/50 between the two spouses.

Equitable distribution states, on the other hand, require that a couple's marital property is divided "equitably or fairly," not necessarily equally. Sometimes a 50/50 division of assets may not produce equal standards of living after the divorce, and in equitable distribution states, the law aspires to a fair result.

Remember that marital property not only includes assets but debts. Debts will be divided, too, and the division of debt follows the rules for division of assets. In most community property states, both spouses will be held equally responsible for the repayment of debt incurred during the marriage, regardless of who got the benefits from the debt.

A Cautionary Word or Two about Hidden Assets

Divorce, by definition, is a time of heightened mistrust between soon-to-be ex-spouses, and it is not unusual for one or both parties to hide assets. Assets have a way of disappearing after divorce proceedings start. Unethical, for sure, but it happens, so beware, and understand what to look for.

Essentially, when a spouse attempts to conceal property or devalue an asset, that is called hiding assets. There are four ways to hide assets:

- Denying the asset exists
- Transferring the asset to a third party
- Claiming the asset was lost or dissipated
- Creating false debt

Some common tricks for hiding, undervaluing, or disguising assets include:

- Stashing cash in a safe-deposit box
- Underreporting income, deferring salary, delaying bonuses and commissions, or delaying signing contracts
- Creating phony debt by colluding with family or friends to set up phony loans
- Transferring stock or investment accounts into the name of family members, business partners, or dummy corporations
- Opening custodial accounts in the name of one or more children

This is not a comprehensive list. When people want to hide something, they will think outside of the box and come up with all kinds of creative ways to do so, unfortunately.

The first place to look to discover hidden assets is past tax returns. If you look through the past five years of tax returns and unearth discrepancies year-to-year, this should raise red flags. Review all federal and state tax returns, W2s, and 1099s. Pay close attention to the schedules on tax returns, which can point to the existence of assets:

- **Schedule A—Itemized Deductions:** This form may identify unlisted assets or sources of income that aren't disclosed elsewhere. For example, the deduction of property taxes may reveal the existence of a hidden property (or properties such as real estate or a boat).

- **Schedule B—Interest and Dividends:** This form identifies assets that generate interest and dividends. If you've already taken inventory of these types of assets that you know about, use this list to compare and identify new or undisclosed assets—or the disappearance of assets.

- **Schedule C—Profit or Loss from Business:** This form may include a depreciation schedule, which can reveal additional assets purchased by a related business entity, and any depreciation expense can be added back to determine actual income.

- **Schedule D—Capital Gains and Losses:** This schedule includes capital gains and losses from securities and other investments, including stocks, bonds, and real estate. Like interest and dividends, reported capital gains and losses can help identify new assets or the disappearance of previously disclosed assets.

- **Schedule E—Supplemental Income and Loss:** This section reports income (or losses) from rental properties, royalties, partnerships, and S corporations, which can all point to related and potentially hidden assets.

If you don't think that your spouse is going to be transparent and voluntarily disclose all financial information without any shenanigans, you or your attorney will need to use a formal, legal process to get information and documents. This is called the discovery process, and it provides several methods of getting information, which vary slightly from state to state but for the most part include all of the following:

- **Document demands.** Your attorney can ask your spouse to produce specific documents, such as tax returns, financial statements, loan applications, and account records.

- **Written questions** called "interrogatories" or "requests for admission." Using these discovery tools, your spouse must answer questions in writing, or admit specific statements that you believe are true.

- **Inspection demands.** You can ask to inspect property such as a safe-deposit box or a wine collection.

- **Testimony** given under oath.

What if discovery doesn't work and your spouse is not forthcoming with documents and answers? Here are some options available to you:

- **Forensic accountant.** Forensic accountants are specialized accountants in the areas of fraud. Their occupation requires them to do extensive investigative work in determining whether there has been a fraud or concealment. These individuals go above and beyond what your regular accountant or CPA does. Forensic accountants may also choose to conduct a lifestyle analysis. A lifestyle analysis lists all your marital living expenses and connects these expenses to all known sources of income, assets, and loans. It can determine whether or not everything can be traced back to the couple. This process allows the accountant to determine where the missing funds or assets went or if any of the assets were changed in form.

- **Private investigator.** Private investigators can find loans or offshore bank accounts, contact individuals who may have more information, and determine if your spouse bought any property without your knowledge, either for himself or for someone else.

- **IRS document requests.** Tax documents can be requested from the IRS with Form 4564.

If hidden assets are discovered after settlement, contact your attorney right away. When a spouse gets away with hiding assets until after the divorce documents are finalized, it can be more difficult to trace them back to the marriage. Before signing any agreements, your attorney should include a clause that penalizes a spouse who hides marital assets, whether that is discovered before or after the process is complete. In many states, your spouse can be held in contempt of court or found guilty of perjury due to their attempts to conceal assets. The Family Law Act provides that each spouse must make a full disclosure of assets, and harsh penalties may apply if a spouse does not do so.

The Dangers of Long-Term Separation

Not only is divorce emotionally challenging, but it's also a lot of work! Time-consuming, taxing, stressful—who wants to do that? Because divorce is so daunting, due to the massive upheaval it often causes, many people avoid it and just stay separated for years—they live apart without any legal separation agreement. This is a bad idea! Why? Because during a long separation without a legal separation agreement, you have no control over what your spouse is doing with marital assets—including hiding them (see "A Cautionary Word or Two about Hidden Assets" on page 224). There are so many risks to a prolonged legal separation without an agreement, and it can affect your eventual settlement. Your spouse could lose his job or experience a plethora of changes that can influence alimony or child custody. If you choose to go down the prolonged separation route, have a legal separation agreement drawn up that covers who pays for what during separation and who is responsible for which debts. Make absolutely sure it gives you access to liquid assets and provides for indemnification if your spouse racks up debt during separation. If you just float through a separation indefinitely, you are putting yourself at great risk.

Child Custody and Child Support

Child custody and child support are very important aspects in any divorce, because they determine what is in the best interests of the children in the family and address their long-term financial security. Although a full discussion of these issues is beyond the purview of this book, I would like to highlight that while each state has its own guidelines for determining child support, all use a predetermined formula of some sort to calculate the amount to be paid. There are many factors that influence this amount, but the main driving factors depend on the income of both parents and how much time a child spends with each parent. As is the case with all aspects of divorce, child support can be amicably agreed to, but if that isn't possible, the courts will intervene and determine the amount of child support. Child support payments are usually made until the child reaches age eighteen. If someone defaults on their child support payments and just doesn't pay, it is a big deal. Nonpayment of child support can create serious legal problems for the nonpayer, and courts can enforce the order in many ways to compel payment. In extreme cases, failing to provide child support can result in the interception of the nonpayer's tax refund, the seizure of property, the garnishment of wages, or jail time. If there are major changes in a parent's life, such as a job loss or serious illness, it is possible to petition the court for a modification of a child support payment.

After Divorce: Stepping into the Light!

Sometimes divorce can be like a death. To my mind, though, it can also ultimately lead to a rebirth. As I have said repeatedly, divorce is an emotional roller coaster that leaves you drained. It's okay to take some time to mourn the loss of the relationship, the family patterns, and your previous lifestyle. Give yourself permission to take some time. Seek support through close friends, family, and/or professional therapy. Stop feeling sorry for yourself—you are not a victim, and you do not need to let your divorce define you. It's okay to grieve and feel sad at unexpected times; you are human, after all. But don't give up. Make yourself a role model for others; and pursue your reincarnation with optimism, resilience, hope, faith, and excitement.

In my opinion, the most important thing you can do for yourself is to become financially independent—be the master of your own fate and the captain of your own ship. That's the whole reason I wrote this book! Being economically dependent on someone is a double-edged sword, and it comes with a cost. Follow your passions, get a job, and embrace your own empowerment. Expand your universe with new friends and new professional endeavors, and look at your new life as an awesome opportunity! After mourning and feeling sorry for myself for a couple of years, and out of necessity, I made getting a job my job. I reinvented myself, and struggled financially for a while as I gained experience in my profession. And then, boom! Things started to change for the better personally, professionally, and financially. I was and still am in charge of my destiny, and it feels great!

THE UPSHOT

Divorce is a process, and whether amicable or contentious, it is a life-changing occurrence that has ripple effects through most aspects of your life. Nobody can prevent some of the twists and turns in a divorce proceeding or foresee the unexpected developments. But by preparing prior to the divorce, ensuring you are knowledgeable about the options for divorce proceedings, retaining competent advisors, and having the knowledge to ask pertinent questions, you can obviate some of the pitfalls of the divorce process.

CHAPTER 11

Estate Planning

"Only put off until tomorrow what you are willing to die having left undone."

—Pablo Picasso

IT IS HUMAN NATURE to procrastinate and to avoid topics that naturally make us feel uncomfortable or highlight our mortality. Nobody likes to think about their own death, because it isn't exactly a fun line of thought. But fun or not, it is going to happen, so why not plan for it and make sure your legacy, however big or small, goes to the heirs of your choice in the smoothest and most tax-effective manner possible? If you have worked hard over your life, don't you want your money and possessions to go to the people you care about most? If you have children, don't you want to select who will be their guardians if they are suddenly left without parents? Estate planning is the final piece of control that you can claim in order to have financial independence—even after you pass.

Important at Any Age or Wealth Level

Many people spend more time researching vacation destinations and the latest restaurants than they do estate planning. The thing is, without estate planning, you don't get to choose who gets everything you have worked so hard for. Estate planning isn't only for the rich. If you don't have a plan that organizes your affairs after you pass, there could be long-lasting negative effects that impact your loved ones—even if you don't have a large IRA or investment account, an expensive home, or art or jewelry to pass on.

The COVID-19 pandemic sharpened people's focus on health, wealth, and unexpected occurrences that can affect our longevity. Sometimes we get diagnosed suddenly with an illness, or a death occurs due to unforeseen circumstances. If there isn't a plan in place, it can take your loved ones months to sort through the details of your life, confront unexpected realities about your financial situation, and deal with legal maneuverings of probate. Probate is the legal process that occurs after someone dies; and it involves paying outstanding debts and taxes, inventorying the deceased person's property, and distributing anything left over by the terms of a will or state law if there is no will.

Most millennials have been busy focusing on building their careers and savings, starting a family, or buying a house. But for many, the pandemic was a wake-up call about estate planning, as the disease claimed the lives of people of all ages. For those with aging parents, it is important to explore with them what planning they have done; otherwise, you will be dealing with a mess if nothing is in place. As a member of the sandwich generation myself (providing for both kids and parents), I saw that my parents didn't have much in the way of estate planning, so I helped them create a plan covering healthcare directives, powers of attorney, and distribution of property so that I know and understand their wishes.

According to Caring.com, two out of three adults still don't have a will despite the advent of the pandemic, and in 2021 only 32.9 percent of adults in the U.S. had a will in place.[1] I don't want you to be part of that 67 percent, so let's get to what you have to do to create an estate plan.

Estate Planning: The Why, the What, and the How

The Why

There are a few key reasons why you want to have an estate plan.

First, it protects your beneficiaries and heirs. If something happens to the family's breadwinner(s), there needs to be a plan as to how the family will function, where they will live, and who will get what. You don't have to be super-wealthy to have real estate, or a few investments, and both of these assets will be passed on to heirs. Without an estate plan designating who gets what, courts will decide who gets your assets; and that process will incur fees, can take years, and can cause unbelievable family strife and arguing. Courts don't know which family members are responsible or irresponsible, nor will they automatically rule that a surviving spouse inherits everything.

Second, if you have young children, you need to prepare for the unthinkable event that both you and your spouse or co-parent could pass before the children are eighteen. By preparing a will, you can name guardians for your children in the event you both pass. If you don't have this in place, a court will decide who raises your children!

Third, estate planning will enable you to reduce all or part of federal and state estate taxes and state inheritance taxes. If there is no plan, it is possible your heirs could owe quite a bit in estate taxes, which will reduce what they actually walk away with from their inheritance.

Fourth, estate planning allows you to customize how you distribute your property after your death. Perhaps one child did more caregiving for you, or you gave one child more for education or other expenses, and you don't want to divide your estate exactly equally but rather customize it—an estate plan can be crafted to do this. It can also set forth any charitable giving you want to do post-death.

Fifth, and maybe most important, it will eliminate or at least reduce family strife and arguments over your property and money. We all have

233

heard the stories of families squabbling over inheritances, to the point where they end up in court. It is important to nip this in the bud by clearly stating in your estate plan who gets what and choosing who will control your finances and property in the event you become mentally incapacitated or after you die. If you have been married multiple times and have children by different spouses, the need for an estate plan is especially urgent.

There are many stories about celebrities who failed to do any estate planning and died without leaving directions for the distribution of their fortune to heirs—Prince, Aretha Franklin, Amy Winehouse, and Michael Jackson, to name a few. Famous people are just like us; they don't want to think about their own death and always believe there will be time to make these arrangements. However, if they unexpectedly pass, the result is family infighting and legal battles to determine designated heirs of the estate. Ric Ocasek, the lead singer of the Cars, unexpectedly passed away in 2019 at age seventy-five while recuperating from surgery. He had split from his famous supermodel wife, Paulina Porizkova, and she had filed for divorce. When Ocasek died, however, they were still married, and even though he had written a new will in 2019 before his surgery, disinheriting Porizkova, the supermodel went to court and claimed under New York law that she had a right to an "elective share" of his estate. Even though she'd been cut out of the estate by Ocasek, she was granted a settlement and received money from his estate, which was not his wish.[2]

People who are not celebrities will also suffer unfortunate consequences when they do no estate planning. I read a heartbreaking story about a young family in Fort Myers, Florida. A young husband and wife died, leaving children ages five, eight, and eleven without parents. The family was completely unprepared for the tragedy. Their relatives didn't have enough money for burial expenses or the medical and psychological care the children required, and they had to decide who would now be guardians for the children, as there was no will specifying the parents' wishes on that front.[3] A simple will and estate plan could have reduced some of this stress and confusion, and provided some funding for the costs.

The What

Your personal situation will dictate what paperwork needs to be drafted and signed to implement your estate plan. Below is a list of basic documents that may be included in an estate plan:

- Will
- Revocable living trust
- Financial power of attorney
- Healthcare proxy
- Beneficiary designation forms (e.g., IRA, life insurance, 401[k])
- Real estate title documents
- Trusts you created and funded during life (e.g., irrevocable life insurance trust)

Before we explore the various documents you may need in more detail, let's talk about probate. Probate is the legal process that happens after a death. It includes proving in court that the deceased person's will is valid, inventorying the deceased person's property, having the property appraised, paying debts and taxes, and distributing the remaining property by the terms of the deceased's will or by state law if the deceased dies intestate (without a will). Typically, probate requires paperwork and court appearances by lawyers. The lawyer's fees and court costs are paid by the estate, thus reducing the amount that the heirs will receive from the estate.

The probate process works like this: after your death, the person you named in your will as executor (if you die intestate, a judge will appoint this person) files papers with the probate court. The executor establishes the validity of your will with the court; and then presents the court with lists of your property, debts, and heirs. Your relatives and creditors are then notified of your death. Your executor will manage your assets during the probate process, which can take up to a year. The executor may have to sell some of your property to generate funds to pay your outstanding debts during this time, or, if your will makes cash bequests but your estate is comprised mainly of artwork, your collection may need to be appraised and sold to generate the cash for the bequests. Once the executor pays your debts and taxes, the property is divided up to the specified heirs and transferred to the new owners.

WILLS

Dying without a will is called dying "intestate"—literally, it is defined as "not having made a will before passing." If you die intestate, your state's laws of descent and distribution will determine who receives your property by default. These laws vary from state to state, but typically the distribution would be to your spouse and children, or, if you don't have a spouse or children, to other family members. Generally, a state's plan often reflects the legislature's guess as to how most people would dispose of their property, and it builds in protections for certain beneficiaries, particularly minor children.

However, the state's plan may or may not reflect your actual wishes, and some of the law's built-in protections may not be necessary if there is a harmonious family setting. A will allows you to alter the state's default plan to suit your personal preferences. It also permits you to exercise control over myriad personal decisions that broad and general state default provisions cannot address.

A will provides for the distribution of certain property owned by you at the time of your death, and generally you can dispose of your property in any manner you choose. Your right to dispose of property as you choose, however, may be subject to the forced heirship laws of most states that prevent you from disinheriting a spouse and, in some cases, children. A will does not address the transfer of certain types of assets, called nonprobate property (see the information that follows), which, because of title or contract (such as a beneficiary designation), pass to someone other than your estate on your death.

The provisions of a will include selecting the executor, designating a guardian for minor children or dependents, transferring assets to designated heirs, directing that certain people do not receive an inheritance (disinheritance), and designating the source of funds for estate taxes. Inventory your valuable property before making a will and include pets, antiques, art, books, appliances, china, crystal, silver, jewelry, coins, stamps, collectibles, vehicles, tools, investments, retirement accounts, real estate, royalties, copyrights, patents, trademarks, cash accounts, and any business interests. This is not a comprehensive list, but simply one to point you in the right direction and jog your memory.

Certain property passes outside your will and probate, and that property should not be included in your will. This type of property includes:

- Property with a right of survivorship, such as that held in joint tenancy, community property with right of survivorship, or tenancy by the entirety.
- Property held in a revocable living trust (discussed below).
- Property for which you have already named a beneficiary, which includes:
  » Property held in transfer-on-death form, which could include investment accounts and bank accounts, and, in some states, real estate and vehicles.
  » Proceeds from a life insurance policy or an annuity for which you have a named beneficiary.
  » Money in an IRA, 401(k) plan, or other retirement plan, or money in a pension plan. In these plans, you name beneficiaries, and the assets are transferred to the beneficiary immediately upon your death.

Wills should be signed in the presence of witnesses, and certain formalities must be followed or the will may be deemed to be invalid. In many states, a will that is formally executed in front of witnesses with all signatures notarized is deemed to be "self-proving" and may be admitted to probate without the testimony of witnesses or other additional proof. A later amendment to a will is called a codicil and must be signed with the same formalities as the will. Caution is advised when using a codicil because, if there are ambiguities between its provisions and the prior will it amends, problems can ensue.

While a testamentary (witnessed) will is likely the best avenue, two other types of wills get varying degrees of recognition and validity. Holographic wills are those written and signed by you, the testator and creator of the will, but are not witnessed. Such wills are often used when time is short and witnesses are unavailable; for example, when the testator is trapped in a life-threatening accident. Holographic wills are not recognized in some states, however, and in the states that permit them, the will must meet minimal requirements, such as proof that the testator wrote it and had the mental capacity to do so. That said, the absence of witnesses often leads to challenges to a holographic will's validity. Oral wills, in which the testator speaks their wishes before witnesses, are the least recognized type of will by courts due to the lack of a written record.

Pour-over wills are commonly used in conjunction with creating a trust. A pour-over will ensures that any assets that were not funded into your revocable living trust should be transferred to the trust upon your death. It names your trust as the beneficiary of any property it doesn't already hold. A pour-over will is a safety net for your trust (discussed below).

TRUSTS

A trust, or revocable living trust, is a document that determines how your assets are handled after you die—just like a will. But a living trust covers three stages of your life: when you are alive and well, when you are alive but incapacitated, and after your death. The primary benefit is that living trusts avoid the probate process, reduce the chances of court disputes, and keep your documents and affairs private. It is in many ways a more efficient and streamlined way of transferring assets upon your death.

A revocable trust is basically a replacement for a will with respect to distribution of assets. Rather than having your asset distribution after death being directed by the court through probate administration, your assets are directed to a private entity, called a trust. A revocable trust is called revocable because it can be amended or revoked at any time during your life. Please note that a trust is *not* a vehicle for naming a guardian for your children or specifying your funeral preferences; those wishes need to be set forth in a will. Therefore, it is recommended to have both a trust and a will.

Revocable trusts provide great flexibility for ownership of assets and allow you and your heirs to achieve goals that cannot be achieved otherwise. You can customize how you distribute your assets after death by establishing certain conditions or ages for receipt of inheritance.

When you create the trust, you are called the grantor. The trust will have a trustee, who is considered the legal owner of the trust property, and designated beneficiaries, who are considered equitable owners of the trust. When you are alive, you will be the grantor, the trustee, and the beneficiary of your revocable trust. You can add property to your trust by holding investment accounts, real estate, and other assets in the name of your trust, and all income or dividends will pass through to you directly and be taxed to you directly. You have total control over the trust and the property/assets held by it while you are alive. Upon the grantor's death (i.e., your death), the revocable trust morphs into an irrevocable trust (it can no longer be changed), and the property in the trust passes to the grantor's (your) beneficiaries under the terms and conditions of the trust. This happens without probate.

As previously mentioned, trusts are not only for the wealthy. Many young parents with limited assets choose to create trusts for the benefit of their children in case both parents die before all their children have reached an age the parents feel indicates sufficient maturity to handle property (which often is older than the age of eighteen or twenty-one). Perhaps you don't want your children to have access to their inheritance until they are thirty-five or forty, because you want them to have matured enough to be able to responsibly manage the inheritance. This can be written into the trust. Also, the trust assets can be held as a single undivided fund used for the support and education of minor children according to their individual needs, with eventual division of the trust among the children when the youngest has reached a specified age. This type of arrangement is advantageous over an inflexible division of property among children of different ages without regard to their level of maturity or individual needs at the time of the distribution.

When creating your estate planning package with a revocable trust, it should also include a pour-over will, a power of attorney, and healthcare directives.

POWERS OF ATTORNEY

In my opinion, every adult should have a power of attorney prepared. The COVID-19 pandemic is a good example of a sudden situation arising in which you could fall ill unexpectedly and be unable to handle financial and legal matters for yourself. Then what? If you don't have a power of attorney and you become unable to manage your personal or business affairs, it may be necessary for a court to appoint one or more people to act on your behalf. Depending on your state law, people appointed are referred to as guardians, conservators, or committees.

A power of attorney allows you to choose who will act for you if you are unable to do so yourself, and it allows you to define the limits of authority, if any. Simply put, a power of attorney is a legal document that authorizes a trusted person to act on your behalf. There are two relevant powers of attorney. A financial power of attorney is a legal document that gives someone the power to handle your financial affairs. A durable power of attorney is a variation of a financial power of attorney that gives legal rights to another person to handle any of your nonhealth or nonmedical affairs. "Durable" means that even if you become incapacitated, the power of attorney remains in effect.

A power of attorney is accepted in all states, but the rules and requirements differ from state to state. The power of attorney may give temporary or permanent authority to act on your behalf. It may take effect immediately, or only upon the occurrence of a future event, usually a determination that you are unable to act for yourself due to mental or physical disability. This is called a "springing" power of attorney. A power of attorney may be revoked, but most states require written notice of revocation to the person named to act for you.

MEDICAL DIRECTIVES

There are two types of medical directives that you should be aware of: living wills and durable medical powers of attorney. Although these two documents are often confused, because they come into play during similar circumstances, they have different purposes.

A living will, also known as a healthcare directive, is limited to deathbed wishes, and is used to declare your desire to not have life-prolonging measures taken if there is no hope for recovery. It is a legal document that details the type and level of medical care you want to receive when you can't communicate your wishes; and it addresses whether you want life-sustaining procedures such as resuscitation, assisted breathing, or tube feeding or dialysis, for example.

A durable medical power of attorney is broader than a living will, covers all healthcare decisions, and lasts as long as you are incapable of making decisions for yourself. You appoint a person and grant them the authority to make medical decisions for you in the event you are unable to express your preferences about medical treatment. Usually, you would want to also appoint one or more alternate persons in the event your first-choice proxy is unavailable. You should confirm prior to appointing someone as your power of attorney that they are in fact willing and able to carry out your wishes. Choose someone you trust, and have a candid and direct conversation with them about what you would like done in certain circumstances. I know it isn't a fun conversation, and most people really don't want to talk about it, but you are doing yourself a disservice if you don't discuss your wishes, and you will be putting your proxy in a stressful situation if they have no idea as to what you might want done.

Medical professionals will make the initial determination as to whether you have the capacity to make your own medical treatment decisions. Having a living will and a durable medical power of attorney will give your physician direction and will avoid familial disagreements about treatment if you are incapacitated. Making your wishes known in advance and designating one person to make decisions on your behalf will reduce stress at a very stressful time.

WHAT ABOUT LIFE INSURANCE? WHEN DO YOU NEED IT?

Life insurance can also be an element of estate planning. If you haven't accumulated sufficient financial assets to provide for loved ones or heirs after your passing, life insurance is a good option, as it will provide financial support to your surviving dependents or beneficiaries after your death. It can also be used to provide funds for paying estate taxes for those who have large estates.

Who should buy life insurance? If you don't have enough assets accumulated to provide support for your dependents in the event of your sudden death, you should buy life insurance. A few examples of people who may need life insurance are:

- **Parents with minor children.** If a parent unexpectedly dies, the loss of their income or caregiving contributions could create financial problems, and life insurance can make sure the children have the financial resources they will need until they can support themselves.

- **Parents with special-needs adult children.** For children who require lifelong care and will never be self-sufficient, life insurance can make sure their needs will be met after their parents pass away.

- **Adults who own property together.** Whether you are married or not, if you own property with someone and the death of one adult means that the other could no longer afford loan payments, upkeep, and taxes on the property, life insurance will ensure the surviving party can keep the property and pay for it and its related expenses.

- **Elderly parents who want to leave money to adult children who are their caregivers.** Many adult children sacrifice by taking time off work to care for an elderly parent who needs help. This help may also include direct financial support. Life insurance can help reimburse the adult child's costs when the parent passes away.

- **Young adults whose parents incurred private student loan debt or cosigned a loan for them.** Young adults without dependents rarely need life insurance, but if a parent will be on the hook for a child's debt after the child's death, the child may want to carry enough life insurance so their parents can pay off the debt if they (the child) predeceases the parents.

- **Young adults who want to lock in low rates.** The younger and healthier you are, the lower your insurance premiums. If you are in your twenties or thirties and think you might have dependents in the future, it might be a good idea to buy an insurance policy when you're younger and can get a great, low rate.

- **Families who can't afford burial and funeral expenses.** Funeral costs have escalated steadily since the 1980s, and today an average funeral can cost up to $9,000 or more, depending on whether the body is buried or cremated. Getting a small life insurance policy can ensure that your loved one has a proper funeral and is honored in death without the hassle and stress of struggling to pay for it if there isn't sufficient money in the estate at the time of your loved one's passing.

- **Wealthy families who expect to owe estate taxes.** Life insurance can be purchased to provide funds to pay estate taxes, which keeps the full value of the estate intact.

If you're interested in getting life insurance, there are different types to explore: term life insurance, whole life insurance, universal life insurance, and variable universal life insurance. Consult with a reputable insurance broker as to the particular type of insurance that will satisfy your specific needs.

The How

Although it comes with some cost, I recommend finding a qualified estate planning attorney to draft or update any of the documents discussed above. You can find an attorney by seeking recommendations from your friends and family or from your trusted advisors, such as your financial advisor or accountant. Once you find an estate planning attorney, it will be helpful in advance of your first meeting to collect copies of your current financial and legal documents.

That said, you can also go the DIY route for simpler estate planning, such as creating a will or trust. If later you need more complex estate planning because you have a small business, have acquired more wealth, or want to leave money to charity, you can then hire an estate attorney. A simple will and living will (advanced directives, discussed below), coupled with naming beneficiaries on retirement accounts and insurance policies, are good first steps to setting up your estate plan.

> **Online Resources for Creating Wills:**
> Nolo
> USLegalWills.com
> Trust & Will
> TotalLegal
> DoYourOwnWill.com
> Rocket Lawyer

In addition to creating your estate plan, you should regularly revisit your plan to ensure it continues to reflect your wishes. I recommend revisiting your estate plan whenever there is a change in your circumstances or the circumstances of a loved one (e.g., marriage, divorce, birth, death, a change in personal finances or health, or moving to another state). Even if there have been no major changes in your life, it is best to revisit your plan every three to five years to ensure that it is in line with current law and still accurately reflects your wishes. .

THE UPSHOT

Although planning for your ultimate demise is probably not one of your favorite topics, and it can be daunting and unnerving if you let it be so, it is really very important that you think about what happens to your loved ones and your property after you exit stage left permanently. During your life, you strive to be responsible and caring, so why not also be so in death? Do you want your heirs subjected to a court's division of your property if you die without a will? A judge who knows nothing about you or your life or your family will make formulaic decisions about who gets what from what you worked your entire life to accumulate. If you are rendered incapacitated and can't make your own medical decisions, do you want your already stressed-out family trying to figure out what you want and trying to come to some agreement, all while your life is on the line? Why not prepare a living will and durable medical power of attorney and save everyone from suffering intense stress. It will ensure that your wishes are executed for your medical care because you have appointed someone you trust as your power of attorney, someone with whom you have already discussed your medical care wishes.

With a little bit of planning and effort, the process can be streamlined. It can make the experience of illness and death less stressful for those you love and guarantee that your wishes are fulfilled. Peace of mind is worth its weight in gold.

CONCLUSION: SAY YES

SAY YES! And then say yes again, and again! Yes to being master of your fate and CEO of your life. Yes to being a boss. Yes to freedom and independence. Yes to engaging willingly and enthusiastically with your finances and your money!

It is never too early or too late to get your financial act together and to invest in yourself. I completely changed my life at fifty-six years of age because it was either get it together or live at a much lower standard than I wanted to. I wasn't exactly a spring chicken, but in today's day and age we are living longer; and we need to have a very long-term vision, remain fluid, and be ready to pivot when necessary. I repeat, it is never too early or too late. Whatever stage of life you are in, getting clarity about your finances and taking control of your financial future are the most important things that you can do for yourself, your health, and your mental state.

Financial freedom is about maintaining your power. Do you want other people making financial decisions for you? Do you want other people deciding what your life looks like now and in retirement? Don't you want to have a vote in that and understand all aspects of your financial choices and decision-making? Yes, you do! When you are in control of your finances and you understand how to manage your personal finances whatever your wealth level, you will feel empowered, confident, and independent—you can make informed decisions about your life and exercise freedom of choice. When you aren't stressed about money and you are in control, you feel better, you sleep better, and you look better because you exude a calm confidence.

I want all women to find financial grace and elegance. By following the guidance in this book, you can implement strategies and use the tools available to you to become financially organized, knowledgeable, and proactive. You will see a positive change in your life. Confidence begets confidence. Once you get your financial house in order, follow preventive strategies and keep your eye on long-term, progressive goals. There isn't anything you can't conquer. Keep your eyes wide open, don't succumb to fear, and be courageous—professionally and personally.

Commit to the right essentials. Be excited about your opportunity to empower yourself.

A few gentle reminders:

- **Be excited** about getting financially organized and pro-active.

- **Don't live in denial.** Remember: ignorance is *not* bliss.

- **Don't make excuses.** There is no time like now to change. Lead yourself with intention and purpose, and be prepared to make adjustments in your life. Pivot when the situation requires you to do so.

- **Be resilient.** Life is a journey that is far from linear. Stay strong in hard times. Practice perseverance, endurance, and patience with steadfast commitment.

- **Be proactive.** You are your own fairy godmother. You need to take responsibility for making your life better.

- **Live without fear.** Nothing good comes from paralyzing fear. Worrying doesn't help, either; it's a negative distraction. Believe in your problem-solving abilities and resilience. You got this.

- **Practice gratitude and count your blessings daily.** This keeps everything in perspective.

- **Set realistic goals and be consistent.** Take one step at a time. Baby steps are okay. Don't try to conquer everything at once or you will get overwhelmed. Small, consistent, and doable steps will get you to the finish line without a breakdown, or without giving up because you are frustrated.

- **Live within your means.** I know this is boring, but if you do this, you will increase your assets and your means will keep growing—*stay* within your means to *grow* your means.

- **Be intentional with your personal and financial self-care.** Life is a long game (hopefully), so take care of your physical, mental, and financial self. In other words, love yourself first.

Your financial journey may not always be easy, and you may be challenged by the task of taking control, but nothing worth achieving is simple or easy. Essentially, this comes down to your mindset and your determination to be the master of your universe, and your own boss.

This book can serve as a road map to being your best financial self. You absolutely can conquer all!

ACKNOWLEDGMENTS

WHEN I DECIDED to write this book because I passionately wanted to encourage and empower women to take control of their financial destinies, I had no idea of the scope of the undertaking I was signing up for. It truly was a team effort that involved many people to whom I am so very grateful.

I could not have completed this book without the support, encouragement, and care of my husband, Mark Powell. Thank you, Mark, for your unwavering belief in me and your patience with my unyielding schedule and commitment to this endeavor. You make each day a beautiful one, and I am beyond blessed to have you as my wingman.

I would like to extend my deepest gratitude to David Bahnsen, my partner at the Bahnsen Group, for mentoring me in my wealth management career and for encouraging me to always be my authentic self. Thank you, David, for inspiring me to find my voice and to engage in thought leadership through blogs, podcasts, and by writing this book. Your example has been a guidepost to me.

Thanks to my mom, Annamae Davis, who imparted her strong will, independent nature, boundless energy, and optimistic spirit to me. You are an unstoppable force of nature who showed me by example how to be a strong woman and to believe that I could accomplish anything in this life.

Thanks to my dad, William Davis, who encouraged me to reach for the stars and to persist in all my endeavors, even when things were bumpy along the way. My dad has stood by me through my ups and downs in life and never wavered in his commitment to helping me accomplish my goals. His work ethic, humble nature, and loving spirit have guided me, and his belief in me has kept me going.

I am so grateful to the many women who have heard my message and encouraged me to continue to spread the word of the fiscal sisterhood. I want to give special thanks to Sheefteh Khalili, who heard my message and joined the movement to inspire women. Sheefteh has contributed vision to my mission, and she is a huge source of support to me—I'm so incredibly grateful for her belief, guidance, and contribution to expanding *The Fiscal Feminist* platform.

I want to thank the talented women at Wonderwell, my publisher, for all their input, guidance, patience, and feedback. Maggie Langrick believed in my message, and from our first conversation she guided me with her expertise through my maiden voyage as a book author. Many thanks to my editors Allison Serrell and Ariel Curry, whose insights and suggestions were invaluable.

Finally, I would like to thank Kenny Molina for his dedicated help. Kenny, many thanks for your meticulous and timely research, your belief in the message, and your ongoing encouragement. You are part of the movement!

NOTES

Chapter 1—The Evolution and the Revolution: Women's Financial Health, Past and Present

1   Kate Moore, *The Woman They Could Not Silence: One Woman, Her Incredible Fight for Freedom, and the Men Who Tried to Make Her Disappear* (Naperville, IL: Sourcebooks, 2021).

2   Amanda Leek, "How to Invest Like ... Hetty Green: The World's Richest Woman," *The Telegraph*, June 22, 2016, www.telegraph.co.uk/money/special-reports/how -to-invest-like--hetty-green-the-worlds-richest-woman/.

3   Kat Eschner, "The Peculiar Story of the Witch of Wall Street," *Smithsonian Magazine*, November 21, 2017, www.smithsonianmag.com/smart-news/peculiar -story-hetty-green-aka-witch-wall-street-180967258/.

4   Carlos Lozada, "How Harvard, Princeton and Yale Discovered Women," *The Washington Post*, October 14, 2016, www.washingtonpost.com/news/book -party/wp/2016/10/14/how-harvard-princeton-and-yale-discovered-women/.

5   The Equal Credit Opportunity Act," U.S. Department of Justice, September 24, 2021, www.justice.gov/crt/equal-credit-opportunity-act-3.

6   Matthew K. Fenton, "A History of Sexual Harassment Laws in the United States," WendzelFenton.com, January 1, 2018, www.wenzelfenton.com/blog/2018/01/01 /history-sexual-harassment-laws-united-states/.

7   "Equally Insured? What You Need to Know About Women and Health Insurance Coverage," Coverage.com, April 23, 2020, www.coverage.com/insurance/health /equality-nears-what-you-need-to-know-about-women-and-health-insurance -coverage/.

8   Liz Elting, "Why Pregnancy Discrimination Still Matters," *Forbes*, October 30, 2018, www.forbes.com/sites/lizelting/2018/10/30/why-pregnancy-discrimination -still-matters/#7567619c63c1.

9   "Pregnant Workers Fairness," A Better Balance, n.d., www.abetterbalance.org /our-campaigns/pregnant-workers-fairness/.

10 Jessica Silver-Greenberg and Natalie Kitroeff, "Miscarrying at Work: The Physical Toll of Pregnancy Discrimination," *The New York Times*, October 21, 2018, www.nytimes.com/interactive/2018/10/21/business/pregnancy-discrimination -miscarriages.html.

11   "U.S. Senate Must Act On House-Passed Pregnant Workers Fairness Act To Ensure Overdue Protections for Pregnant Workers," Center for American Progress, September 17, 2020, www.americanprogress.org/press/statement/2020/09/17/490492/statement-u-s-senate-must-act-house-passed-pregnant-workers-fairness-act-ensure-overdue-protections-pregnant-workers/.

12   "Women Have Fundamentally Different Journeys to Financial Wellness Merrill Lynch Study Reveals," Business Wire, April 19, 2018, www.businesswire.com/news/home/20180419005028/en/Women-Have-Fundamentally-Different-Journeys-to-Financial-Wellness-Merrill-Lynch-Study-Reveals.

13   Gretchen Livingston and Kim Parker, "8 Facts About American Dads," Pew Research Center, June 12, 2019, www.pewresearch.org/fact-tank/2019/06/12/fathers-day-facts/.

14   Kathleen Elkins, "Here's How Much Men and Women Earn at Every Age," CNBC, July 18, 2020, www.cnbc.com/2020/07/18/heres-how-much-men-and-women-earn-at-every-age.html.

15   Richard Fry, "U.S. Women Near Milestone in the College-Educated Labor Force," Pew Research Center, June 20, 2019, www.pewresearch.org/fact-tank/2019/06/20/u-s-women-near-milestone-in-the-college-educated-labor-force/.

16   Dani Matias, "New Report Says College-Educated Women Will Soon Make Up a Majority of U.S. Workers," NPR, June 20, 2019, www.npr.org/2019/06/20/734408574/new-report-says-college-educated-women-will-soon-make-up-majority-of-u-s-labor-f.

17   "Education and Lifetime Earning," Social Security, n.d., www.ssa.gov/policy/docs/research-summaries/education-earnings.html.

18   Kelley Holland, "Gender Pay Gap Hurts More Than Your Paycheck," CNBC, April 11, 2016, www.cnbc.com/2016/04/11/gender-pay-gap-hurts-more-than-your-paycheck.html.

19   Rachel Siegel, "Women Outnumber Men in the Workforce for Only the Second Time," The Washington Post, January 10, 2020, www.washingtonpost.com/business/2020/01/10/january-2020-jobs-report/.

20   Emily Barone, "Women Were Making Historic Strides in the Workforce. Then the Pandemic Hit," Time, June 10, 2020, time.com/5851352/women-labor-economy-coronavirus/.

21   Claire Ewing-Nelson and Jasmine Tucker, "Women Need 28 Months of Job Gains at April's Level to Recover Their Pandemic Losses," National Women's Law Center, May 2021, nwlc.org/wp-content/uploads/2021/05/April-Jobs-Day-Final-2.pdf.

22   Jasmine Tucker, "At August's Rate, It Will Take Women 9 Years to Regain the Jobs They Lost in the Pandemic," National Women's Law Center, nwlc.org/wp-content/uploads/2021/09/Aug-Jobs-Day.pdf.

23   Adi Gaskell, "How Discrimination Leads to a Motherhood Penalty in the Labor Market," Forbes, September 7, 2021, www.forbes.com/sites/adigaskell/2021/09/07/how-discrimination-leads-to-a-motherhood-penalty-in-the-labor-market/?sh=52ea8f4016bf.

24   Sara Savat, "Mothers' Paid Work Suffers During Pandemic, Study Finds," Washington University in St. Louis, July 13, 2020, source.wustl.edu/2020/07/mothers-paid-work-suffers-during-pandemic-study-finds/.

25 Courtney Connley, "More Than 860,500 Women Dropped Out of the Labor Force in September, According to New report," CNBC, October 2, 2020, www.cnbc.com /2020/10/02/865000-women-dropped-out-of-the-labor-force-in-september-2020 .html.

26 "Raising Kids and Running a Household: How Working Parents Share the Load," Pew Research Center, November 4, 2015, www.pewresearch.org/social-trends /2015/11/04/raising-kids-and-running-a-household-how-working-parents-share -the-load/.

27 Julie Hyman, "Study: Women Bear the Brunt of Caring for Aging Parents," Yahoo!, January 11, 2020, www.yahoo.

28 "Women and Financial Wellness: Beyond the Bottom Line," Merrill/Age Wave, August 2021, mlaem.fs.ml.com/content/dam/ML/Registration/Women-Age -Wave-White-Paper.pdf, 21.

29 Women and Financial Wellness: Beyond the Bottom Line," Merrill.com, n.d., www.ml.com/women-financial-wellness-age-wave.html; "Women and Financial Wellness," 21.

30 Department of Economic and Social Affairs, Population Division, "World Popula- tion Ageing, 2019," United Nations, 2020, www.un.org/en/development/desa /population/publications/pdf/ageing/WorldPopulationAgeing2019-Report.pdf.

31 "Women and Financial Wellness: Beyond the Bottom Line," AgeWave, agewave.com /what-we-do/landmark-research-and-consulting/research-studies/women-and -financial-wellness/.

32 "Women and Financial Wellness: Beyond the Bottom Line," AgeWave, p. 16.

33 Janice Co, "National Retirement Index: Planning for Retirement—Women in Two- Income Households at Greatest Risk" Prudential, June 2019, prudential.assetserv.com /prudential/download/file?assetId=8291886&external=true.

34 Dorothea Schäfer, "Investments: Women Are More Cautious Than Men Because They Have Less Financial Resources at Their Disposal," DIW Berlin, Weekly Report 1, 2010, s. 1–4, www.diw.de/de/diw_01.c.454137.de/publikationen /weekly_reports/2010_01/investments__women_are_more_cautious_than_men _because_they_have_less_financial_resources_at_their_disposal.html.

35 "BlackRock Annual Global Investor Pulse Survey," BlackRock, March 7, 2016, ir.blackrock.com/news-and-events/press-releases/press-releases-details/2016 /BlackRock-Annual-Global-Investor-Pulse-Survey-American-Women-Feeling -Better-about-Their-Financial-Futures-but-Keen-Focus-on-Day-to-Day-Finances -May-Deter-Longer-Term-Financial-Goals/default.aspx.

36 Jessica Farronato, "'Men Buy, Women Shop': The Sexes Have Different Priorities When Walking Down the Aisles," Wharton, November 28, 2007, knowledge.wharton.upenn.edu/article/men-buy-women-shop-the-sexes-have -different-priorities-when-walking-down-the-aisles/.

37 Amy Livingstone, "Men, Women, and Money: How the Sexes Differ with Their Finances," MoneyCrashers, November 29, 2021, www.moneycrashers.com/men -women-money-sexes-differ-finances/.

38 "Women More Like to Give and Give More Than Men, Study Finds, Philanthropy News Digest, October 21, 2010, philanthropynewsdigest.org/news/women-more -likely-to-give-and-give-more-than-men-study-finds.

Chapter 2—Women's Challenges in the Workforce

1   Kierra Sheffield, LinkedIn post, October 2021, www.linkedin.com/posts
    /kierrasheffield_thank-you-god-from-unemployment-to-working-ugcPost
    -6848312625596522496-sXXH/.

2   Janet L. Yellen, "The History of Women's Work and Wages and How It Has
    Created Success for Us All, Brookings Institution, May 2020, www.brookings.edu
    /essay/the-history-of-womens-work-and-wages-and-how-it-has-created-success
    -for-us-all/#:~:text=Between%20the%201930s%20and%20mid,factors
    %20contributed%20to%20this%20rise.

3   "Women in the Workforce: United States (Quick Take)," Catalyst, October 14, 2020,
    www.catalyst.org/research/women-in-the-workforce-united-states/.

4   Mitra Toossi and Teresa L. Morisi, "Women in the Workforce Before, During
    and After the Great Recession," U.S. Bureau of Labor Statistics, July 2017,
    www.bls.gov/spotlight/2017/women-in-the-workforce-before-during-and-after
    -the-great-recession/pdf/women-in-the-workforce-before-during-and-after-the
    -great-recession.pdf.

5   Yellen, "The History of Women's Work."

6   "Labor Force Participation Rate, female (% of female populations ages 15+),"
    World Bank, June 15, 2021, data.worldbank.org/indicator/SL.TLF.CACT.FE.ZS.

7   Felix Richter, "COVID-19 Has Caused Huge Amount of Lost Working Hours,"
    World Economic Forum, February 4, 2021, www.weforum.org/agenda/2021/02
    /covid-employment-global-job-loss/.

8   Eleni X. Carageorge, "Covid-19 Recession is Tougher on Women," U.S. Bureau of
    Labor Statistics, September 2020, www.bls.gov/opub/mlr/2020/beyond-bls/covid
    -19-recession-is-tougher-on-women.htm.

9   Anu Madgavkar, Olivia White, Mekala Krishnan, Deepa Mahajan, and Xavier
    Azcue, "Covid-19 and Gender Equality: Countering the Regressive Effects,
    McKinsey Global Institute, July 15, 2020, www.mckinsey.com/featured-insights
    /future-of-work/covid-19-and-gender-equality-countering-the-regressive-effects.

10 Anu Madgavkar, Olivia White, Mekala Krishnan, Deepa Mahajan, and Xavier
    Azcue, "Covid-19 and Gender Equality: Countering the Regressive Effects,
    McKinsey Global Institute, July 15, 2020, www.mckinsey.com/featured-insights
    /future-of-work/covid-19-and-gender-equality-countering-the-regressive-effects.

11 Alisha Haridasani Gupta, "Why Some Women Call This Recession a 'Shecession,'"
    The New York Times, May 9, 2020, www.nytimes.com/2020/05/09/us
    /unemployment-coronavirus-women.html.

12 Patricia Cohen and Tiffany Hsu, "Pandemic Could Scar a Generation of Working
    Mothers," The New York Times, June 3, 2020, www.nytimes.com/2020/06/03
    /business/economy/coronavirus-working-women.html.

13 "Certain Challenges Are More Likely to Push Women Out of the Workforce,"
    in Women in the Workplace 2020 (report), Lean In, 2020, leanin.org/women
    -in-the-workplace-report-2020/impact-of-covid-19.

14 "Covid-19 Could Push Many Mothers Out of the Workforce: In their words," in
    Women in the Workplace 2020.

15 "One in Three Mothers May Be Forced to Scale Back or Opt Out," in *Women in the Workplace* 2020.

16 "Covid-19 and Gender Equality: Countering the Regressive Effects," McKinsey Global Institute, July 15, 2020, www.mckinsey.com/featured-insights/future-of-work/covid-19-and-gender-equality-countering-the-regressive-effects.

17 Madgavkar et al., "Covid-19 and Gender Equality."

18 *Women in the Workplace* 2020.

19 "Senior-Level Women Are Facing Heightened Pressure Both at Work and at Home," in *Women in the Workplace* 2020.

20 *Women in the Workplace* 2020.

21 "Senior-Level Women Are Facing Heightened Pressure Both at Work and at Home" in *Women in the Workplace* 2020.

22 Jill Orr, "I Can Bring Home the Bacon, but the Rest Is On You," An Exercise in Narcissism (blog), February 27, 2012, jillsorr.com/2012/02/27/i-can-bring-home-the-bacon-but-the-rest-is-on-you/.

23 Matt Krentz, Emily Kos, Anna Green, and Jennifer Garcia-Alosnso, "Easing the COVID-19 Burden on Working Parents," Boston Consulting Group, May 21, 2020, www.bcg.com/publications/2020/helping-working-parents-ease-the-burden-of-covid-19.

24 Jess Huang, Alexis Krivkovich, Ishanaa Rambachan, and Lareina Yee, "For Mothers in the Workplace, a Year (and Counting) Like No Other," McKinsey & Company, May 5, 2021, www.mckinsey.com/featured-insights/diversity-and-inclusion/for-mothers-in-the-workplace-a-year-and-counting-like-no-other.

25 Maressa Brown, "Here Are the States with the Most—and the Fewest—Stay-at-Home Parents During the Pandemic, *Parents*, March 29, 2021, www.parents.com/news/places-with-the-most-stay-at-home-parents/.

26 "Cost of Care for Single Mothers," Single Mother Guide, February 20, 2021, singlemotherguide.com/cost-of-child-care/.

27 Leila Schochet, "The Child Care Crisis Is Keeping Women Out of The Workforce," Center for American Progress, March 28, 2019, americanprogress.org/article/child-care-crisis-keeping-women-workforce/.

28 Michelle Budig, "The Fatherhood Bonus and the Motherhood Penalty: Parenthood and the Gender Gap in Pay," Third Way, September 2, 2014, www.thirdway.org/report/the-fatherhood-bonus-and-the-motherhood-penalty-parenthood-and-the-gender-gap-in-pay.

29 Misty L. Heggeness and Jason M. Fields, "Working Moms Bear Brunt of Home Schooling While Working During Covid-19," United States Census Bureau, August 18, 2020, www.census.gov/library/stories/2020/08/parents-juggle-work-and-child-care-during-pandemic.html.

30 Dina Gerdeman, "How Gender Stereotypes Kill a Woman's Self-Confidence," Harvard Business School, February 25, 2019, hbswk.hbs.edu/item/how-gender-stereotypes-less-than-br-greater-than-kill-a-woman-s-less-than-br-greater-than-self-confidence.

31 Anthony Martinez and Cheridan Christnacht, "Women Are Nearly Half of US Workforce but only 27% of STEM Workers," United States Census Bureau, January 26, 2021, www.census.gov/library/stories/2021/01/women-making -gains-in-stem-occupations-but-still-underrepresented.html.

32 Dina Gerdeman, "How Gender Stereotypes Kill a Woman's Self-Confidence."

33 Katty Kay and Claire Shipman, *The Confidence Code: The Science and Art of Self-Assurance—What Women Should Know* (New York: Harper Collins, 2014), 3.

34 Hau L. Lee and Corey Billignton, "The Evolution of Supply-Chain-Management Models and Practice at Hewlett-Packard," *Interfaces* 25, no. 5 (1995): 42–63.

35 Gustavo Razzetti, "Why Good Enough Is Better Than Perfect," Ladders, June 22, 2019, www.theladders.com/career-advice/why-good-enough-is-better-than -perfect.

36 Laura Berlinsky-Shine, "These Are the 25 Best Careers for Women, Fairygodboss.com, fairygodboss.com/career-topics/best-careers-for-women.

37 William Bridges, *Transitions: Making Sense of Life's Changes* (Boston: Da Capo Lifelong Books, 2004), 135.

38 Amy Wilkinson, "Want to Switch Career Lanes (or Make a Total U-Turn)? Here's How, Even When You're Far on One Path," Well + Good, January 28, 2019, wellandgood.com/changing-career-paths-how-to/.

39 Michal Biron, Renee De Reuver, and Sharon Toker. "All Employees Are Equal, But Some Are More Equal Than Others: Dominance, Agreeableness, and Status Inconsistency Among Men and Women," *European Journal of Work and Organizational Psychology* 25, no. 3 (2015): 430. doi 10.1080/1359432X.2015.1111338.

40 Katie Shonk, "Women and Negotiation: Narrowing the Gender Gap in Negotiation," Harvard Law School, August 24, 2021, www.pon.harvard.edu/daily/business -negotiations/women-and-negotiation-narrowing-the-gender-gap/.

41 Suzanne de Janasz and Beth Cabrer, "How Women Can Get What They Want in a Negotiation," *Harvard Business Review*, August 17, 2018, hbr.org/2018/08/how -women-can-get-what-they-want-in-a-negotiation.

42 Simonetta Lein, "10 Inspiring Women Entrepreneurs on Overcoming Self-Doubt and Launching your Dream," Entrepreneur, July 13, 2020, www.entrepreneur.com /article/352948.

43 "Woman Owned Businesses Are Growing 2X Faster On Average Than All Businesses Nationwide," American Express, September 23, 2019, about.americanexpress.com /all-news/news-details/2019/.

44 Falon Fatemi, "The Value of Investing in Female Founders," *Forbes*, March 29, 2019, www.forbes.com/sites/falonfatemi/2019/03/29/the-value-of-investing-in-female -founders/?sh=50e461225ee4; and First Round, 10years.firstround.com/.

45 "Letter from Sharon Miller, Head of Small Business," Bank of America Business Advantage, 2019 Women Business Owner Spotlight, about.bankofamerica.com /assets/pdf/2019-Women-Business-Owner-Spotlight.pdf.

Chapter 3—The Elusive Paradox: Money and Relationships

1   Amanda Clayton, "I've Counseled More Than 500 Couples and This Is the NO. 1 Money Mistake That Ruins Relationships," www.cnbc.com/2019/05/07/the-big gest-mistake-that-destroys-relationships-according-to-financial-therapist.html.

2   Catey Hill, "This Common Behavior is the No.1 Predictor of Whether You'll Get Divorced, MarketWatch, January 10, 2018, www.marketwatch.com/story/this -common-behavior-is-the-no-1-predictor-of-whether-youll-get-divorced -2018-01-10.

3   Jeffrey Dew, Sonya Britt, and Sandra Huston, "Examining the Relationship Between Financial Issues and Divorce," *Family Relations* 61, no. 4 (October 2012): 615–28, onlinelibrary.wiley.com/doi/abs/10.1111/j.1741-3729.2012.00715.x; "Divorce Study: Financial Arguments Early in Relationship May Predict Divorce," HuffPost, July 15, 2013, www.huffpost.com/entry/divorce-study_n_3587811.

4   Ken Honda, "There are 7 Money Personality Types, Says Psychology Expert— How to Tell Which One You Are (and the Pitfalls of Each)," CNBC, April 28, 2021, www.cnbc.com/2021/04/28/7-money-personality-types-and-the-pitfalls-of -each.html.

5   Gary Chapman, *The Five Love Languages: How to Express Heartfelt Commitment to Your Mate* (Chicago: Northfield Publishing, 1995).

6   Tomi Toluhi, "Why Couples Really Fight Over Money," Tomi Talks, June 7, 2016, www.tomitalks.com/2016/06/07/why-couples-really-fight-over-money/; Bobbie Salow, "Discovering Your Partner's Money Language," Morey & Quinn, n.d., www.moreyandquinn.com/blog/86-discovering-your-partners-money-language.

7   Rianka Dorsainvil, "Why Communicating About Money Is Key to a Healthy Relationship and Financial Future," *Forbes*, August 28, 2019, www.forbes.com /sites/riankadorsainvil/2019/08/28/why-communicating-about-money-is-key-to -a-healthy-relationship-and-financial-future/?sh=152d98d3749b.

8   James Paxton, "5 Ways to Prevent Money from Ruining your Marriage," Finance $ Education, March 19, 2018, www.financecareeducation.com/5-ways-to-prevent -money-from-ruining-your-marriage.html.

9   Jennifer Ryan Woods, "10 Ways To Prevent Money From Ruining Your Marriage," *Forbes*, July 5, 2015, www.forbes.com/sites/jenniferwoods/2015/07/06/10-ways -to-prevent-money-from-ruining-your-marriage/?sh=4376425744c9.

10   Dennis Jacobe, "One in Three Americans Prepare a Detailed Household Budget," Gallup, June 3, 2013, news.gallup.com/poll/162872/one-three-americans-prepare -detailed-household-budget.aspx.

11   WM Americas News, "UBS Study of Women Investors Reveals the 'Divide and Conquer' Approach to Managing Finances Is a Multi-Generational Problem," UBS, March 6, 2019, www.ubs.com/global/en/media/display-page-ndp/en -20190306-study-reveals-multi-generational-problem.html.

12 Jennifer Brown, Nari Rhee, Joelle Saad-Lessler, and Diane Oakley, "Shortchanged in Retirement: Continuing Challenges to Women's Financial Future," National Institute on Retirement Security, March 2016, papers.ssrn.com/sol3/papers.cfm ?abstract_id=2779813.

13 "Three Questions with Implications to Your Financial Future," Wharton, February 11, 2015, knowledge.wharton.upenn.edu/article/three-questions -major-implications-financial-well/.

14 Who's the Better Investor: Men or Women?, Fidelity, May 18, 2017, www.fidelity.com/about-fidelity/individual-investing/better-investor-men-or -women/.

15 "Breadwinner Mothers by Race/Ethnicity," Institute for Women's Policy Research, April 2020, iwpr.org/wp-content/uploads/2020/05/QF-Breadwinner-Mothers -by-Race-FINAL-46.pdf.

16 Wendy Wang, "The Happiness Penalty for Breadwinning Moms," Institute for Family Studies, June 4, 2019, ifstudies.org/blog/the-happiness-penalty-for -breadwinning-moms. The survey was conducted September 13 to 25, 2018, with a nationally representative sample of 2,025 adults ages eighteen to fifty in the United States via the Knowledge Panel of Ipsos. It is part of the IFS/Wheatley Institution 2018 Global Family and Gender Survey. Respondents were asked whether they earn more money than their spouse, their spouse earns more, or they earn about the same. Analyses in this report are based on married heterosexual adults. Results for married men and women who make about the equal amount of the money as their spouses are not shown because of the small sample sizes.

17 Sasha Ann Simons, "More Couples Are Embracing Female Breadwinners, Despite Decades-Old Stigma," NPR, February 18, 2020, www.npr.org/local /305/2020/02/18/807050015/more-couples-are-embracing-female-breadwinners -despite-decades-old-stigma; "Historical Income Table for Families," U.S. Census Bureau, www.census.gov/data/tables/time-series/demo/income-poverty/historical -income-families.html.

18 Wang, "The Happiness Penalty for Breadwinning Moms."

19 Wang, "The Happiness Penalty for Breadwinning Moms."

20 Marta Murray-Close and Misty L. Heggeness, "Manning Up and Womaning Down: How Husbands and Wives Report Their Earnings When She Earns More," U.S. Census Bureau, June 6, 2018, www.census.gov/content/dam/Census/library /working-papers/2018/demo/SEHSD-WP2018-20.pdf.

21 Kim Parker and Renee Stepler, "Americans See Men as the Financial Providers, Even As Women's Contributions Grow, Pew Research Center, September 20, 2017, www.pewresearch.org/fact-tank/2017/09/20/americans-see-men-as-the-financial -providers-even-as-womens-contributions-grow/.

22 Daniel Carlson, Amanda J. Miller, and Stephanie Rudd, "Division of Housework, Communication, and Couples' Relationship Satisfaction," *Journal of Health and Social Behavior*, June 1, 2020, doi.org/10.1177/2378023120924805.

23 "Modern Marriage," Pew Research Center, July 18, 2007, www.pewresearch.org /social-trends/2007/07/18/modern-marriage.

Chapter 4—The Blessing and the Curse: Technology

1   Patty, "How Was Ellevest Started," Ellevest, support.ellevest.com/hc/en-us/articles /360016869254-How-was-Ellevest-started-.
2   Shawn M. Carter, "Social Media May Be Making You Overspend—and It's Not Just Because of the Ads," CNBC, March 15, 2018, www.cnbc.com/2018/03/15 /social-media-may-make-you-overspend-and-its-not-just-because-of-ads.html.
3   "2018 Allianz Generations Ahead Study—Quick Facts #3," Allianz, www.allianzlife.com/-/media/files/allianz/pdfs/newsroom/2018-allianz -generations-ahead-fact-sheet-3.pdf.
4   "New Data Shows FTC Received 2.2 Million Fraud Reports from Consumers 2020," Federal Trade Commission, February 4, 2021, www.ftc.gov/news-events /press-releases/2021/02/new-data-shows-ftc-received-2-2-million-fraud-reports -consumers-.
5   "U.S. Identity Theft: The Stark Reality," Giact, March 2021, giact.com/identity /us-identity-theft-the-stark-reality/.
6   "Cybersecurity Breaches to Result in over 147 Billion Records Being Stolen by 2023." Juniper Research, August 8, 2018, www.juniperresearch.com/press /cybersecurity-breaches-to-result-in-over-146-bn.

Chapter 5—Five Steps to Financial Freedom

1   Rachel Ellen, "9 Inspiring Financial Stories, Chicken Soup for the Budgeter's Soul," YNAB, January 14, 2021, www.youneedabudget.com/9-inspiring -financial-stories/.
2   "Make a Budget" (worksheet), Federal Trade Commission, September 2012, www.consumer.ftc.gov/articles/pdf-1020-make-budget-worksheet.pdf.
3   "Do We All Really Spend More with a Credit Card," Free Money Finance, September 3, 2008, www.freemoneyfinance.com/2008/09/do-we-all-reall.html.
4   Claire Greene and Scott Schuh, "The 2016 Diary of Consumer Payment Choice," Federal Reserve Bank of Boston, 2017, www.bostonfed.org/publications/research -data-report/2017/the-2016-diary-of-consumer-payment-choice.aspx.
5   Joydeep Srivastava and Priya Raghubir, "Monopoly Money: The Effect of Payment Coupling and Form on Spending Behavior," *Journal of Experimental Psychology*: Applied 14, no. 3 (2008): 213–25, www.apa.org/pubs/journals/releases /xap143213.pdf.
6   Geoffrey Gerdes, Claire Greene, Xuemei (May) Liu, and Emily Massaro, "The Federal Resrve Payments Study: 2020 and 2021 Annual Supplements," Federal Reserve, December 2021, www.federalreserve.gov/paymentsystems/2019 -December-The-Federal-Reserve-Payments-Study.htm#:~:text=In%202018%2C %20for%20the%20first,to%2042.6%20billion%20check%20payments.
7   "First Quarter 2020 Results," Paypal Holdings Inc., May 6, 2020, s1.q4cdn.com/633035571/files/doc_financials/2020/q1/Q1-20_PayPal _Earnings-Release_Final.pdf.

8   Alex Gailey, "This 32-Year-Old Paid Off $7,000 of Credit Card Debt in 7 Months. Here's What She Learned," NextAdvisor, September 27, 2021 time.com/nextadvisor /credit-cards/how-32-year-old-paid-off-7k-in-credit-card-debt.

9   "Debt Snowball & Avalanche Payoff Calculator," DoughRoller, tools.doughroller.net /debt-snowball-calculator.

10   "Credit Card Payoff Calculator," Mentor, www.mentormoney.com/calculators /credit-card-payoff-calculator/.

11   "Personal Loan Calculator," Bankrate, www.bankrate.com/calculators/managing -debt/loan-calculator.aspx.

12   Jessica Dickler, "Fewer Women Now Pay Their Credit Card Balances in Full," CNBC, September 3, 2019, www.cnbc.com/2019/09/03/fewer-women-now-pay -their-credit-card-balances-in-full.html.

13   Louis DeNicola, "How Long Do Late Payments Stay on My Credit Reports," Experian, January 14, 2020, www.experian.com/blogs/ask-experian/how-long -do-late-payments-stay-on-credit-reports/2.

14   Kenneth Terrell, "Half of Adults Don't Have Emergency Savings, AARP Finds," AARP, October 8, 2019, www.aarp.org/money/budgeting-saving/info-2019 /emergency-funds.html.

15   "Report on the Economic Well-Being of U.S. Households in 2019," Board of Governors of the Federal Reserve System, May 2020, www.federalreserve.gov /publications/2020-economic-well-being-of-us-households-in-2019-dealing -with-unexpected-expenses.htm.

16   "Pew Finds American Families Ill-Equipped for Financial Emergencies," Pew Research Center, November 18, 2015, www.pewtrusts.org/en/about/news-room /press-releases-and-statements/2015/11/18/pew-finds-american-families-ill -equipped-for-financial-emergencies/.

17   "Retirement Security Amid COVID-19: The Outlook of Three Generations," in the 20th Annual Transamerica Retirement Survey, Transamerica Center for Retirement Studies, May 2020, /transamericacenter.org/retirement-research /20th-annual-retirement-survey.

18   Molly Triffin, "How Their Emergency Fund Saved Them," HerMoney, December 2, 2019, hermoney.com/save/emergency-fund/how-their-emergency-savings -saved-them/.

19   Catherine S. Harvey, "Unlocking the Potential of Emergency Savings Accounts," AARP Public Policy Institute, October 2019, www.aarp.org/content/dam/aarp/ppi /2019/10/unlocking-potential-emergency-savings-accounts.doi.10.26419ppi .00084.001.pdf.

20   Arloc Sherman, Claire Zippel, Robert Gordon and Danilo Trisi, "Widespread Economic Insecurity Pre-Pandemic Shows Need for Strong Recovery Package," Center on Budget and Policy Priorities, July 14, 2021, www.cbpp.org/research /poverty-and-inequality/widespread-economic-insecurity-pre-pandemic-shows -need-for-strong.

21 Kim Parker, Julianna Menasce Horowitz, and Anna Brown, "About Half of Lower-Income Americans Report Household Job or Wage Loss Due to COVID-19," Pew Research Center, April 21, 2021, www.pewresearch.org/social-trends/2020/04/21 /about-half-of-lower-income-americans-report-household-job-or-wage-loss-due -to-covid-19/.

22 Theodore Roosevelt, *American Ideals: And Other Essays, Social and Political.* Quoted at www.goodreads.com/work/quotes/2828082-american-ideals.

Chapter 6—The Linchpin: Funding Your Retirement (Start Early!)

1   Simon Moore, "How Long Will Your Retirement Really Last?" *Forbes*, April 24, 2018, www.forbes.com/sites/simonmoore/2018/04/24/how-long-will-your -retirement-last/?sh=3ac0c9097472.

2   Jia Haomiao Jia and Erica Lubetkin, "Life expectancy and active life expectancy by marital status among older U.S. adults: Results from the U.S. Medicare Health Outcome Survey (HOS), *SSM Population Health* 12 (December 2020), www.sciencedirect.com/science/article/pii/S2352827320302792.

3   Grace Enda and William Gale, "How Does Gender Equality Affect Women in Retirement?" Brookings, July 2020, www.brookings.edu/essay/how-does-gender -equality-affect-women-in-retirement/.

4   "Women 80% More Likely to be Impoverished in Retirement," National Institute on Retirement Security, March 1, 2016, www.nirsonline.org/2016/03/women-80 -more-likely-to-be-impoverished-in-retirement/.

5   Matthew S. Rutledge, Alice Zulkarnain, and Sara Ellen King, "How Much Does Motherhood Cost Women in Social Security Benefits," Center for Retirement Research at Boston College, October 2017, crr.bc.edu/wp-content/uploads/2017/09 /wp_2017-14.pdf.

6   Enda and Gale, "How Does Gender Equality Affect Women in Retirement?"

7   Enda and Gale, "How Does Gender Equality Affect Women in Retirement?"; Grover J. Whitehurst, "Why the Federal Government Should Subsidize Child Care and How to Pay for It," Brookings, March 9, 2017, www.brookings.edu /research/why-the-federal-government-should-subsidize-childcare-and-how-to -pay-for-it/

8   "Policy Basics: Top Ten Facts About Social Security," Center on Budget and Policy Priorities, August 13, 2020, www.cbpp.org/research/social-security/top-ten-facts -about-social-security.

9   Lieber and St. John, "How to Win At Retirement Savings."

10 Rob Lieber and Todd St. John, "How to Win At Retirement Savings," *The New York Times*, n.d., www.nytimes.com/guides/business/saving-money-for-retirement.

11 Ellen Stark, "5 Things You Should Know about Long-Term Care Insurance," *AARP Bulletin*, March 1, 2018, www.aarp.org/caregiving/financial-legal/info -2018/long-term-care-insurance-fd.html.

12   Sarah Berger, "3 in 10 Americans Withdrew Money from Retirement Savings amid the Coronavirus Pandemic—and the Majority Spent it on Groceries," MagnifyMoney by Lending Tree, May 13, 2020, www.magnifymoney.com/blog /news/early-withdrawal-coronavirus/.

Chapter 7—Investing: The Catalyst for Financial Independence

1   "U.S Bank Survey Says Women Are Leaving Money and Influence on the Table," U.S. Bank, March 5, 2020, www.usbank.com/about-us-bank/company-blog /article-library/us-bank-survey-says-women-are-leaving-money-and-influence -on-the-table.html.

2   "Women's Retirement Outlook Is Becoming Even Riskier amid COVID-19," TraansAmerica Center for Retirement Studies, September 17, 2020, transamericacenter.org/docs/default-source/retirement-survey-of-workers /tcrs2020_pr_women-and-retirement-amid-covid19.pdf.

3   Kathy Lynch, "Women Hold Too Much Cash, Study Says," *Financial Advisor*, January 22, 2015, www.fa-mag.com/news/women-hold-to-much-cash--study -says-20499.html.

4   Jean Chatzky, "Why Women Invest 40 Percent Less Than Men (and How We Can Change It), NBC News, September 25, 2018, www.nbcnews.com/better/business /why-women-invest-40-percent-less-men-how-we-can-ncna912956.

5   Fidelity Investments Survey Reveals Only Nine Percent of Women Think They Make Better Investors Than Men, Despite Growing Evidence to the Contrary," Fidelity Investments, May 18, 2017, newsroom.fidelity.com/press-releases/news -details/2017/Fidelity-Investments-Survey-Reveals-Only-Nine-Percent-of -Women-Think-They-Make-Better-Investors-than-Men-Despite-Growing -Evidence-to-the-Contrary/default.aspx.

6   Catey Hill, "This Is the Little-Known Way Money-Savvy Women Are Joining Together to Earn Thousands," *Real Simple*, n.d., www.realsimple.com/work-life /money/millie/women-investing-group-millie.

7   Pooneh Baghai, Olivia Hayward, Lakshmi Prakash, and Jill Zucker, "Women as the Next Wave of Growth in US Wealth Management," McKinsey & Company, July 29, 2020, www.mckinsey.com/industries/financial-services/our-insights /women-as-the-next-wave-of-growth-in-us-wealth-management.

8   Baghai, Hayward, Prakash, and Zucker, "Women as the Next Wave of Growth in US Wealth Management."

9   James Chen, "Annualized Total Return," Investopedia, September 3, 2021, www.investopedia.com/terms/a/annualized-total-return.asp.

10   "How Two Reactions to Volatility Could have Led to a $932,774 Difference in Results," Hartford Funds, March 19, 2020, www.hartfordfunds.com/insights /investor-insight/client-seminars/beyond-investment-illusions/reactions-to -volatility.html.

11   "How Two Reactions to Volatility."

12   "Day Trading: Your Dollars at Risk," U.S. Securities and Exchange Commission, April 20, 2005, www.sec.gov/reportspubs/investor-publications /investorpubsdaytipshtm.html.

13   "Impact Investing," Global Impact Investing Network, n.d., thegiin.org/impact -investing/.

Chapter 8—Your Home: Should You Buy or Rent?

1   "Homeowners vs Renters Statistics," iPropertyManagement, October 17, 2021, ipropertymanagement.com/research/renters-vs-homeowners-statistics #:~:text=Meanwhile%2C%20the%20number%20of%20households ,percentage%20of%2037.0%25%20in%201965.

Chapter 9—Hidden Financial Risks and How to Protect Yourself: Cohabitation, Marriage, and Roommates

1   Juliana Menasce Horowitz, Nikki Graf, and Gretchen Livingston, "Marriage and Cohabitation in the U.S.," Pew Research Center, November 6, 2019, www.pewresearch.org/social-trends/2019/11/06/marriage-and-cohabitation -in-the-u-s/.

2   Benjamin Gurrentz, "Cohabiting Partners Older, More Racially Diverse, More Educated, Higher Earners," United States Census Bureau, September 23, 2019, www.census.gov/library/stories/2019/09/unmarried-partners-more-diverse-than -20-years-ago.html.

3   Gurrentz, "Cohabiting Partners."

4   Nikki Graf, "Key Findings on Marriage and Cohabitation in the U.S.," Pew Research Center, November 6, 2019, www.pewresearch.org/fact-tank/2019/11/06/key -findings-on-marriage-and-cohabitation-in-the-u-s/#:~:text=Over%20the %20same%20period%2C%20the,t%20plan%20to%20get%20married.

5   "Divorce Statistics and Divorce Rate in the USA," Divorce Statistics, n.d., www.divorcestatistics.info/divorce-statistics-and-divorce-rate-in-the-usa.html.

6   Jessica Sayers, "10 Things to Consider Before Becoming a Stay-at-Home Mom," Moms.com, October 7, 2019, www.moms.com/stay-at-home-mom-plan/.

Chapter 10—Divorce: Breaking Up Is Hard to Do

1   Erin McDowell, "The Average Cost of Getting Divorced Is $15,000 in the US— But Here's Why It Can Be Much Higher," Business Insider, August 1, 2019, www.businessinsider.com/average-cost-divorce-getting-divorced-us-2019-7.

2   As told to the author.

Chapter 11—Estate Planning

1   Daniel Cobb, "For the First Time, Caring.com's Will Survey Finds That Younger Adults Are More Likely to Have a Will Than Middle-Aged Adults," Caring.com, n.d., www.caring.com/caregivers/estate-planning/wills-survey/.

2   Jimmy Verner, "Death Before Divorce Puts Disinheritance Wishes of Cars Singer Ocasek on Legal Detour," Legacy Assurance Plan, January 14, 2020, legacyassuranceplan.com/articles/estate-stories/death-before-divorce-Ric-Ocasek/.

3   Tom Alberts, "Tragedies Involving Young Families Are Heartbreaking Reminder of Importance of Estate Planning—at Any Age," Legacy Assurance Plan, May 10, 2019, legacyassuranceplan.com/articles/estate-stories/unexpected-stories/.

GLOSSARY

401(k) plan (Traditional): a retirement savings and investing plan offered by employers that gives tax breaks to the employee on their contribution. It is named after a section of the U.S. Internal Revenue Code. Contributions made are taken out of the employee's paycheck before income taxes are taken out; the contribution reduces the employee's taxable income and lowers income taxes. The employee contributes a percentage of income to the plan, which is directly deposited into an investment account. The money can grow in the account tax-free.

403(b) plan: a retirement account for employees of nonprofit organizations and the government. Participants include teachers, school administrators, professors, government employees, nurses, doctors, and librarians. Employees have pre-tax money deducted from their paycheck and paid into an investment retirement account. All growth and earnings on the investment is tax-free.

alternative investment: an investment that doesn't fit into one of the traditional categories of investments such as stocks, bonds, or cash. Alternative investments are uncorrelated to the stock and bond markets, which means they often move in a different direction from those markets. This makes them a good tool for portfolio diversification and a good inflation hedge. Examples of alternatives are liquid hedge funds, hedge funds, private equity funds, real estate investment trusts, art, and gold.

asset allocation: an investment strategy that involves dividing up an investor's portfolio among different asset categories such as stocks, bonds, cash, and alternatives. This mix of assets is based on the investor's risk tolerance, goals, and timeline. Over the course of an investor's life, their asset allocation may change as their risk tolerance, goals, and time horizon changes.

asset: a resource or item of economic value that an individual or corporation owns or controls that is used to produce positive economic benefits. An asset is something that can generate future cash flow, reduce expenses, or improve sales.

bear market: a prolonged period when broad market prices fall at least 20 percent concurrently with widespread pessimism and negative investor sentiment. Although bear markets are often associated with declines in an overall market, individual securities can also experience a bear market if their prices decline by 20 percent over a sustained time. A market correction is a market decline that is more than 10 percent but less than 20 percent—the difference between a bear market and a correction is the size of the decline. Although there have been a few bear markets, the market spends more time in bull markets than bear markets. It's called a bear market because bears attack their opponents by swiping their paws downward.

bonds: a type of security that represents a loan made by an investor to a company or government that pays the investor a rate of return over a certain amount of time. A bond could be thought of as an IOU between the lender and borrower that includes the details of the loan and its payments. Owners of bonds are creditors of the issuer. Bond details state the date when the principal of the loan is due to be paid to the investor and the terms for variable- or fixed-interest payments made by the borrower.

bull market: a continuous period in the stock market or other traded exchange market (such as bonds, real estate, currencies, and commodities markets) when prices are on the rise or are expected to rise and continue to rise. The term *bull market* is most often used to refer to the stock market but can be applied to anything that is traded. Because prices of securities rise and fall continuously during trading, the term *bull market* is typically reserved for extended periods in which large portions of securities prices are rising. Bull markets can last for months or years. One of the longest bull markets ran from December 1987 until March 2000. A commonly used metric for a bull market is when stock prices rise by 20 percent after two declines of 20 percent each. The term *bull* is used because when bulls attack their opponents, they thrust their horns up.

certificate of deposit (CD): commonly known as a CD, this is a type of savings account you can open at most banks or credit unions that requires you to lock up your deposit for a specific period of time until a maturity date. It usually pays higher interest than a regular savings account, but you will pay a penalty if you withdraw it early.

compounding: the process when an investment's value increases because it is generating earnings from its initial investment (principal) and the accumulated earnings on the initial investment over time. An asset's earnings, from either capital gains or interest, are reinvested to generate additional earnings. Compounding differs from linear growth, where only the principal earns interest each period.

exchange-traded fund (ETF): a fund that can be bought and sold on an exchange just like a stock can be. It can be bought and sold throughout the day. ETFs track an index, sector, commodity, or other asset and can even be structured to track specific investment strategies.

individual retirement account (IRA) (Traditional): a tax-advantaged investment account that allows you to save for retirement. Contributions are usually tax-deductible. Any person with earned income can open an IRA. There are contribution limits, and growth and earnings are tax-free within the IRA. An IRA investor gets taxed on distributions.

investment portfolio: a basket of assets including stocks, bonds, exchange-traded funds, mutual funds, commodities, cash, cash equivalents, and alternatives. A portfolio also may contain a wide range of assets including real estate, art, and private investments.

liquidity: refers to the ease and ability to convert securities and other assets into cash. If this can be done quickly and without restrictions, the asset will be called a liquid asset.

money market fund: a mutual fund that invests in cash or debt securities that are short-term and have low credit risk (such as U.S. Treasuries). Money market funds offer investors the option of an investment that is very liquid with a low level of risk. Money market funds are also called money market mutual funds.

mutual fund: a mutual fund pools money collected from many investors to invest in securities like stocks, bonds, money market instruments, and other assets. Mutual funds are managed by portfolio managers, who allocate the fund's assets to match the investment objectives stated in its prospectus. Each share represents an investor's partial ownership in the fund. Mutual funds are "redeemable" and can be sold at any time with payment being made within seven days.

power of attorney: a legal authorization that gives a person you designate the power to act on your behalf as your agent or attorney-in-fact to make decisions about your property, finances, investments, or medical care.

revocable living trust: a legal document created by you (the grantor) during your lifetime that puts your assets (investments, bank accounts, real estate, and valuable personal property) in a trust for your benefit during your lifetime and spells out what happens to these assets upon your death. You can change or cancel the trust anytime during your lifetime.

risk-adjusted return: a measure of how much risk is involved in an investment's return. It is an indicator of how much risk are you willing to take on to get a certain return. The risk is measured in comparison with that of a risk-free investment, such as U.S. Treasuries. It is usually expressed as a number or rating; and risk-adjusted returns are applied to individual stocks, investment funds, and entire portfolios.

robo-advisors: low-cost digital platforms that use computer algorithms and advanced software to create and manage an investment portfolio for you. There is little or no human interaction. Typically, robo-advisors have people complete surveys and answer questions about their financial situation and future goals and then use the data to offer advice and automatically invest client assets. Due to their low costs, there are low minimum investment requirements and, in some cases, people can begin investing in minutes. Robo-advisors usually have five to ten portfolio choices ranging from conservative to aggressive. The algorithm will recommend a portfolio based on your answers to the questions.

Roth 401(k): a retirement savings and investment plan offered by employers that is funded with after-tax dollars. That means that you pay taxes on your paycheck first and then invest the money. This is different from a traditional 401(k) plan, which deducts your contribution from your gross pay before taxes. With a Roth 401(k), because you pay taxes first, you will take less home in your paycheck now, but when you retire, withdrawals from the account will be tax-free, unlike traditional 401(k) withdrawals, which are taxed at ordinary income rates.

Roth IRA: an individual retirement account that is funded with after-tax dollars; there are no current tax benefits, unlike the deduction you get when you contribute to a traditional IRA. Contributions and earnings grow tax-free, and all future withdrawals are tax-free, which differs from traditional IRA withdrawals, which are taxed at ordinary income rates. Just like with a traditional IRA, you have to earn income to contribute to a Roth IRA.

stock: (also known as an equity) a security that represents the ownership of a fraction of a corporation. The owner of stock is entitled to a proportion of the corporation's assets and profits equal to how much stock they own. Units of stock are called *shares*.

will: sometimes called last will and testament. A will is a legal document that specifies who will inherit your assets and possessions after your death. It also addresses custody of dependents (i.e., who will be guardian to minor children).

INDEX

Please note that page numbers in italics in this index indicate illustrative material.

ABOUT THE AUTHOR

Jessica Schramm

KIMBERLEE DAVIS is the host of *The Fiscal Feminist*, a podcast and platform about women and their relationship with money and finance. Her mission is to help all women of all ages and wealth levels embrace their responsibility to themselves to achieve solid financial footing in both calm and turbulent times. Kimberlee has more than twenty-five years of finance, legal, and corporate experience and is a Certified Divorce Financial Analyst®. Currently, she is a Managing Director and Partner at The Bahnsen Group, a private wealth management firm. She is the proud mother of three daughters, Allison, Claire, and Merrill.